# GUSTAVUS III

## AND HIS CONTEMPORARIES

# GUSTAVUS III

## AND HIS CONTEMPORARIES

## 1746–1792

### AN OVERLOOKED CHAPTER OF
### EIGHTEENTH CENTURY HISTORY

### By R. NISBET BAIN

*FROM ORIGINAL DOCUMENTS*

" *Gustavus of Sweden, a shining sort of man.*"—CARLYLE

### IN TWO VOLUMES
### VOL. II.

LONDON
KEGAN PAUL, TRENCH, TRÜBNER, & CO. Ltd.
PATERNOSTER HOUSE, CHARING CROSS ROAD
1894

Robert Nisbet Bain

# GUSTAVUS III
## and His Contemporaries
## (1742-1792)

An Overlooked Chapter
of 18th Century History

(From Original Documents)

Volume Two

**BERGMAN PUBLISHERS**
224 WEST TWENTIETH STREET / NEW YORK, N.Y. 10011

First published: London, 1894
by Kegan Paul, Trench, Trübner & Co., London

Published, 1970, by
BERGMAN PUBLISHERS
224 West Twentieth Street
New York, N.Y. 10011

———

Standard Book Number: 87503-28-9
Library of Congress Catalog Card Number: 68-58419

———

This edition has been reproduced in its entirety
from an original copy in the Harvard College Library

———

Printed in the United States of America

# CONTENTS

## CHAPTER XVII.

## CHAPTER XVIII.

# CONTENTS

## CHAPTER XIX.

## CHAPTER XX.

## CHAPTER XXI.

## CHAPTER XXII.

CONTENTS

## CHAPTER XXV.

## APPENDIX.

# GUSTAVUS III.

## AND HIS CONTEMPORARIES

### CHAPTER XVII.

#### *WAR AND TREASON.*

Gustavus's constitutionalism a mistake—Advances in the direction of absolutism—Death of Creutz—Retirement of Liljencrantz—Toll supreme — New men — Ruuth — Wallqvist—Nordin—Disturbed state of Europe—Death of Frederick the Great—The Dutch war —Collapse of France—Turkey declares war against Austria and Russia—Anglo-Dutch-Prussian league—Difficulties of Russia— Gustavus resolves to attack her—Secrecy of his plans—Conferences with Ruuth and Toll—Toll's plan of campaign—Gustavus crosses the Baltic—Insolent ultimatum to Catherine—Her rage and courage—Naval battle of Hogland—First symptoms of mutiny —Warnings and disgrace of Toll—Mutiny begins at Hussala— Retreat of army to Liikala—Deputation of the Finnish regiments to the Empress—Sprengtporten and Jägerhorn—The Confederation of Anjala — Gustavus will not treat with rebels — Escapes to Sweden.

FROM all that we know of the character of Gustavus III., we may safely say that if, at this point of his career, he could have seen his way to retreat within the bounds of a strictly limited constitutional monarchy with honour and safety, he would have gladly done so.. But, in truth, such a retreat was scarcely possible. It was Gustavus's unalterable conviction, based upon the experience of a lifetime, that the Swedish nation, demoralised by half a century of

anarchy, corruption, and slavish dependence on foreign
Powers, could not be safely trusted with complete self-
government, and that a strong monarchy was the only safe-
guard of the national independence.   To establish such a
monarchy had been the dream of his youthful ambition, and
the successful revolution of 1772 was a deliberate first step
in that direction.   But then a prodigy took place.   The victor
suddenly stopped short in mid-career, and surrendered all
the fruits of his victory to the vanquished by presenting
them with a brand new liberal Constitution.   The world
loudly applauded him.   French philosophers wept for joy.
Great French ladies predicted the dawn of a new era at
the sight of a young monarch sacrificing his legitimate
prerogatives for the sake of his people.   We opine, on the
contrary, that this much-lauded act of magnanimity was
really a serious political blunder.   In the then condition
of Sweden, it was essential that the Executive should be
strong indeed, and altogether independent of the Legislature.   Yet Gustavus deliberately placed himself at the
mercy of the Estates by not only relinquishing to them
the power of the purse, but also solemnly engaging not to
declare war without their consent.   It has well been said
that the knowledge Russia possessed that her north-western
frontier could not be attacked without the permission of
the Swedish Riksdag was worth more to her than an army
corps.   All this Gustavus must have clearly foreseen when
he gave his people the free gift of a liberal Constitution ;
but a skilful actor's love of theatrical display, a young
ruler's belief in the sincerity of popular gratitude, above
all, the confidence of genius in its own resources, conspired
to blind him to the danger of such a step.   In 1772,
indeed, the possibility of any future disagreement between
King and people was barely conceivable, yet no more than
fourteen years had elapsed, and Gustavus suddenly found

himself caught between two desperate alternatives: he must either break his self-imposed obligations and ride rough-shod over his own Constitution, or he must henceforth abide by the strict letter of the law, be content to remain a purely constitutional king, and allow his country to become the prey of her neighbours. As the lesser of two evils, he resolved to curtail the liberty in order to save the independence of the nation. He knew only too well that he was staking everything on the issue, but he faced the situation without flinching for an instant, and was to emerge, not without honour, from the dangers that were closing in upon him.

But the passage from semi-constitutionalism to semi-absolutism was so cautious and gradual, all legal forms were so carefully retained long after they had lost their force, that very few people were really aware of the great change that was silently going on.

The King's first care was to dexterously remove from the administration all the friends of the old system, and surround his throne with men of his own choosing, with sufficient intelligence to enter into his designs and sufficient enterprise to carry them into effect. The man whom he chiefly relied upon at this time was Toll.

Toll's promotion had at first been slow, and his position was for a long time ambiguous and precarious. The King seems to have had little personal sympathy with the most resolute and inscrutable of his servants, but the frequency with which he employed him was the best tribute to Toll's extraordinary abilities. At the end of 1782 Toll was sent to Warsaw to negotiate a marriage between the King of Poland and Gustavus's sister. The project, which was kept so secret that the Princess herself never knew anything about it, foundered on the jealousy of Stanislaus' own sisters; but the happy mixture of tact and nerve which

Toll displayed on the occasion, and the masterly report[1] which he sent home on the political situation of Poland, raised him still higher in his master's favour. In the autumn of the same year we find Toll at Berlin attentively studying the army of Frederick the Great, which all the world then regarded as the *ne plus ultra* of military efficiency. Toll, however, was rather disgusted than dazzled by what he saw. The sharp eyes of the future Field-Marshal detected flaws and blemishes where every one else saw absolute perfection, and, with truly prophetic insight, he hinted at the possibility of a collapse of Prussia, as a military power, at no very distant date. In 1785 Toll was sent on a secret mission to Copenhagen, with the twofold object of spying out the nakedness of the land and bringing about a domestic revolution there. The ability he showed on this occasion amazed even Gustavus himself. " I have always taken you, my dear Toll," wrote the King, " for a man who could successfully execute everything in-trusted to him, but I frankly confess that I did not expect such diplomatic dexterity from you." On his return, honours and responsibilities were thrust upon him. He superseded Count Sparre as War Minister; he was one of the secret Council of Four which practically ruled Sweden during the King's absence in Italy, and the deaths of his two most distinguished colleagues, Trolle (spring, 1784) and Creutz (30th October 1785), left him nearest to the throne, without either rival or equal. Creutz was the last of the Swedish Chancellors. The post remained vacant after his death. The importance it conferred was now considered too great for a subject, and Gustavus, who wished to have his hands as free as possible, determined to be henceforth his own Foreign Minister. As, however the abolition of such an ancient office would have caused

[1] *Relation om Ställungen i Polen aar* 1782.

too much commotion and alarm, it was provisionally put into commission.

A further step towards the doing away with Ministerial responsibility and the uniting of all the departments of State in one hand was the dismissal of the last real Minister of Gustavus III., Secretary Liljencrantz. That great financier had long been tolerated as a necessary evil; but his blunt remonstrances against extravagance and his staunch advocacy of economy had always been unpalatable. His stiff, awkward manners and his tiresome prosiness also tried the King's patience severely. His immense personal credit had, indeed, enabled him for a time to raise foreign loans on marvellously favourable terms for Sweden, but he was too sound a financier not to see that even his credit was limited, and every day he became more querulous and impracticable. So at last the King shook him off as an encumbrance by exalting him to the high but harmless dignity of a senator. It was Gustavus's invariable practice never to part on ill terms with old and faithful servants. His disgraces were always, ostensibly, promotions.

Liljencrantz's retirement left Gustavus practically his own Finance Minister; but, as it was necessary, for the sake of appearances, that Liljencrantz should have a nominal successor, the portfolio of the department was thrust upon Baron Erik Ruuth, a friend and *protégé* of Toll's, who, however, would only consent to take over the perilous charge on receiving an assurance in writing from the King that he was not responsible for the disposal of the funds passing through his hand. The very next day, Toll, whose nominal rank of Colonel was ridiculous, considering his power, and a cause of much murmuring among his subaltern generals and admirals, was made a major-general, and at the same time appointed his Majesty's first Adjutant-

General.   He was now indisputably the highest subject
in the land.

But although the chief, Toll was by no means the only
royal counsellor.   It is just about this time that we find
near to the King two clergymen whose political genius
Gustavus himself had been the first to discover and employ, whom he raised from obscurity to be the supports
of his throne, and on whom he was to lean more and more
as his former friends fell away from him, namely, Carl
Gustaf Nordin, long afterwards Bishop of Hernösand, and
Olof Wallqvist, already Bishop of Wexiö.

When Wallqvist first attracted the King's attention
(1780), he was the special preacher at the fashionable St.
Clara Church at Stockholm.   Struck by his eloquence,
Gustavus at once took him by the hand; appointed the
young man (he was then only twenty-five) one of his
chaplains; made him a canon before he was thirty, and a
bishop at thirty-two, and finally placed him at the head of
the newly appointed Commission for reforming the ecclesi-
astical administration of the country.   Thus at thirty-four
Wallqvist had nothing more to hope for but the primacy,
which would infallibly have been his also had the Archbishop died during the King's lifetime.

Yet Wallqvist's genius was fully equal to his fortune.
His knowledge of human nature, energy, firmness, and a
dauntless self-confidence which rose with his difficulties,
made him indispensable to Gustavus, while his insinuating
address and seductive manners won even the hearts of
Gustavus's bitterest enemies.[1]   Wallqvist's presence was
imposing.   His stature was tall, his frame vigorous and
athletic.   His eye was sparkling, penetrating, piercing.
His voice was tender and insinuating when he would

---

[1] "Wallqvist," said one of the Opposition, "has mildness in his eye, upright-
ness on his tongue, honour on his lips, and ambition in his heart."

appeal to the feelings of his audience, loud and sonorous when he would rebuke or convince. Fearlessness, however, was his chief characteristic, and in moments of peril or anxiety he was calmness personified.

There was one brother clergyman, however, whom, as the masterful, energetic young prelate himself confessed to the King, he feared so much " that no protection is good enough against him, save your Majesty's alone." This dreaded rival was Prebendary Nordin, a shy, reticent and pensive person, who, to the world at large, seemed harmless and insignificant enough. But Wallqvist, with the instinct of genius, recognised beneath this humble exterior, qualities less brilliant and enterprising perhaps, but every whit as keen and as ambitious as his own. Nordin was the son of a poor army chaplain, who gave him an excellent education and then left him to his own resources. After taking his degree at Upsala, he was appointed Professor of Eloquence Philosophy and Theology at the little northern city of Hernösand, where he devoted his spare time to the study of history, and the first fruits of his researches was the discovery that many of the oldest and most cherished Scandinavian MSS. were clever forgeries, whereupon he became suspicious of all ancient documents. Like Hardouin, he got to believe that a very great deal of what is called classical literature was compiled by anonymous authors at a much later date, and he used frequently to disturb and startle the Gustavan Academicians by his audacious paradoxes. Like many other sceptics, however, he clung to the positive in religion, and always held that the fundamental truths of revealed religion were necessarily above and beyond all dispute. He could not conceive a Church without dogmas. He was no friend of Luther's, and thought that the Reformation in Sweden, as elsewhere, had gone much too far. His theological standpoint was, in fact, that of an English High Churchman, while Wallqvist was broad. In politics he was a royalist from pure conviction. A strong monarchy was his political ideal. To him a Parliament seemed little better than a mob. It was to the King alone that he looked for good government. In 1782 the name and fame of this obscure country schoolmaster reached the ears of the King, who summoned him to the capital, and half an hour's private conversation convinced Gustavus that Nordin's proper place was by his side. He employed him, however, quite differently to Wallqvist. While the bishop took his seat at the Council Board and publicly defended the royal measures, his unpretentious colleague was the King's private adviser on both political and religious matters and his suggestions were acted upon in nine cases out of ten. Both Wallqvist and Nordin were what the Opposition called " the willing tools of despotism," and it was in no small measure owing to their co-operation that Gustavus triumphed over the Nobility in the deadly struggle of 1788–89. But the methods of the two men were as diverse as their characters. Wallqvist was always for storming the enemy's position, Nordin preferred stealthily undermining it. And yet the hostility of the quiet prebend was sterner and more thorough than the hostility of the dashing prelate. Wallqvist, fighting man as he was, always treated and negotiated up to the very last moment, whereas, when once Nordin had made up his mind to fight, he was deaf to all concession and compromise.[1]  It was due almost entirely to Wallqvist and Nordin that the scandalous abuses of the Swedish

---

[1] The favourite Armfelt was once asked which he thought was the most loyal of the two, Wallqvist or Nordin. "Well," replied he, "if his Majesty ordered Nordin to set Stockholm on fire, he would obey at once and hold his tongue, however loudly folks might shriek. Wallqvist, too, would obey such an order with equal alacrity, but if there was any row about it, he would shriek his loudest also, and even help to put out the flames."

Church were reformed, and an end put to the simony which had disgraced Schröderheim's administration.

Meanwhile the state of Europe had become such as no Swedish statesman could regard with indifference. The death of Frederick the Great (August 1786) had completely upset the equilibrium of Continental politics. He left behind him, indeed, a compact and prosperous state, an overflowing treasury, and an army of 150,000 men ; but this splendid heritage was utterly thrown away upon his successor, Frederick William II. That sensual and superstitious prince, the natural prey of sycophants and harlots, seemed bent upon undoing in a moment the work which three generations of laborious princes had barely accomplished. The treasures amassed by his predecessor were speedily dissipated in useless wars and shameful prodigalities, while the vacillating and pettyfogging policy of the new Government soon made the Court of Berlin the laughing-stock of Europe. At first, however, the prestige of Prussia enabled the new King at the very outset to gain an important political triumph. In 1786 the deposition of the Stadholder, William V., Prince of Orange, by the Dutch popular party for alleged maladministration had been the signal for a civil war in the Netherlands. Frederick William II. espoused the cause of the Stadholder, and demanded instant satisfaction from the States. Holland, relying on the support of France, with whom she was connected by a whole catena of treaties, rejected the demands of the King of Prussia and war began. But the Court of Versailles looked on with the most supreme indifference while a Prussian army in 1787 overran Holland and reinstated the Stadholder at the Hague. The supineness of France on this occasion was only explicable on the assumption of her utter exhaustion, and so the other European Powers explained it. " France ! " cried the Emperor

Joseph, "is about to fall, and it is doubtful whether she will ever rise again." France, therefore, was regarded as a negligeable quantity, and Catherine II. considered the time to have arrived for the accomplishment of her favourite project, the partition of the Ottoman Empire. For the last four years Potemkin, with feverish haste, had been building fleets, fortresses, dockyards, and arsenals in Southern Russia, and converting the whole Crimea into a basis for offensive operations against Turkey; and in the beginning of 1787, Catherine, surrounded by a brilliant court, and with all the Foreign Ministers in her train, quitted her capital for the shores of the Black Sea to inspect the labours of her mighty satrap. Her journey resembled a triumphant progress. Tartars, Calmucks, Khirgiz, and Circassians assembled in their thousands to do homage to "the great mother." Palaces combining the gorgeousness of barbarism with the luxury of civilisation awaited her at every halting-place. Brand new cities sprang up in a single night along the line of route. At Kaniev, her former lover, King Stanislaus of Poland, at Kaimki, her present admirer, the Emperor Joseph, swelled her suite. The quays of Kherson, the harbour of Sebastopol, and the magnificent fleet that rode upon its waters, filled the foreign guests with amazement. Potemkin received a perfect ovation. It was difficult to believe that a single man could have done so much in so short a time. That Catherine was bent upon war there could be no doubt, though, as she herself expressed it, she had as yet only one foot in the stirrup. It was her object to make the world believe that her trip to the south was a mere picnic of princes and statesmen. But nobody was deceived, and the Ministers of the hostile Powers lost no time in warning the Porte. The French Ambassador, Segur, advised the Turks to strengthen Ochakov and concentrate

an army of 150,000 on the Danube.   But the Turks needed
little prompting.   They knew that so long as Russia held
the Crimea, the Ottoman Empire was "like a house with
open doors   The intrigues of the Russian consuls in
Moldavia were also no secret, and the meeting of Catherine
and Joseph at Kherson pointed ominously to a contemplated
partition of Turkey between them.   So the Divan anticipated an invasion by throwing the Russian Ambassador,
Bulgakov, into the Seven Towers,[1] and issuing a manifesto
to the Powers demanding the restitution of the Crimea, and
declaring the expulsion of the Russian consuls from Jassy,
Bucharest, and Alexandria.   Catherine was completely taken
by surprise.   But though she wept for vexation in private,
to the world at large she was contemptuously confident.
Yet her difficulties, in reality, were overwhelming.   Neither
her fleets nor her armies were quite ready, and her over-
worked generalissimo, Potemkin, collapsed altogether.   For
weeks he sat still with folded arms, and when a storm in
the Black Sea suddenly destroyed his fleet, his disorder
took the form of religious monomania.   When the Empress
commanded him to fight, he tearfully exhorted her to put
her trust in God and announced his intention of retiring
into a monastery.   Suvarov's brilliant repulse of the advancing Turks at Kinburn somewhat revived the fainting
giant, however, and in the spring of 1788 his fleet destroyed a Turkish squadron off Ochakov, and proceeded
to invest that fortress.   But for the next six months the
Turkish Kapudan-Pasha held the whole Russian army at
bay behind the walls of Ochakov; and although Austria
had declared war against the Porte simultaneously with
Russia, more than twelve months passed before a single
Austrian soldier could cross the Danube.   Nor was this

---

[1] The usual mode of declaring war in those days.   Bulgakov employed his
two and a half years' confinement in translating into Russian twenty-seven
volumes of the Abbé de la Poste's *Voyages Français*.

all.   Russia's difficulties became, of course, the opportunities of her enemies, and she had an enemy in almost
every European Power.   France and Spain raised the
question whether Russian warships had any right in the
Mediterranean ; Poland began to assume a tone of independence; and England, Prussia, and Holland entered into
a defensive alliance, which was clearly directed against the
Tsarina.

And if the Western Powers had one reason to be jealous,
Sweden had twenty reasons to be seriously alarmed at the
progress of Russia.   If Catherine emerged victorious from
the Turkish war, Sweden would be lost.   Gustavus was
well aware that his government existed only on suffer-
ance.   The treaties of Nyslott and Åbo gave Russia the
right of interference in Sweden's domestic affairs.   The
treaty of Copenhagen expressly bound Denmark and Russia
to overthrow the Constitution of 1772 at the very first
opportunity.   With the example of Poland before him, it was
plain to the King of Sweden that only a well-timed attack
upon his powerful neighbour, when she could be taken at a
disadvantage, could free him from the diplomatic meshes
in which he was involved.   It was equally plain to him
that he could never expect a more favourable opportunity.
The north-western frontiers of Russia lay open before him.
So little did Catherine anticipate a rupture with Sweden,
that she had withdrawn her troops to the south, except
an inadequate garrison of 6000 men in St. Petersburg.
Gustavus's mind was made up.   He resolved to attack
Russia at once, and surprise the Empress in her very
capital.

It was with the speed and secrecy of a conspiracy that
Gustavus pushed on his warlike preparations.   Toll alone
was privy to his master's designs, though both Wallqvist
ᵃnd Nordin suspected them.   All the machinery of diplo-

WAR AND TREASON                13

macy was set in motion to draw into his plans every European Power hostile to Russia. Secret negotiations were
entered into with the Courts of London, Paris, Berlin,
Madrid, Warsaw, and Constantinople simultaneously. The
King composed his own despatches to his representatives
abroad, and opened with his own hand those he received
from them. The result of all these negotiations was confidentially communicated to Toll and Ruuth at a series of
cabinet councils held during the earlier part of 1788, at
which they were the only persons present. At the very
first of these conferences the King gave his reasons for
assisting Turkey against Russia. As France, he said,
was no longer to be counted upon as a useful ally, while
Russia was clearly aiming at a supremacy in the North
which meant the absorption of all her neighbours, it behoved
Sweden to look elsewhere for support. He had therefore
sounded the Ottoman Porte, and found it willing to pay
Sweden an annual subsidy of 1,000,000 piastres for the
next ten years. He further represented that the Porte
had already claimed the fulfilment of the treaty which had
existed between Sweden and Turkey ever since 1739, by
which each Power engaged to assist the other in case either
of them were attacked by Russia. In reply, Toll declared
that it was impossible to commence, still less carry on, a
war with the scanty funds actually in hand. Absolutely
nothing could be done, he opined, till the expenses of such
a costly undertaking had at least been guaranteed by a
definite treaty. Ruuth, also consulted, and well aware of
the unsatisfactory state of the finances, assumed, as a matter
of course, that his Majesty would undertake nothing till he
was not only perfectly sure of obtaining the money for it,
but actually had a part of it in hand ; whereupon the King
replied that all his calculations were based upon the cer-
tainty of obtaining the necessary subsidies from foreign

Powers. Then, but not till then, both Ministers agreed that a war was desirable.[1]

The army and the commissariat had been left entirely to Toll, and at the first conference he reported that the whole army would be perfectly ready to take the field early in spring at the cost of about £3800 a day. At a subsequent conference, Toll, at the royal command, drew up a plan of campaign which the King at once adopted. It was audaciously simple. Military critics, both Russian and Swedish, agree that, with a fair trial, its success must have been instantaneous and decisive. Assuming the Swedish fleet to be strong enough to defeat and blockade the Russian Baltic squadron, Toll proposed to land 20,000 men at Oranienbaum, eighteen miles from St. Petersburg, and make a sudden dash on the Russian capital, which, in the panic and confusion thence ensuing, could either be taken by a *coup-de-main* or bombarded into a capitulation. Cronstadt was to be treated in the same fashion, while a detached corps, starting simultaneously from Savolax in Northern Finland, was to unite with the main army at St. Petersburg. "*If*," concluded Toll significantly, "if England preserves a strict neutrality, . . . if Denmark does not suddenly turn round and attack us ; and *if* Prussia regards with indifference the reconquest of Livonia by Sweden, then the enterprise against Russia seems pretty certain of success." This array of "*ifs*" clearly shows that Toll, though in favour of war, feared that the King was going too fast, and would have stopped him if he could. At a subsequent conference Gustavus pressed for the commencement of the war in May, but Toll objected that he could not collect sufficient forage by then. The King accused him of inventing obstacles, and insisted on the

---

[1] Compare Toll's Memoirs and Geijer, *Gustav. Papp.* There can be no doubt that the King misled and deceived both Ministers on the question of subsidies.

danger of a postponement ; but Toll was immovable, so the
rupture was finally put off till July.

So well was the secret kept, that every one felt quite
sure of peace long after war had actually been decided
upon.[1] Towards the end of May, however, sinister rumours
began to circulate. Russian troops were said to be massing
in Finland, and the Swedish frontier was insecure. At
first there was a general panic, but the firm and confident
tone of the Government and its vigorous defence measures
speedily restored confidence. The military preparations
were pushed on with a speed and energy which astonished
the Foreign Ministers and confounded the King's enemies.
The dockyards were open from daybreak to sunset. The
King, who visited the men two or three times a day, was
everywhere received with enthusiasm. He seemed to be
in the best of humours, and was frequently heard to say,
"If I am driven to defend my realm, I'll show the world
that I'm man enough to defend it well." In April a military
envoy was sent, with an ostentatious affectation of the utmost
secrecy, to St. Petersburg, to demand a categorical explanation of the Russian armaments. He returned to Stockholm
with the most pacific assurances. The anxiety on the part
of the Empress to avoid a rupture was more than Gustavus
had bargained for, and embarrassed him considerably ; but
he had now gone too far to retreat. The equipment of
the fleet was pushed hastily on, and in the beginning of
June twelve liners, six frigates, and a host of smaller
vessels were ready to put to sea. The Duke of Sudermania had already been declared High Admiral, with two

[1] Nordin tells us, however, that the King sent for him, and had a long conversation with him as to the expediency of war in general, when Nordin said,
amongst other things, that war, and the misfortunes attending it, were often
a sort of moral tonic to a nation at large, and "that all radical improvements
in national character take place during the severest wars." These reflections
had a great effect upon the King.

gallant and experienced seamen as his Vice-Admirals,
Wrangel and Clas Wachtmeister.    On the 29th the King
informed the Senate that Russia was mobilising 200,000
men on the shores of the Baltic, and that he could no
longer answer for the Empress's good intentions.    The
Senate, deceived by these false tidings, unanimously advised
his Majesty to take the most vigorous defensive measures
and meet force by force.    On Midsummer Day, 1788 (the
anniversary of the day on which Gustavus Adolphus, 150
years before, had landed on German soil to take part in the
Thirty Years' War), Gustavus III. embarked for Finland,
and arrived at Helsingfors, the capital, on July 2, 1788.

The host which now quitted Sweden was superior in
numbers and equipment to any host which Sweden had put
in the field since the Thirty Years' War.    Nothing short
of a miracle seemed able to save the Russian capital.    For
the first time in her life Catherine II. was completely taken
by surprise.    Though repeatedly warned of the designs
of her restless neighbour, she had always ridiculed them.
" Do you really think this madman will attack me ? " she
asked her private secretary, Khrapovitsky,[1] incredulously.
But intercepted despatches from Poland suddenly opened
the eyes of the Empress to her danger, and almost simultaneously a note from Gustavus himself fell upon the Court
of St. Petersburg like a bombshell.    Never since the foundation of the Empire had a Russian monarch received such
an insolent and dictatorial missive.    The French Ambassador at St. Petersburg declared that the Padishah himself
would not have dared to address such language to the
meanest of his Pashas.    If Gustavus had just won six
pitched battles, he could not have offered Catherine peace
on more humiliating terms ; he demanded the cession of
Carelia and Livonia to Sweden, the restoration of the

---

[1] Khrapovitsky, *Dnevnik.*

Crimea to Turkey, and the instant disbandment of the Russian forces. Catherine was beside herself with rage. She wept and swore in turns. She reviled Gustavus as only a voluble lady of choleric temperament and a perfect command of the Bilingsgate of three languages can revile those who have offended her. But though she lost her temper, she never lost her head. Her courage rose with her difficulties, and while her trembling court hourly expected the bombardment of the capital, she vigorously set about defending it. To those who urged flight she haughtily replied that she would show the King of Sweden what a high-spirited woman at the head of a devoted people could do with even the fag-ends of a great empire. Her military preparations were pushed on with the most determined energy, and in a few weeks a new army and a new fleet stood between the Swedes and the Russian capital. Nevertheless her hasty levies would have proved but a sorry defence had she not suddenly found a potent ally where she least expected it. Just as the triumph of the Swedish arms seemed inevitable, a mutiny so extraordinary that it has no parallel in history, so scandalous that no man of honour can read the pitiful story without indignation, broke out in the Swedish camp, and ruined in an instant the hopes built upon the arduous labours of the last sixteen years.

On July 2, 1788, Gustavus arrived at Helsingfors, impatient to carry out Toll's plan of attack. Fortune seemed to favour him as she had never done before. He was at the head of a fine army of 40,000 men, only thirty-six hours' sail from the defenceless Russian capital. But, as Toll had all along insisted, it was essential to the success of such a *coup-de-main* that the Swedes should have the absolute command of the Baltic. Everything therefore now depended on the action of the fleet. On July 5, the Duke of Suder-

mania, as Lord High Admiral, hoisted his flag, and, quitting
Carlscrona, went in search of the enemy.    On the 17th,
the anniversary of the great three days' battle of Warsaw
which had laid Poland at the feet of Charles X. a century and
a half before, the rival fleets encountered each other off the
island of Hogland.    The Russian fleet, commanded by the
veteran Scotchman Greig, supported by a staff of experienced British and Norwegian naval officers, consisted of one
huge ship of 108 guns, eight seventy-fours, eight sixty-
sixes, and eight frigates, while the Swedish fleet could only
muster four seventy-fours, eleven sixties, and seven frigates ;
thus the Russians had a preponderance of nearly 250 guns,
and a favourable wind enabled them to make the most of
their superiority.    The Russian Admiral in his huge three-
decker, carrying nearly forty more guns than any single
Swedish ship, and attended by another vessel of seventy-
four guns, bore down upon the Swedish flagship and raked
her fore and aft.    Captain Balthasar Horn of the *Vasa*,
followed by the *Honour* and the *Fatherland*, at once threw
himself between the Russian and Swedish flagships, but the
same instant fell mortally wounded on the deck.    Raising
himself on one arm, the dying man cried to his second in
command, Lieutenant Liljenstraale, " Liljenstraale, I charge
you before God not to strike the flag ! "    Liljenstraale vowed
he would never do so, and was as good as his word.    The
action now became general, and raged its fiercest round the
Swedish flagship.    The Duke of Sudermania in this, his
first battle, displayed an imperturbable *sang-froid.*    The
cabin near which he stood was carried away by a cannon-
ball, his officers were struck down by his side, and his
cocked-hat was pierced through by a shot from the enemy's
rigging ; but he never moved a muscle of his face, and
remained on deck throughout the action.    During the
engagement the Swedish fleet gradually drifted close ashore,

so that the Admiral had to reconstruct his line of battle, in
consequence of which a seventy-four, the *F,...ce Gustavus*,
was surrounded and ultimately captured, a loss more
than compensated, however, by the capture of a Russian
seventy-four, which ventured too far into the Swedish
lines, and had to strike her flag. The battle, though
indecisive, was not inglorious to the Swedes. For six
hours they had sustained a contest with greatly superior
forces. The Russian loss, too, was heavier than the
Swedish. Greig, who was himself wounded, put it down
at 1000 men, while the Swedes had only 130 killed and
334 wounded. Yet the battle of Hogland was rather a
re˘erse than a triumph. It proved that the Russian fleet
was as strong, if not stronger, than the Swedish, and in
the face of this obstinate fact the original plan of campaign
fell at once and completely to the ground. The Russian
capital, therefore, could now only be approached by land.
It was not the fleet, but the army that had to strike the
decisive blow.

And if the officers of the Swedish army had only done
their duty, the chances of success of an attack by land would
have been scarcely less certain than the chances of an attack
by sea. The nearest road along the coast was indeed
long and difficult, but so feeble and defenceless were the
Russian frontier fortresses that they were prepared to
surrender at the very first summons, while the handful
of volunteers and irregulars which Count Mushkin-Pushkin
had hastily collected could not have kept back the invaders
for half an hour. But the Swedish officers had not the
slightest intention of doing their duty. On the contrary,
most of them were already secretly banded together in
a conspiracy which aimed at nothing less than stopping
by any means and at whatever cost, a war which, if
successful, would infallibly increase the royal power and

prestige, and proportionately diminish their own. Gustavus seems to have been quite unconscious of the danger
threatening him till he was warned by Toll. The moment
he arrived at Helsingfors, the quick eye of the resolute
Minister detected something amiss, and he solemnly adjured
the King to repress with the most exemplary severity the
very first symptoms of a mutiny, which he prophesied was
not very far off. Gustavus, however, paid little heed to
Toll's warnings, and ordered the Finnish division of the
army to march at once to the frontier. This command was
the signal for the first outbreak of insubordination. Major
Count Kalling, one of the ex-Cap leaders, offered his resignation the same day. Toll instantly urged the King to
make an example of an officer so forgetful of honour and
duty as to desert his colours on the very eve of action, by
cashiering him in the presence of the whole army as a
poltroon and deserter. Such counsel was as wise as it
was audacious, and, by deterring Kalling's accomplices,
would doubtless have proved efficacious and saved the
King an infinity of trouble and anguish. Unfortunately,
Gustavus was weak enough to temporise, and, instead of
ignominiously discharging Kalling on the spot, accepted
his resignation and let him go. The result was as Toll
had anticipated. No less than fifty officers imitated
Kalling's example, declaring that they could not participate
in a war commenced without the consent of the Riksdag.
In fact, it was only by the most humiliating entreaties
and concessions that the remainder of the officers were
restrained from deserting *en masse.* This first success naturally stimulated the mutineers to proceed still farther.
The general discontent grew louder and bolder every day.
Complaints were made that the soldiers were obliged to
sleep on the damp earth; that the dragoons had no provisions
and the guards no muskets; that no magazines had been

provided along the line of march; that the heavy artillery was still in port; that no bridges had been built; that the whole commissariat had hopelessly broken down, and every one united in laying the blame upon Toll, who, with superhuman energy, was struggling night and day to make good other men's blunders and reduce the chaos around him to something like system. We know now that most of these complaints were either fictitious or exaggerated, and that the hitches and flaws which really came to light were due entirely to the precipitancy with which the King, despite the earnest protests of his War Minister, had insisted on carrying out his only half-matured plans. None knew this better than Gustavus, but the unanimity with which both his friends and his foes reviled Toll suddenly suggested to him an expedient for making his peace with the army. He resolved to sacrifice his too faithful Minister to satisfy the malcontents—an expedient as fatal as it was dishonourable. So when, on July 23, the King departed with the army for the frontier, Toll was left behind. His disgrace, however, did not involve his dismissal : he was much too indispensable for that. It was as Commissary-General that he remained for another month in Finland, and when the outbreak of the Danish war demanded his presence in Sweden, he departed thither as Commander-in-Chief of the South. But he had no longer any influence over affairs, and he never saw the King's face again.

Meanwhile, young Gustaf Armfelt had had a lively engagement with the enemy at Summa, a little place just within the Russian border; whereupon, to save his nephew from being cut off, General Carl Gustaf Armfelt, who commanded the Finnish regiments, 2000 strong, crossed the boundary river, Kymmene, and encamped at Hussula, a small village six miles to the north-east of the Russian fortress of Fredrikshamn; while Admiral Ankarsvärd, with the

22

galley-flotilla,[1] having on board the Swedish regiments, 8700 strong, under Siegroth, invested the fortress from the sea side, and a combined attack was fixed for the following day.   At the Russian capital, Fredrikshamn was already given up for lost, and Levishov, the commandant, was prepared to surrender at the first summons, when a sudden outbreak of mutiny in the Swedish camp at Hussula, in which Catherine saw the hand of Providence,[2] paralysed Gustavus and saved the fortress.

It was the Finnish regiments that revolted first.   On July 31, Colonels Montgomery, Hästesko, and Von Otter appeared in the King's tent at Hussula, and, after drawing an appalling picture of the utter demoralisation and destitution of the army, bluntly declared that both officers and men were weary of the war, and that, to prevent a general mutiny, there was nothing for it but to disband the forces and call a Riksdag.   The rebels treated "the little gentleman with the red heels"[3] with scarcely disguised insolence, and Hästesko is said to have even gone the length of button-holing the King, and threatening him with the loss of his crown; while Montgomery played the bully, and swore like a trooper.[4]   So far, however, from showing the white feather, as they had anticipated, the King came out of his tent and ordered that all the disaffected regiments should be drawn up in camp; then, riding along the ranks, he addressed them in a spirited harangue, appealing to their fidelity and honour, and concluding by asking his valiant Finns point-blank whether they would follow him to battle.   "We'll follow thee to the death!" cried all

---

[1] *Skärgardsflotta*, for navigating the narrow rocky channels in the Gulf of Finland; while the *orlogsflotta*, or great fleet, kept the open sea.

[2] Khrapovitsky, *Dnevnik*.

[3] Gustavus usually wore high red-heeled shoes, made expressly for him at Paris.

[4] He admitted as much at the subsequent court-martial.

the soldiers with one voice. Gustavus then made them swear that they would follow him so long as he could wield a sword; then, turning to Hästesko and Von Otter, he said, "You hear that the soldiers are eager to fight and do their duty; do yours!" For the moment the mutineers were put to silence; but as soon as the King's back was turned they fell foul of their own troops, and cursed them for born fools. Lieutenant Gadolin shook his fist in the face of his regiment and cried, "You shall be dragged to the shambles for this, you blockheads!" Lieutenant Wilhelm vowed that he would cut down with his own hand those of his soldiers who escaped the Cossacks; while the other officers reviled the King in chorus, and kicked and cuffed their soldiers for listening to him. Fresh pressure was then brought to bear upon the King, and finally, with tears in his eyes, Gustavus reluctantly gave orders for the army to retire northwards upon Liikala; while the galley-flotilla, with the Swedish regiments on board, retreated from before Fredrikshamn to Sveaborg, and the royal headquarters were transferred to Kymmenegaard, a hamlet lying on an island in the delta of the Kymmene.

Thus the whole plan of campaign had ignominiously collapsed, and the unfortunate monarch, deserted by his allies, betrayed by his own countrymen, and exposed to the derision of his mortal enemies,[1] hid his head at Kymmenegaard in an agony of grief and shame. The handful of devoted friends whom personal affection still kept to his side regarded his cause as altogether hopeless. Yet, even in this desperate situation, Gustavus did not lose heart. That he was deeply dejected for a time, his letters to his intimate friends abundantly show; but the rapidity with

[1] Catherine II.'s delight at the discomfiture of " cet execrable Falstaff," as she now called Gustavus, knew no bounds. Khrapovitsky, *Dnevnik*.

which he recovered his usual spirits was astonishing.
Only a week after the catastrophe of Hussula, we find him
endeavouring to inspire the crestfallen Armfelt, who never
deserted him,[1] with something of his own hope and courage.
"'Tis for feeble souls to complain," he wrote ; "the strong
conceal their misfortunes in their heart of hearts while
they seek to repair them." And all the time he was busy
devising means for extricating himself from his awkward
predicament. With characteristic sagacity he divined from
the first that Russia would prefer using fraud to force,
and that her long-spun-out intrigues to further divide the
nation would give him time and opportunity to recover
his authority.

But although the King never despaired of ultimate
success, his position for the next three weeks was so
forlorn and ignominious, that even his bitterest enemies
were half inclined to pity him ; he was forced to look on
in helpless rage while his army proceeded from simple insubordination to downright treason.

The Finnish regiments had no sooner reached Liikala
than the second act of this disgraceful drama began.

Among General Armfelt's officers was one Colonel Johan
Anders Jägerhorn, a close friend and worthy disciple of
the renegade Göran Sprengtporten.[2] This Jägerhorn belonged to a clique of fanatics who had long been dreaming
of an independent Finland, and now thought they saw an
opportunity of realising their ideas, and he proposed that
the army should send a deputation to the Tsarina, both to
assure her of their pacific intentions and to get at her real
sentiments towards them. Hästesko, Von Otter, and a
Baron Klingspor, who was supposed to stand high in the

---

[1] The Empress attempted to corrupt Armfelt also, by having conveyed to
him a letter with a draft for £2000, the price of his stipulated desertion.

[2] Sprengtporten had changed his nationality, and now held a commission in
the Russian army.

royal favour, were easily won over to this proposal, little
expecting what lurked behind it; but, as none of them
was of sufficient importance to present himself to the
Empress as the plenipotentiary of the army or the nation
without making the whole affair ridiculous, it was necessary to win over the Finnish commander-in-chief, General
Armfelt, who had a high reputation for patriotism, and
whose personal authority could not fail to overcome the
scruples of the timid and wavering. Besides, Armfelt's
signature at the bottom of a memorial would be the best
guarantee to the Empress of the *bona fides* of the conspirators. Old Armfelt, a brave and honest but incredibly
simple and credulous man, was easily persuaded that the
whole affair was right and proper, especially after Klingspor
(who was himself duped by Jägerhorn, and knew nothing
of the proposed separation of Finland) positively assured
him that such a patriotic step, so far from displeasing the
King, would be the best means of extricating his Majesty
from his painful and embarrassing situation. So the poor
old simpleton, who, after all, was only the commander of a
small corps of scarcely 2000 men, was actually induced to
take the unheard-of step of opening negotiations with the
enemy without previously communicating with headquarters.
A note drafted by Jägerhorn and revised by Armfelt was then
addressed to the Empress, in which, after apologising for commencing a war with the motives of which they had not been
sufficiently acquainted beforehand, the undersigned generals
and commanders begged to humbly assure her Imperial
Majesty that it was the conscientious desire of the whole
nation that eternal peace and friendship should subsist
between the two realms, which happy state of things had
only been disturbed by certain unruly heads who used the
war as a cloak for their personal designs. Passing at a
bound from crawling servility to presumptuous audacity,

the petitioners then coolly suggested that the safest guarantee for a durable peace would be the restitution by
Russia of the territory won from Sweden by the treaty
of Åbo fifty years before, and they concluded by humbly
requesting her Imperial Majesty's answer to their proposals
as soon as possible, so that they, "the representatives of
the nation," might decide whether they should lay down
their arms or take them up, to defy danger and death
on behalf of the fatherland! This remarkable document
was secretly signed at midnight on the 9th August by
Armfelt, Hästesko, Otter, Klingspor, and three other officers,
and Jägerhorn posted off with it at four o'clock the following morning. Absurdly enough, the document was written
in Swedish, the conspirators forgetting, in their haste, that
the Empress knew not a single word of that language.
The same day General Armfelt received orders from the
King to retire within the Swedish border, and recrossing
the Kymmene, pitched his camp at Anjala.

Jägerhorn reached the Russian capital on August 11,
and three days later had an audience of the Empress. It
is more than probable, though not absolutely certain, that
Catherine had no hand in the promotion of this conspiracy,
and though mightily exultant over it, she sagaciously suspected, from the first, that the power of the conspirators was
by no means equal to their goodwill, and therefore treated
their ambassador with a discreet reserve which was the reverse of flattering. It was plain to her that Jägerhorn, who
now boldly offered peace on condition that Russian and
Swedish Finland were erected into an independent state,
was exceeding his instructions, and she summoned Göran
Sprengtporten from Olonetz to St. Petersburg to throw a
little more light on the matter. Jägerhorn himself had previously communicated with Sprengtporten, and offered him,
on his own responsibility, the supreme command of the

rebel army, and Sprengtporten, after a preliminary interview with Jägerhorn, easily persuaded the Empress that
that gentleman's mission was *bona fide*. Catherine, however, was much too wary to compromise herself by an open
alliance with an unknown and possibly insignificant clique
of conspirators. While commending, therefore, the good
intentions of the " Finnish nation," she hinted that a Finnish Riksdag under Russian protection must first be held
to settle all preliminaries, and promised that a Russian
army would be in readiness to cross the border at the
first invitation, "to establish and uphold that civil and
political liberty which all good patriots wished for, or
ought to wish for." The value of the document containing these benevolent words was considerably impaired by
the fact that it was a mere unsigned draft. But that and
500 ducats was all that Jägerhorn could get, and he returned somewhat crestfallen to Anjala.

Ever since the retreat from Fredrikshamn, Gustavus,
surrounded by wavering friends and open foes, had been
practically imprisoned in his yacht, the *Amphion*, at
Kymmenegaard. On the 9th of August he first heard
of the treasonable intrigues of General Armfelt's army
from Colonel Hastfehr, the commander of the northern
brigade at Savolax, who sent the King a letter he had
received from General Hentzel, the Russian commandant
of Viborg, informing him of the conduct of the Finns,
and inviting him to follow their example. The King,
thunderstruck at this intelligence, at once sent the letters
of Hentzel and Hastfehr to General Armfelt, at the same
time demanding a full explanation. The King's letter
filled the conspirators at Anjala with consternation, and
compelled them to show their hands, for retreat was now
impossible. Accordingly, they proceeded to draw up a
declaration which is not the least extraordinary feature of

this extraordinary conspiracy. It was subscribed by General Armfelt and thirty-four officers, and set forth that the signatories were not merely soldiers but citizens; that love of their country and loyalty to their King constrained them to turn to the Empress, and inform her of the sentiments of the nation; that they considered honest Swedes much better qualified than any foreign Power to mediate between the two crowned heads; that, continuing as they had begun, and putting their whole trust and confidence in the most high God, who knew the purity of their intentions, they solemnly engaged, in the interests of their common fatherland, to stand by each other in upholding this solemn confederation; and, finally, in case her Imperial Majesty would not consent to an honourable peace, they would extort it from her by force of arms. Perhaps nothing shows so clearly the utter infatuation and imbecility of General Armfelt than that he should actually have sent his royal master this certificate of his open rebellion accompanied by a letter not merely justifying but applauding his own treasonable conduct.[1] The very day on which the Anjala declaration was signed, General Meierfelt, who was sent by the King to supersede Armfelt, arrived in the rebel camp. The conspirators received him politely, but gave him distinctly to understand that they would obey no orders which might in any way lead to hostilities. They then proceeded to draw up a formal act of confederation, which was subscribed within a week by 113 officers.

Meanwhile Jägerhorn had returned to Anjala, and the confederates was not a little disconcerted to find that he was quite empty-handed, for the ambiguous anonymous document which he brought with him naturally counted

---

[1] As if to accentuate the insult of sending such a document to the King at all, it was sent to him not by an adjutant, in the usual way, but by an itinerant peasant postman.

for nothing.  He was escorted back to camp by a company of Cossacks, and announced that Göran Sprengtporten was on the frontier, and anxious for an interview with General Armfelt.  Armfelt met the arch-traitor accordingly, but the suggestion then made by Sprengtporten, that the Russians and Finns should unite to erect Finland into an independent principality, horrified the honest but simple old Swede, and they parted in mutual dudgeon.  The confederates were now all at sixes and sevens.  Some of them wished to make their peace with the King, and repudiated the idea of dissevering Sweden from Finland, and finally a fresh declaration, signed as before by old Armfelt and his merry men, containing a garbled but rose-coloured version of Catherine's reply to Jägerhorn, was sent to the King through Lieutenant-Colonel Leijonhufvud, with the humble request that he would convene a Riksdag as the only means of mending matters.

The 20th August, the anniversary of the revolution of 1772, had now arrived, and to his friends and foes alike the situation of Gustavus seemed altogether hopeless.  "The King," wrote Armfelt at this time, "is on the brink of destruction.  All who wish him well are agreed that he has no other alternative but to cast himself into the arms of the nation and frankly admit that he has made a mistake."  Gustavus, indeed, had not the slightest power to check the progress of the mutiny or bring the mutineers to book, yet honour forbade his flying from Finland,[1] and to open negotiations with the Empress under such circumstances he rightly regarded as " an act of political suicide." His one remaining hope was that the Danes might declare war against him.  A Danish invasion would imperatively require his presence in Sweden, and therefore justify his

---

[1] " To run away from traitors," said he to Armfelt, " would be a *lâcheté* which would only increase their audacity."

departure from Finland, and he was clear-sighted enough
to perceive that such a contingency "would open the eyes
of the Swedes to the reality of their danger, and rally the
people round the throne." [1]    When, therefore, the news
reached him that the Danes, at the instigation of Russia,
had actually declared war against Sweden, he exclaimed,
"We are saved!" and set out at once for Stockholm,
leaving his brother Charles commander-in-chief in his
stead.    At the little seaport of Lovisa he met Leijonhufvud, the delegate of the Anjala confederates, with
General Armfelt's latest declaration.    Gustavus returned
him the document unopened, and dismissed him with the
curt message, "I do not treat with rebels!"    He already
saw his way to his ultimate triumph, and his native energy
and courage came back to him.

[1] That his friends, however, could not see so far as he did, is perhaps not
surprising.    "So far from acknowledging the wisdom of his arguments," says
Armfelt, "I thought that despair and misfortune had turned his head.    But
the event was to show that he was wiser than I."

# CHAPTER XVIII.

## THE DANISH INVASION AND THE RISING OF THE DALESMEN.

Desperate situation of Gustavus—Royalist reaction begins—Gustavus departs to raise the Dales—Description of the Dales—Gustavus at Mora—At Falun—Enthusiasm of the Dalesmen—Twenty thousand volunteers—G. Armfelt made General of the Dalesmen —Panic at Stockholm—Danger of Gothenburg—Advance of the Danes—Gustavus saves Gothenburg—Intervention of Prussia and England in his favour—The Hon. Hugh Elliot—His spirited exertions—Compels the Danes to accept an armstice—Impatience of the Dalesmen—Danes evacuate Sweden—Rage of Catherine II. at Gustavus's deliverance—Her abuse of George III. and Frederick William.

It was little better than a ragged [1] and forlorn fugitive that Gustavus returned to his capital, which he had quitted only two months before with all the pomp and circumstance of war and the full assurance of a swift and easy triumph. Never had Swedish king been in such evil case. The army was in open mutiny; the fleet was blockaded in Sveaborg; a Russian squadron occupied the Gulf of Bothnia; a combined Russo-Danish squadron swept the Cattegat; a Danish army under the Prince of Hesse had actually crossed the border and was advancing upon Gothenburg, in rank the second, in wealth the first, city in the kingdom. Confusion reigned in the capital, panic in the provinces. A perplexed Senate, a treacherous nobility, a stupefied population were

---

[1] " You may judge of my condition when I tell you that I travelled all the way from the Russian frontier to this place [Stockholm] in the same shirt."— *Gustavus to Wallqvist.*

anxiously watching every movement of a defenceless King. Peace and a Parliament was the universal cry. Even his friends and relations united in imploring him, with tears, to summon a Riksdag, as the one means of saving the realm from swift and utter destruction. But Gustavus on this point was inflexible. He saw clearly enough that a Riksdag at that moment would be the ruin of his power, and he also saw what, strangely enough, seems to have escaped the attention of every one else, that the tide of public opinion had turned again, and was beginning to run very strongly in his favour. In fact, a royalist reaction had really set in. The essentially martial and patriotic instincts of the Swedish people had revolted against the conduct of the noble officers. To receive pay for defending the Fatherland in time of peace, and to hastily quit the service with a retiring pension the moment war began ; to desert the King on the very field of battle and negotiate with the enemy instead of fighting him, seemed to the robust common-sense of the nation at large the most infamous baseness and treachery. The subtle distinctions drawn by these same officers between offensive and defensive warfare, between the obedience due to a sovereign and the obedience due to a Parliament, excited universal derision ; and when the deserters, who flocked to the capital in scores, actually began to abuse the King and talk of changing the Constitution, the popular indignation knew no bounds. The coffee-houses and wine-cellars were placarded with lampoons and squibs, fiercely denouncing the "be-periwigged gentry;" the deserting officers were hustled and hooted by the mob ; and when the news of the Confederation of Anjala reached Stockholm, it was unsafe for any one in uniform to show himself in the streets without a police escort. On the other hand, the first appearance of the King in Stockholm after his return from

Finland was the signal for an imposing popular demonstration, and the burgesses of the capital were with difficulty
restrained from harnessing themselves to his carriage. The
people were evidently with him, and to the people he determined to appeal, and first and foremost, as he himself
finely expressed it, to that portion of the people which
"had the right, by long prescription, to be the bulwark of
the realm against the Danes"—to the peasantry of the
Dales. Yet most of the King's friends were filled 'with
the utmost dismay at the step he now contemplated. "It
is impossible," wrote the shrewd Rosenstein, the Crown
Prince's Governor, "it is impossible that such a good
statesman as your Majesty can wish to invite the interference of the peasantry in the adjustment of our domestic
affairs, a peasantry, too, which has always proved, sooner
or later, such a scourge to those who would make a tool
of it." The sagacious Nordin, also, whom the King
seems to have previously consulted on the matter,
was very dubious as to the wisdom of such an experi-
ment. But though it is evident from the King's own
correspondence that he was well aware of the risk he
ran, he felt that in his desperate straits he must venture
something, and he believed himself strong enough to
control the bands that might obey his summons. So
on September 11, 1788, accompanied only by Baron Essen
and five attendants, he left the capital and hastened to
the Dales to rouse the hardy peasantry in defence of
their country, as Gustavus Vasa had done more than 250
years before.

*Dalarne*, or the Dales,[1] the name given to the basin of
the Dal rivers in Central Sweden, is a rude and rugged

---

[1] The province is very often and very erroneously called Dalecarlia (*i.e.*,
Dalemanland). We might just as well call the Highlands of Scotland
"Highlandia." The ancient name of the district was *Järnbäraland*, *i.e.*,
"iron-bearing land."

tableland extending from the Norwegian frontier right across the Peninsula, and rising higher and higher as it approaches the lofty Dövrefield.   The climate is rigorous, the soil poor and scanty, yet the Dales are the most prosperous and populous part of Sweden.   Beneath the barren soil lie treasures untold.   The hills, the valleys, the very bogs and fens abound with minerals of every description. The iron of Hedemora and the copper of Falun are still accounted the best in the world.   The silver deposits of Löfvas are inexhaustible ; amethysts and topazes are to be found everywhere, and the poorest peasant there eats his humble fare off porphyry tables.   The scenery of the Dales is wild, sombre, and majestic, and the ruggedness of the landscape, the severity of the climate, is reflected in the character of the people.   Accustomed all their lives to rigorous, unceasing labour in inhospitable regions and beneath a cheerless sky, the Dalesmen came to be the most dogged, thrifty, and self-reliant portion of the Swedish population, and learnt, while enriching their country in times of peace, to defend her in times of war.

It was to the men of the Dales, then, that Gustavus now turned in his hour of need, and to the superficial observer it might well have seemed that such a man could look for little success in such a quarter.   What sympathy, what possible point of contact could there be, it might plausibly have been urged, between this subtle and refined prince, this delicate sybarite, this master of finesse, who was nothing if not exquisite and ceremonious, and a rude and simple peasantry who looked upon the luxuries and refinements of life with suspicion and contempt, and whose primitive manners and brutal straightforwardness were proverbial ?   But, as a great critic[1] has acutely observed, Gustavus III., despite his fondness for artificial combina-

[1] Geijer, *Gustav. Papp.*

tions, was always simplicity itself in times of crisis. He knew too that the patriotism of the Dalesmen was as intense and self-sacrificing as his own, and he trusted to his natural eloquence, which had never yet failed him, to do the rest.

The little town of Mora was the first place in the Dales that he visited. There he donned the distinctive garb of the Dales, a short black jacket, grey hose, and round cap with a silver lining, and after attending divine service at the quaint little stone church with the copper roof so picturesquely situated on Lake Seljan, harangued the villagers from the self-same mound in the churchyard from which Gustavus Vasa had addressed their forbears more than 250 years before on a similar errand. His success was even more striking than the success of his great ancestor. At a subsequent general assembly of the entire male population, the magistrates expressed themselves content with the statements of the King, and declared it the bounden duty of every loyal Dalesman to stand by him in his present dire need, and spare neither life nor limb in so righteous a cause. Before separating, the assembly agreed to raise at its own expense a corps of 1200 volunteers, who were to be entirely at the King's disposal. After appealing with equal success to the men of Leksand and Great Tuna, the King, 17th September, arrived at Falun, the capital of the Dales. Here a perfect ovation awaited him. A corps of mounted volunteers met him outside the town, and escorted him through triumphal arches to the mouth of the great copper-mine, where he was received by the chief miner, Berndtsen, at the head of his staff. All the public buildings were illuminated, and the large tower directly opposite the mine bore in letters of fire the inscription: "*Ave! rex, pater, protector, civis!*" The miners, with lighted torches in their hands, formed a double row from the pit's mouth to the house where the King resided, and

during his passage through the town a salute of 128 guns
was fired.   The Municipality gave a great ball in his
honour, at which the King was accessible to every one,
and on the 20th September Gustavus descended the great
mine, and drank to the prosperity of the miners of Falun
at the bottom of it, at a greater depth than any of his
ancestors had ever descended before.   When the King
reappeared in his begrimed miner's blouse, the people,
breaking all bounds in their enthusiasm, unyoked the
horses from his carriage, and dragged it through the
town, shouting "Long live the King!"   At Falun the
King received deputations from all the other districts of
the Dales.   The number of volunteers already amounted
to 20,000 men, but want of arms and ammunition obliged
Gustavus to select for the present only 6000, whom he
divided into two brigades.   Two old Carolines, Captains
Willenkrona and Föberg, both over eighty years of age,
patriotically offered their services to drill and instruct the
raw recruits, and the peasants themselves elected their own
officers.   Antiquated muskets from Charles XII.'s days
were the only firearms with which Gustavus could provide
his raw levies, but the deft and handy Dalesmen speedily
converted them into serviceable weapons.   In the science
of shooting they required little instruction.   Most of them
were as good marksmen as they were mechanics.

The King's correspondence shows how deeply he was
touched by the devotion of the Dalesmen.   In a letter to
Ruuth, contrasting their enthusiasm with the treachery of
the army, he says : "It makes my heart bleed to think
that a few factious officers should be the sole cause of the
imminent ruin of the State."   A fortnight later he thus
writes to Armfelt : "At Marienstadt I witnessed a sight
which brought the tears to my eyes.   A band of peasants
approached my carriage and asked me how I was.   Then

they said, 'We well know that you have had great reverses. God be merciful to *us* if aught befall *you!* but God will help you in the long-run.' Such pure affection, so naïvely expressed, pierced me to the very heart, especially when I reflected that they would be quite defenceless if the enemy advanced."

Meanwhile Gustavus was pushing on his defensive preparations with unceasing vigour. His first care was to find a fit general for his peasant army, and without a moment's hesitation he fixed upon young Armfelt. The choice was in every way a happy one. Young, handsome, vivacious, with easy manners and no end of pluck, Armfelt was certainly the right man to carry the people along with him. He was also one of the few officers who could look back upon the last six weeks without a blush. Amidst the general defection of the army he had remained unalterably loyal to his King. No wonder then if "the bonny general," as the common people called him, took the hearts of the peasantry by storm. "They welcome me almost as if I were a god," he writes to his wife; "all the old peasants, men and women, begin to cry the moment I open my mouth." Armfelt, besides being raised to the rank of Brigadier-General, received such ample powers that for the next six weeks he was practically Viceroy of Central Sweden.

Meanwhile in Stockholm the greatest anxiety prevailed. The most distracting rumours filled the air. Every one looked upon the ruin of the realm as inevitable. The arrival of an insolent and irresistible army of Danes and Russians was confidently expected every moment. To men in such a panic the solitary courage and serene self-confidence of the King savoured of infatuation. In his peasant host they did not place the smallest confidence, and they argued, not unreasonably, that the Danes had only to follow the example of the Russians and use the Swedish army as an instrument to destroy the Swedish State. But what alarmed them most of all was the pressing danger of Gothenburg. " Our fate depends on Gothenburg," wrote Rosenstein to the King, "and we implore the Almighty to defend it !`. . . The destruction of Gothenburg means the ruin of half the kingdom. It will take half a century at least to repair such a loss. No conquests, however considerable, no peace, however advantageous, would make up for it."

And certainly, if Gothenburg was to be saved, not a moment was to be lost. On September 24, 12,000 Danes, under the Prince of Hesse, crossed the border, and, after surprising and capturing a small Swedish force of 1000 men at Qvistrum, advanced rapidly and unopposed through Bohuslän upon Gothenburg, occupying on its way the fortresses of Venersborg and Elfsborg. General Durietz, the commandant of Gothenburg, gave the city up for lost, openly discouraged anything like resistance as absurd, and, hastily packing up all his valuables, prepared for instant flight. The Danes were now only a day's march from the wealthy and defenceless city, and the inhabitants went to bed with the firm conviction that they would awake prisoners of war in the morning.

But help was already nigh at hand. At midnight, a strange and solitary horseman, drenched to the skin, presented himself at the gates of the town and loudly demanded admission. The timid garrison kept him waiting for nearly an hour before they ventured to raise the drawbridge ; but the stranger had no sooner passed through than a group of burgesses, who met him near the quays with lanterns and torches, recognised Gustavus. Their loud cries of " Long live the King ! " brought every one to the doors and windows of the houses, and by the time Gustavus reached the

Governor's house he was surrounded by a mixed mob, cheering vociferously, and throwing their caps into the air. Their amazement at seeing him there was not unreasonable. They fancied he was still at Carlstad, on the other side of Lake Wener, and his presence there seemed little short of a miracle. But to save the commercial capital of his kingdom, the physically frail and delicate monarch had braved almost incredible hardships, riding in forty-eight hours 250 miles, the last sixty miles of which had been an incessant gallop across country on dray-horses and farmyard hacks in the teeth of driving hailstorms.

On the following morning the King inspected the fortifications. He found the cannons full of dust, and most of them unmounted. The arsenal was in hopeless disorder. Gustavus at once dismissed General Durietz from his post of Governor, and appointed in his stead General Count Sparre, a veteran of seventy, renowned for his exploits under Marshal Saxe and Prince Eugene. All the defensive preparations now took quite another complexion. Fresh earthworks were thrown up; the ramparts were planted with fresh cannon; a corps of 1200 volunteers was raised from among the citizens, and the East Indian merchants gave up their splendid horses to the artillery. The dragoons, the lifeguards, the local militia, and the first companies of the Dalesmen kept pouring in day after day, so that in less than a week the King had a garrison of 7000 men at his disposal. The morale of the townsmen was excellent. Since Gustavus's arrival every trace of fear and irresolution had disappeared. In his speech to the Municipality, he described in the liveliest colours how the honour and safety of the realm depended on the success with which Gothenburg might sustain a siege, but, at the same time, did not disguise from the citizens any of the horrors of war. The burgesses replied with spirit that they were ready to suffer a bombardment rather than surrender at discretion; whereupon all the bullion in the Bank was buried, the non-combatant part of the population was sent away, the garrison was mustered by the King personally, and every preparation made for facing the enemy. A few days later, General Haxthausen with two trumpeters was sent by the Prince of Hesse to summon the city to surrender. He was led blindfold to the Governor's house, where he was much surprised to find the King of Sweden in the midst of a brilliant staff. Gustavus, with a smile, asked the bewildered officer whether he really supposed that such a city would surrender at the first summons? He was then shown all round the place, and the last thing he saw as he passed through the Swedish lines was the burning of the new bridge over the Göta, whereby the Danes were completely cut off from the city.

But although Gothenburg was saved, the position of Gustavus, if not desperate, was still highly critical. The Danish forces lay at the gates, and he had only undisciplined levies to oppose to them. The gentry of South Sweden, so far from hastening to his assistance, maintained an attitude of suspicious reserve. Fortunately he was no longer acting alone. He had found friends where he least expected them. England and Prussia, both alarmed at the ambition of Russia, had warmly approved and secretly encouraged Gustavus's warlike diversion; and when Russia had retaliated by inducing Denmark to invade Sweden under the terms of the Treaty of Copenhagen, the neutral Powers also felt bound to interfere on behalf of the King of Sweden, who was really doing their work in the north. They were not disposed, 'tis true, to go the length of an actual war with Russia; but they were quite determined that Sweden should not be sacrificed. The initiative was

taken by the Hon. Hugh Elliot, the British Minister at
Copenhagen, a man of peculiar but very decided abilities.
An eminently martial temperament seemed to have cut him
out for a soldier; but circumstances had made him a diplomatist, and, at an age when ordinary young men have
only begun to think of a profession, he was already at the
head of his.[1] Elliot had received only very general instructions to prevent by every means in his power a
change in the relative position of the Northern Powers,
coupled with secret information from his colleague, Mr.
Ewart of Berlin, that a Prussian army of 16,000 would
invade Holstein the moment the Danes crossed the Swedish
frontier, but this was quite enough for him to act upon.
A two hours' interview with the Danish Premier, Bernstorff,[2] convinced him that ordinary diplomatic methods were
useless here; so, under the pretext of drinking the waters
of Medevi,[3] he crossed over to Sweden, and, after tracking
Gustavus from place to place for eleven days, caught him
at last at Carlstad on his way to Gothenburg. The first
interview between the Swedish monarch and the English
diplomatist was characteristic of both. "You find me," cried
Gustavus, "like James II. when he was obliged to fly his
kingdom and abandon his crown. I am about to fall a
victim to the ambition of Russia, the treachery of Denmark,
and the factiousness of my own nobility." " Sir," replied
Elliot, "lend me your crown, and I will restore it to you
with all its lustre." In reality, however, Gustavus's position was now so much improved that he could afford to
make merry at his own expense. Overwhelmed as he was
with affairs, he still found time for a little relaxation, and

---

[1] For the history of Elliot's mission, see "Memoirs of the Right Hon. Hugh
Elliot," by the Countess of Minto; and Ahnfelt's *Svenska Hofvets . . lif*,
vol. iv.

[2] Khrapovitsky's *Dnevnik*, September 23, 1788.

[3] Toll to the King in Del. I. of *Grefve J. C. Töll*.

it was in the perusal of the "Thousand and One Nights"[1] that he forgot for a time "the violence of the Scythians and the intrigues of the Cimbri," as he humorously styled the Russians and the Danes. "I resemble the princess in the fairy tale," he wrote to Armfelt, "who encounters all sorts of adventures with nothing but a smock and a casket of diamonds, while England and Prussia are the beneficent magicians who suddenly swoop down from the clouds to rescue her." Yet the intervention of these "beneficent magicians" was almost as embarrassing as it was welcome. By accepting the mediation of England he ran the risk of offending his old ally France, who had also offered to intervene on his behalf, while to accept the good offices of France was tantamount to rejecting the advances of England and Prussia. "I scarcely know," he writes to Armfelt, "which saint I ought to invoke, but I really believe that St. George will prove the most efficacious." And for St. George Gustavus ultimately decided, and placed himself unreservedly in the hands of Mr. Elliot. It was arranged between them that while the King went on his way to Gothenburg, the English Minister should proceed to the headquarters of the Prince of Hesse and open negotiations for the withdrawal of the Danish troops from Sweden.

Adventurous, indeed, was the quest upon which the

---

[1] That the King could read such a book at such a time was more than his Court and kinsmen could understand. "Cela m'a paru si comique," wrote his sister-in-law, "que lorsque on a les intérêts de l'état à conduire de s'enfoncer à Carlstad et lire ' *Les mille et une nuits,*' que j'en ai ri comme une folle." The King himself, in sending for the book, admits "que ce sont de singulières lectures pour un homme occupé d'affaires aussi serieuses, mais [he adds with much force] ce sont justement celles qui me font plaisir et qu'il me faut quelquefois." Indeed, fairy-tale books seem to have been the favourite reading of statesmen in difficulties just then. Madame Du Deffand tells us that the Duc de Choiseul, after his disgrace, "se fait lire des contes de fées toute la journée." She adds, "C'est une lecture a laquelle nous nous sommes tous mis; nous la trouvons aussi vraisemblable que l'histoire moderne."

English diplomatist had departed. Without a guinea in his pocket to clench his arguments, without a grenadier at his back to enforce his threats, he proposed to throw himself in the way of an irresistibly advancing army and compel a singularly ambitious prince to relinquish his newly won conquests on the very eve of victory. But where success seemed impossible, Elliot nevertheless succeeded, and, after incredible difficulties and a continual running to and fro, he extorted from the Prince of Hesse an armistice for a week, which was ultimately prolonged for a fortnight. But the armistice was no sooner drawing to a close than fresh difficulties arose. It was now not Denmark, but Sweden that required holding back, for the last fortnight had wrought such a beneficial change in Gustavus's affairs that he was now as desirous of war as before he had been desirous of peace. The Dalesmen were all eager for fighting, and Armfelt was every moment in " deadly fear " lest they should break the truce. " They are like raving madmen," he wrote to the King, " and regard *nous autres* as poltroons—the natural result of their ignorance of diplomacy." These representations from his fiery lieutenant were not without their effect upon the King. On October 24 he sent a sharp and sarcastic note to the Prince of Hesse, which was obviously meant to provoke a rupture. Every day the situation became more strained, and towards the end of October a rupture seemed inevitable. But Elliot again intervened decisively on behalf of peace. The Danes, who, since the capture of their transports by a Swedish squadron, were in a deplorable condition, readily listened to him, and a most spirited appeal by Elliot to Gustavus's sense of honour at last brought the Swedish monarch to more moderate counsels. On November 6 the final convention for the evacuation of Sweden was drawn up by Mr. Elliot at Uddevalla, the headquarters of the Prince of Hesse, and a fortnight later not a single Danish soldier remained on Swedish soil.

It was with pardonable pride that the English Minister looked back upon the result of his exertions.  " Six weeks after my arrival in Sweden," he writes, " a victorious army of 12,000 men, animated by the presence of their prince, were checked in their progress by my single efforts, and induced to evacuate the Swedish territories. . . . Perhaps in the annals of history there is not to be found a more striking testimony of deference paid by a foreign prince to a king of England than that the Prince Royal of Denmark [1] manifested on this trying occasion."  There can be no doubt that Elliot's prompt and decided intervention turned the scale in Sweden's favour at a most critical point of her history ; but, on the other hand, but for the raising of the Dales by the King and his forced march on Gothenburg, that city must have been captured by the Danes without a blow, in which case nothing could have stopped the advance of the Prince of Hesse on Stockholm, where the foreign ambassadors might, perhaps, have persuaded him to offer terms of peace, but certainly never could have compelled him to accept an armistice.  On finally parting with Elliot, the King warmly embraced him, pressed upon the English Minister a portrait of himself richly set with brilliants, and warmly eulogised him in an autograph letter to George III.

---

[1] The Danish Crown Prince was a volunteer in the Prince of Hesse's army. There can be no doubt, however, that Elliot sometimes exaggerates both his own exploits and the King's difficulties.  Thus, describing his first interview with Gustavus, he says : " I found his carriage ready to convey him to a place of greater safety, without generals, without troops . . . he was devoid of every means of defence."  It was not to " a place of greater safety," but to the relief of Gothenburg that the King was hastening, and he had no time to take with him the 6000 Dalesmen already at his disposal.  Lady Minto, too, is incorrect in saying that it was "by Mr. Elliot's advice that the King of Sweden resolved to throw himself into Gothenburg."  The relief of Gothenburg had from the first been Gustavus's object.

" In justice to Mr. Elliot," he wrote on this occasion, "I must say that no one could have shown more activity and zeal than he did. . . . He served me as he might have served your Majesty, that is to say, with all the loyalty and firmness of a true-born Englishman."

But though the prompt intervention of England and Prussia saved Sweden, it all but lit the flames of a European war. Catherine II., who had given up Gustavus for lost, was naturally furious at seeing her prey escape her. When the Anglo-Prussian mediation was first offered to her, she cried derisively, "I like their dictatorial tone!"— "Such conduct amongst honest folk is called villainy,"[1] was her comment on Prussia's threatened invasion of Holstein. "As for that d——d Falstaff," as she pleasantly dubbed Gustavus, "he is nothing better than a scoundrel and a poltroon, unworthy of the place he occupies . . . and he [deserves to be] exposed to the derision of Europe." Yet, almost in the same breath, she expressed her admiration of the skill with which he contrived to make a bad case look like a good one; admitted that he knew how to deceive the unwary, and declared that he would not be satisfied till he had set all Europe by the ears. For the "brothers Gegu,"[2] as she nicknamed George III. and Frederick William I., she could not sufficiently express her contempt, and their "absurdities" and "impertinences" were the subjects of her most bitter gibes. Elliot's intervention she called "putting a dagger to Denmark's throat;" and, in the first moment of her wrath, she seemed prepared to risk a war with England, Prussia, and Holland rather than lose her

---

[1] Khrapovitsky.

[2] In her sovereign contempt for George III. and Frederick William of Prussia, Catherine did not even consider them worthy of separate nicknames, but lumped them together under the *sobriquet* of Gegu, *i.e.*, the first syllable of George and the first syllable of Guillaume. Sometimes she made use of the compound epithet Gegu-Falstaff, to include all three of her enemies. George III. she called " *Notre ennemi le plus acharné.*"—*Khrapovitsky.*

hold upon Sweden. "We shall have another war," she said to her private secretary, "circumstances compel us; but the King of Prussia shall be despoiled of all his acquisitions."[1] The Court of Berlin was officially informed that the invasion of Holstein would be regarded by Russia as a *casus belli*, and the suggestion of the French Foreign Minister, Montmorin, to *déjouer* the Western Powers by a Franco-Russian alliance was eagerly listened to. But her wrath exhaled in words after all. Circumstances were against her. France, when the decisive moment came, wouldn't fight, the Russian host was still kept at bay beneath the walls of Ochakov, and not an Austrian soldier had yet crossed the Danube to assist her. Even Poland, instigated by the Prussian and Swedish Ministers, had assumed a dictatorial tone, reformed her Constitution, and demanded the withdrawal of the Russian troops from her territories. Catherine's hands, therefore, were full enough already; and it was even doubtful whether she would be able to make head against her difficulties. So she sheathed her sword, so far as Prussia was concerned, and postponed her vengeance for a more befitting opportunity.

[1] Khrapovitsky. Compare her correspondence with Grimm, *Imp. Russ. Obshch. . . . Sb.* 23.

# CHAPTER XIX.

## THE COUP D'ÉTAT OF 1789 AND THE ACT OF UNITY AND SECURITY.

A Riksdag summoned—Hostility of the first Estate and enthusiastic
loyalty of the three lower Estates—Popular indignation against
the Nobility—The four Talmen—The King's secret agents—
Preparations on both sides—Opening of the Riksdag—The
speech from the throne—The King demands a secret committee
of ways and means—Obstructive tactics of the Nobility—They insult their Marshal—Violent scenes in the Riddarhus—The King's
interview with Wallqvist—He resolves to humble the Nobles—
Anxiety of the King's friends—The King addresses the Estates in
Congress—His vigorous phillipic against the Nobility—The first
Estate banished from the Rikssaal—The Nobility refuses to
apologise to their Marshal as the King commands—Gustavus
lays before the Ofrälse Estates an Act of National Unity and
Security, which practically restores absolutism in Sweden—Dismay
of the lower Estates—Gustavus arrests the leaders of the Nobility
—The Act of Security proposed to the Estates in Congress—
Adopted by the three lower Estates — Adlerbeth's touching
appeal to the King—Obstinate obstruction of the Nobles—The
question of subsidies—Difficulty in passing them—The King
forces the Upper House to adopt them by presiding there in person
—Close of the Riksdag—Speech from the throne.

AND now at last, the Danes disposed of, Gustavus had his
hands free to set his house in order. His first step was
to convoke a Riksdag. So long as the temper of the
nation was uncertain, so long as a Riksdag might afford
Sweden's foreign foes an opportunity of interfering in her
domestic affairs, the King had resolutely shut his ears
against the chorus of timid counsellors who had implored
him again and again to summon the Estates. But now

that he was sure of his people, he hesitated no longer, and on December 8, 1788, a royal proclamation, issued from Gothenburg, invited the Estates of the realm to assemble at Stockholm on the 26th January following.

A Riksdag, indeed, was absolutely indispensable. It was not so·much that the King by this time was completely at the end of his material resources and had nothing to expect from any of his allies, but, more than that, the events of the last three months had convinced him that the existing Constitution was absolutely worthless as an instrument of Government. There was not an abuse or an anomaly which could not find a shelter beneath its ambiguous provisions. It encouraged subjects to rebel against their sovereign ; it justified the mutiny of officers on the very field of battle. On the other hand, it hampered the executive at every step, and made freedom of action absolutely impossible when most imperative. The safety, nay, the very independence [1] of Sweden depended upon its repeal or abolition, and there can be little doubt that Gustavus had now deliberately determined to do away with it. But he clearly foresaw that this could not be done without a life and death struggle with the First Estate, or, in other words, with the whole of the nobility and gentry of Sweden. For such a phenomenon as the

---

[1] " It was the dominating political principle˜of those days," says the eminent Russian historian Soloviev, " for every great Power to endeavour to maintain in every neighbouring Power such a form of government as would enfeeble her the most, and thus make her less dangerous to her neighbours. Thus the neighbours of Poland had long made it a standing article in their conventions to maintain the supremacy of the aristocratic democracy in Poland ; thus, too, Russia, Prussia, and Denmark had pledged each other to maintain in Sweden the Constitution of 1720." In another place he candidly admits that this same "aristocratic democracy" had enfeebled Sweden ever since 1720, and that its abolition by Gustavus III. "was naturally anything but pleasing to the enthusiasts at St. Petersburg." Soloviev, *Istoriya padeniya Pol'shi*, p. 183 *et seq*. The Constitution of 1772 was, of course, but a modification of the Constitution of 1720, and quite as dangerous to Sweden in 1789 as ever its prototype had been in 1772.

Confederation of Anjala meant nothing less than the disaffection of the privileged classes, and the subsequent conduct of the nobility had been still more ominous.  While
the King was wandering from province to province to
rally his people against the invader ; while the burgesses
were turning out to garrison the defenceless cities at their
own expense; while the priests were stimulating the peasantry to take up arms, and the peasantry was assembling in
its thousands round the royal standard, the nobility and
gentry of Sweden stood sullenly aloof, ridiculing the patriotic
exertions of their fellow-citizens, obstructing where they
dared not openly oppose, and industriously circulating
scandalous or terrifying reports.  The technical illegalities
committed by Gustavus provided the "*patriots*" (as, with
unconscious irony, they called themselves) with a plausible
defence as well as an effective weapon ; the coming Riksdag was to be the battle-ground between the malcontents
and the monarch, and the prize to be contended for was
nothing less than the honour and safety of the nation.

On January 26, 1789, the Estates assembled at Stockholm.

From the first, the temper of the four Orders was
unmistakable.  Of the 950 gentlemen who sat in the
Riddarhus during this Riksdag, more than 700 were
*soi-disant* patriots, who defended or excused the Anjala
treason ; nay, many of those very noblemen, who, seventeen years before, had been most ardent royalists, were so
vehemently antagonistic to the King that Fersen himself
seemed moderate in comparison.  On the other hand, the
three lower Orders were heart and soul with Gustavus.
Even among the Clergy, where the Court was weakest,
the Opposition could only reckon upon sixteen deputies
out of fifty-two, while among the 112 Burgesses and the
178 Peasants, the King's enemies could be told upon the

fingers of one hand.  It was only natural, indeed, that
the Burgesses and the Peasantry should compare their
own patriotic conduct during the last three months with
the cowardice and treachery of their noble colleagues, and
such a comparison as naturally led to the reflection that
a military caste which so shamefully shirked its easy
obligations was unworthy of its inordinate privileges.
Moreover, the sincere admiration which the lower Orders
felt for the courage and patriotism of the King was
nourished by a growing belief in his inherent superiority,
and a not irrational hope that he would reward the services of his faithful commoners at the same time that
he chastised the insolence of his presumptuous nobility.
There was, indeed, a very general belief among the Ofrälse [1]
that the King was about to take his own again, and a very
strong opinion that the sooner he did so the better.  These
sentiments were very naïvely expressed in many of the
mandates or *full-makts* which the Ofrälse deputies brought
to town with them from their constituents.  Thus the
deputy from Helsingfors was instructed to vote for any
amount which the King might require for carrying on the
war ; another deputy was charged to insist upon the trial
and dismissal of the rebellious officers.  The hostility of
the Ofrälse to the nobility also expressed itself in countless
scurillous lampoons and ballads, which described the noble
officers as poltroons and the paid spies of Russia.

The last few days of January 1789 were devoted to
purely routine business and the appointment of the Presidents and other officers of the four Estates.  The King
confided the *bâton* of Marshal of the Diet to Count Carl
Emil Lewenhaupt ; the Primate, Dr. Troil, was by prescription Talman of the Estate of Clergy ; Alderman Anders
Lydberg of Stockholm wielded the mace of office in the

[1] As already explained, the technical title of the *non-noble* Estates.

Estate of Burgesses, while Olof Olsson from Ostrogothland presided over the Peasantry. All four Presidents were men of very inferior ability, and the Marshal of the Diet was next door to a fool. Many people were amazed that the King should have pitchforked such an incompetent man into such a difficult position on the eve of a political crisis. The shrewder heads suspected, however, that the choice was insidiously intended to excite discord among the gentry by leaving them without firm control.[1] That the four Presidents were meant to be mere dummies, moreover, is pretty plain from the care with which Gustavus selected his real though secret managers in all four Estates, for they were all men of exceptional energy and ability. The recently ennobled Johan Magnus Nordin, the Prebendary's brother, feared and hated by the Opposition for his unshakable loyalty and impenetrable astuteness, looked after the King's interests in the first Estate. The Peasantry were skilfully handled by their secretary, Judge Ahlman, a most determined foe of the aristocrats. The King was so sure of the Burgesses that he left them pretty much to themselves; but for the guidance of the Estate of Clergy, which Prebendary Nordin, in a secret interview with the King, had compared to ice which may be walked upon but not driven over, he reserved his incomparably ablest coadjutor, Bishop Wallqvist, who, throughout this stormy Riksdag, acted as a mediator between a justly incensed monarch and an irreconcilable nobility with a consummate tact and an imperturbable good-humour which the most painful and trying circumstances could not ruffle or disturb.

And while intrusting the management of his majorities to competent hands, the King spared no pains to keep the

---

[1] It is said that the royalist Rosenstein, soon after the Riksdag began, anxiously told the King that the Riddarhus was chaotic, and that this was largely due to the incompetence of the Marshal of the Diet, whereupon Gustavus whispered, "So much the better."—*Adlerbeth.*

rank and file in a good humour by ministering to their creature comforts. He opened and maintained clubs for all four Estates, the Estate of Peasants being particularly well provided for. Every peasant deputy on arriving in town found furnished lodgings ready for him, and eating-houses where he could get his meals gratis. Gustavus had also opened two large clubs for the nobles; but they preferred to partake of the hospitality of Baron Carl de Geer, one of the Opposition leaders, and the wealthiest peer in Sweden, who kept open house during the session for all the poorer gentry. The Opposition was managed by a committee of seven, which met every day at Frietz-sky's house.

The Riksdag was formally opened on February 21, when the King, the Court, the Senate, and all four Estates, headed by their Presidents, with the maces of office borne before them, went in state to the Cathedral, where Wall-qviśt preached a plain and soothing sermon from the text, "Eschew evil and do good, seek peace and ensue it." From the Cathedral the Estates proceeded to the Rikssaal, or Hall of Congress, where Gustavus addressed them from the throne with his usual eloquence,[1] and with a moderation and forbearance which showed how eager he was to avoid extremities. He began with a touching picture of the danger of the realm and the machinations of Sweden's foreign enemies; then, turning towards the Estate of Peasants, he thus addressed them, with the liveliest emotion: "It was reserved for you, my faithful Dannemän,[2] to give the first example of loyal devotion, and, arming yourselves of your

[1] " In such pure and noble Swedish," says one who was present, "that it was easy to recognise the founder of the Swedish Academy."

[2] This ancient word had been applied for generations to the substantial yeomanry of Sweden, and had been particularly applied by Gustavus Vasa to the Dalesmen when they rose at his appeal against the Danes. It was certainly the most flattering epithet which a Swedish king could have bestowed upon the Peasantry, and so it was understood.

own free will like your valiant forefathers, to hasten to my help and your country's rescue . . . when the irresistible voice of honour speedily compelled all the other Estates to follow so noble an example. . . . Nay, even that Estate whose peaceful hands are solely dedicated to the service of the Most High, showed that loyalty to one's country and a manful withstanding of one's country's foes go hand in hand with a true fear of God."

The orator then went on to say that peace was his dearest desire ; but the only peace he would accept was a sure, certain, and honourable peace, which could only be obtained by vigorously prosecuting the war to a successful issue. It was for that reason that he had summoned them, and they were to recollect that the fate of their country depended upon the result of their deliberations. This patriotic appeal was followed by an unmistakable note of warning not to listen to the voice of faction or obstruction, and to draw closer the bonds between King and people. " For my part," concluded the orator, " I am willing to forget all personal animosity, all that righteous displeasure which the events of the last few months might so well justify. . . . My only enemies are the enemies of my country. I am your King, but I am also your fellow-citizen, and such titles as these constrain me to sacrifice everything for the common weal."

On the following day, the King, again addressing the Estates in Congress, justified the war with Russia as necessary to the independence of Sweden ; and, after describing at some length the actual situation of European politics, and making the most of the difficulties besetting Russia, urged the Estates to at once take advantage of this favourable state of affairs, and appoint a Secret Committee of thirty members, consisting of twelve noblemen, six priests, six burgesses, and six peasants, to deliberate with him as to the ways and means of maintaining the honour, safety, and independence of the realm.[1]   For this proposition the King demanded urgency ; and the three lower Estates, loyally expeditious, at once proceeded to elect their Committee-men, of whom fifteen out of eighteen were royalists.   Nor did the dutifulness of the Ofrälse Estates stop here.   On the very first day of the session, the burger deputy, Damme, from Gothenburg, moved an address of thanks to his Majesty for saving the kingdom,[2] which was carried unanimously in the three lower Estates.

Very different was the conduct of the Nobility.   No sooner had the royal proposition been brought before the Riddarhus, than Fersen proposed that it should be laid upon the table, the technical expression for postponing its consideration indefinitely.   It was laid upon the table accordingly, whereupon Baron Carl de Geer moved that a humble petition be presented to his Majesty beseeching him to proceed summarily against the unknown and anonymous libellers of the nobility and the officers of the Swedish army, and that the other three Estates be invited to second the petition of the first Estate.   Such a motion at a time when the vast majority of the Swedish officers was so strongly suspected by the nation at large of a treasonable correspondence with the enemies of their country, that the King had been obliged to publicly denounce many of the nobility as rebels and traitors, was an imprudent blunder ; nor did De Geer's manner of presenting it improve it, for in the course of his speech he went out of his way to institute a most insulting comparison between Gustavus

---

[1] It was, in fact, a Secret Committee, the first the King had ever asked for.   Another novelty about it was the presence of the Peasant deputies.   By Article 47 of the Constitution such a Committee was to be always secret.

[2] The significance of this motion lay in this, that it justified the Russian war, and thus shut the door against the complaint of the Nobles that it had been begun illegally.

and one of the most abject of his predecessors. The
Upper House, moreover, showed a tyrannous impatience
of anything like loyalty. The few royalists who attempted
to speak were howled down, and even threatened with
expulsion ; and after a tumultuous three days' debate, in the
course of which swords were freely drawn, the Riddarhus
resolved to invite the three lower Estates to join them
in petitioning the King against the libellers of the noble
officers. As might have been expected, the lower Estates
bluntly refused to fight the battles of the gentry ; but this
rude rebuff, though it must have opened the eyes of the
Nobility to their isolation, made no change whatever in
their obstructive tactics, which were not a little furthered
by the ambiguities of the Constitution of 1772.

We have seen that the King had demanded urgency
for the business of the Secret Committee, and that the
Ofrälse committee-men had already been elected, and were
only waiting for the arrival of their noble colleagues to
consider the royal propositions. The Nobility, however,
showed no hurry in choosing their delegates ; but, on
February 6, Frietzsky, who throughout this Riksdag acted
as the protagonist of the gentry against the Court, moved
that the Secret Committee should first of all be provided
with an *instruktion*, or rules of procedure, although an
*instruktion* in such cases was both unnecessary and unusual.[1]
On the following day, however, just as Frietzsky was
about to begin the debate on his own motion, the Marshal

---

[1] Par. 47 of the Constitution of 1772 empowered the King to demand a
Secret Committee whenever he considered it expedient, but said not a word
about any *instruktion* for such committee. Par. 55 provided that committees
on the affairs of the Bank should always have *instruktions*, but such committees were not Secret Committees, like the present one. In short, the
Estates might refuse to grant the King a Secret Committee, but they had no
right to demand an *instruktion* for it. At the same time, many of the paragraphs of the Constitution being obscure or ambiguous, lent themselves to the
manipulation of skilful special pleaders.

of the Diet read a royal message to the Nobles, forbidding them to discuss the question of an *instruktion* as *ultra vires*, and charging them, instead, to elect their delegates to the Secret Committee, as their colleagues of the lower Estates had already done. The royal message raised a perfect storm of indignation. Frietzsky professed to be hurt and surprised at what had happened. Fersen declared that the Secret Committee had a perfect right to an *instruktion*, while the impetuous Engeström exhorted the House to steadfastly resist this and every other attempt at intimidation. The Marshal of the Diet, equally afraid of disobeying the King and disobliging the Nobility, would have adjourned the sitting to take his Majesty's opinion; but the House contemptuously ignored him by carrying Frietzsky's motion by a large majority. On the 9th the House met again, and the Marshal again urged the Nobles to elect their delegates to the Secret Committee; but Fersen moved, instead, that a deputation should be sent to the lower Estates inviting them also to petition for an *instruktion*. The Marshal, now thoroughly frightened at the obstinacy of the Opposition, refused to put the motion. It was against his oath, he said, which bound him to respect the prerogatives of the Crown as well as the privileges of the House.

A fearful tumult immediately arose. The majority literally howled with rage. A rush was made at the presidential chair; swords were drawn and fists were shaken at the Marshal, and he was overwhelmed with imprecations. One gentleman even went so far as to call him an infamous scoundrel and threaten him with death. Even the steadiest heads forgot themselves for the moment. Frietzsky's language was indescribable ; De Geer reviled the King with a volubility which astonished every one who heard him, while Fersen, trembling like an aspen leaf, fought his way up to the table of the Marshal and roared at him with

the full force of his lungs.[1] It was the first time in his life
that that haughty and sedate patrician had so far forgotten
himself. Finally, Fersen's motion was put and carried,
and a deputation was sent off to the lower Estates forthwith. But the lower Estates refused point-blank to consider the question of an *instruktion* for the Secret Committee,
and so the noble delegates returned empty-handed.

Two days later, Fersen, now a little calmer, and anxious,
as usual, to avoid extremities, demanded and obtained an
audience of the King, but the interview which followed did
more harm than good. Fersen found the King haughty, irritable, and suspicious, while Gustavus himself told Adlerbeth, afterwards, that the Count had had the audacity
to address him as if he (Fersen) were an independent
prince of minor rank addressing another scarcely greater
than himself. "He is the only one of my subjects," added
the King, "with whom it is not beneath my dignity to
cope." Such words, says Adlerbeth, used by a sovereign
of a subject, were of themselves a threat. The same evening Adlerbeth learnt from Nordin that the King had given
orders for the Dalesmen volunteers to march into town.
Thus the only result of Fersen's conversation with the
King was to hasten on the inevitable thunderclap.

Meanwhile, thanks to the obstruction of the Nobles, the
whole machinery of legislation had come to a standstill.

---

[1] See Tham, *Konung Gustaf. III. och Rikets Ständer vid* 1789, *ars Riksdag*. Also Fersen, *Historiska Anteckningar*, and Adlerbeth, *Anteckningar*. The latter discreetly omits all mention of this bear-garden scene, but
admits that the " tone " of the patriots was " offensive." Fersen's own account
of this *row* is absolutely comical in its naïve euphemism. " I was much
moved," he says, " to see the law transgressed and the Estate of Nobility degraded by a senseless Landmarshal, and I delivered my *speech* [*sic*] in as loud a
voice as my chest could bring forth, but with courtesy towards the Landmarshal
personally . . . for whom I had every respect " [*sic*]. Fersen's friends explain
away his menacing gestures by saying that he held a white handkerchief in his
hand, which he flourished about in his excitement.

The Ofrälse deputies had not met for several days.  They
walked about the streets with their hands in their pockets ;
perplexity and disquietude were written on every face.
In the clubs and social gatherings there was an ominous
silence about politics, a sure sign, says Wallqvist, of an
impending change.  And he was right.  The King had
determined upon action.  " There must be no more beat-
ing about the bush," he wrote to Stedingk ;[1] "we must
make straight for the goal and clear the disaffected out
of the way."  His correspondence shows, however, with
what extreme reluctance he laid down the olive branch and
took up the sword.  What decided him was a note handed
to him by the Marshal of the Diet, and attested by forty
members of the Riddarhus, in which Lewenhaupt bitterly
complained of the outrages he had suffered from his fellow-
peers, and appealed to the King for satisfaction.  Two
days after Gustavus's interview with Fersen, Wallqvist
was summoned to the palace, when the King informed
him that he intended to summon the Estates in Congress,
reproach the Nobility, in the presence of the other Orders,
for their neglect of public business and their indecent treatment of their Marshal, and endow the Ofrälse Estates with
privileges similar to those so long usurped by the Nobles.
The King further declared that he meant to make the worst
offenders apologise to the Landmarshal, and, if necessary,
would banish the whole of the first Estate from the Hall of
Congress and come to terms with the Ofrälse Estates in
their absence.

The Bishop of Wexiö was a bold man with a strong
liking for adventure, but the audacity of the royal project
fairly took his breath away.  It was nothing less than a
revolution which the King was aiming at, and the Bishop
knew very well that Gustavus had little or no military force

---

[1] See following chapter for an account of this officer.

to rely upon in case of need. Fifty light dragoons were all the regular troops in the capital; the Burgess Guard could not have stood firm for five minutes against the determined onslaught of nearly a thousand armed noblemen; while the Dalesmen, for all their good-will, were notoriously unruly, and likely, on the whole, to be rather a menace than a defence to the capital. Wallqvist therefore, with affectionate importunity, tried to turn the King from his purpose; but finding all his representations in vain, finally quitted him with a heavy heart. "I went home," he tells us, "full of anxiety for the good cause and for the King's safety. . . . Everything tended to a rupture, and the King was immovable. It seemed to me that he reckoned more upon other people's follies than upon his own resources. Excepting his incomparable personal advantages, he was destitute of everything which such a plan as his imperatively demanded." [1]

Even the dashing Armfelt was much perturbed at the turn things were taking. He had received secret and peremptory instructions to hasten to the Dales, raise there a corps of 1200 men, and quarter them at the Drottningholm Palace, so as to be ready at a moment's notice to march from thence upon the capital. He obeyed with his usual unquestioning loyalty, but he trembled at the possible consequences of the King's rashness, while the restless insubordination of his Dalesmen taxed even his courage and resource to the uttermost.

No wonder, then, if the King's most daring and devoted partisans looked forward to the 17th February, when the Estates were to meet again in Congress, with fear and trembling. Early in the morning the three Ofrälse Estates, headed by their Talmen, marched in procession to the Rikssaal, or grand hall of assembly at the palace, where the

[1] Wallqvist, *Anteckningar.*

Nobles, led, in the absence of their Marshal (who had absented himself from the House on the plea of ill-health), by Count Brahe, the senior peer of Sweden, were already assembled. Presently the King appeared, surrounded by the Senators in their purple and ermine mantles. He was in full regalia, with the crown upon his head and the silver sceptre of Gustavus Adolphus in his hand. An eye-witness has told us that his whole bearing was manly and majestic, yet wary and circumspect. His eyes sparkled and his colour was high, but there was not the slightest trace of embarrassment or hesitation in his gestures or features. He took his seat on the throne amidst the most profound silence, then, turning to the Estates, addressed them in that famous speech which critics of every school and party have unhesitatingly pronounced the unapproachable masterpiece of Swedish oratory.[1]

"Fourteen days have now elapsed," began the orator, "since I informed you from this place of the weighty reasons which made your convention necessary. I told you without reserve of all that had taken place during the last four months . . . I demanded a committee which might take all important matters into consideration. I said that time was pressing, that the enemy was arming, and that prompt measures could alone defend the realm. . . . No more than three days were necessary for appointing such a committee, and the Reverend Estate of Clergy, the Worshipful Estate of Burgesses, and the Honourable Estate of Peasants have obeyed . . . the law with the same devotion for myself and their country . . . which has animated their brethren in the provinces. But ye, my good lords and gentlemen, so far from setting an example to your colleagues of the other Estates . . . have per-

---

[1] No translation, however correct, can give any adequate idea of the energy and simplicity of this wondrous diatribe.

sisted in unnecessary debates on subjects which do not
fall within your scope . . . subjects, moreover, which the
times, our circumstances, and the condition of the country
should have made you pass over in silence, as only tending
. . . to excite uneasiness, cause delay, and thereby promote the intrigues and the interests of our enemies."

Gustavus then severely rebuked the Nobles for their
indecent conduct towards their aged Marshal (Lewenhaupt
was over seventy), and having ordered his attested complaint against them to be read aloud by one of the royal
secretaries, thus proceeded :—

"Who is there who does not here recognise once more
that old spirit of license which has so long been lurking
among us ; which has sought so diligently to turn from
me the hearts of my people ; which has misrepresented
all my doings, yes, even the most innocent, as dangerous ;
which, under the name of Liberty . . . would reinstate
that aristocratic tyranny which I thought I had crushed
at the beginning of my reign ? Who does not recognise once more those self-same persons who, during their
dominion, ruled the land with an iron sceptre ; who cannot bear to look back upon the sixteen years of my
indulgent sway ; who force me to speak a language so
alien to my nature ; and who, finally, when they find it
impossible, ye good and worthy men of the three lower
Estates, to shake your devotion to me . . . try to terrify
you with the word Absolutism—that odious word which
I so freely abjured—and would fain brand as a tyrant
him who, after being for three days the most absolute
monarch in Europe, freely renounced his power . . .
content only to put an end to anarchy and license. I
therefore declare to you from my throne, for the second
time (and I am surprised that I should have to make
such a declaration at all), that I never will accept abso-

lute power, and that if the progress of disorder should place it again in my hands, I never will retain it. I declare that I hold it the highest honour to be the champion of true freedom ; but that I consider it the first of my duties, as the head of the State, to quell and crush license, and not for an instant to suffer that they who laid presumptuous hands upon my father's crown should wrest from me the sceptre. I must not permit a mere fraction of the nation to forward the interests of our enemies by a calculated obstruction."

These last words, uttered with unusual fervour and vehemence, produced such an effect upon the Peasants that they exclaimed with one voice, " God save the King ! " But Gustavus, striking the table before him with his sceptre to enjoin silence, continued as follows :—

" For I declare before you all, that if I am not enabled, and that right speedily, to pay and clothe my army and get my fleet afloat ; I declare that if, in consequence thereof, our coasts are ravaged, Finland is devasted, and this capital is threatened, it will be no fault of mine ; no, it will be their fault who would rather welcome the Russians in Stockholm, and see a Russian ambassador dictate peace to me here, than forego their vindictive ambition . . . and who hope by means of these long delays to force upon me a dishonourable peace—a peace which you, ye good men of the three Estates, would one day reproach my memory with as an infamy, as a crime against the State, and a stigma upon the great name which I have the honour to bear. But rather let this right hand dry up and wither than sign anything which would bring dishonour on my country ! Rather let this crown, the crown of Gustavus Adolphus, be torn from my brows and broken to pieces than that I should not give it back, if not as glorious, at least as unblemished, as he left it ! And let me tell you, my

good lords and gentlemen, that you will be responsible
for it to me and your fellow-Estates if, by reason of your
dissensions and your usurpations, you waste such precious
time, or mislead your fellow-subjects by the panic terrors
you would spread abroad! I have not deserved such
treatment at your hands, my good lords ; nor could I have
imagined such treatment possible from those whom I have
hitherto in so many ways preferred before their fellow-
Estates—those faithful servants who did *not* forsake me in
the hour of need, who left their homes to a man to defend
their country and their King, while ye did nought but blame
and mock their zeal. . . . All these things I have endured
with patience so long as your unruliness did not presume
too far ; but now you compel me to speak out and declare
to you my will, which is that you give due satisfaction to
your Marshal ; that you apologise to him for what you
have done, and that you strike out from your protocols all
record of these illegal and disloyal debates. . . . You will
therefore forthwith depart from hence to the Riddarhus ;
there you will form a deputation, headed by the premier
peer of Sweden, and of this deputation, you Count Axel
von Fersen, you Baron Carl de Geer, and all the rest of
you whose names appear in the Marshal's complaint, will
form part. You will then apologise to him, as in duty
bound, for what has happened, and respectfully conduct
him back to his presidential chair, where he will cause to
be erased from your protocols all record of these irregular
proceedings. . . ."

During the course of this speech, the King had gradually
worked himself up into an extraordinary state of excitement. His eyes flashed, his colour changed, and all his
gestures expressed violent rage. Yet the 900 gentlemen
upon whom his rebukes had fallen were filled rather with
fury than with fear. Never since the foundation of the

monarchy had the Swedish nobility listened to such language from the throne. Their pride was wounded, their honour impugned, their ambition chastised, and their brethren of the lower Estates had been the willing witnesses of their deep humiliation. So intense indeed was their excitement and so manifest their wrath, that the King's friends trembled for the consequences. "Every one's feelings," says Wallqvist, "were wound up to the highest pitch. . . . No one seemed master of himself but the King, who followed the course of events with the utmost composure."

As soon as the King had finished, Fersen rose and asked for leave to speak. Gustavus bade him be silent. The Nobles, he said, were there not to answer, but to obey. Still the Count persisted, and his colleagues, taking courage from the sound of their leader's voice, began to murmur loudly ; but the King again struck the table with his sceptre, and throwing into his voice all the authority he could command, ordered the Nobility to retire at once to their own house as he had bidden them. Then followed what the anxiously observant Wallqvist [1] calls "one of those critical moments which happen only once in a lifetime "— not one of the 900 noblemen stirred from his place, but many placed their hands upon their swords, and every eye was bent on Fersen. There was a pause which seemed interminable, and then the silence was broken by the grey-haired leader of the Opposition, who, giving his hand to Count Brahe, said in a mournful voice, " Let us go ! " Slowly, very slowly, the Nobility moved towards the door. In five minutes the last gentleman had quitted the Riks-saal, and the King was left alone with the three Ofrälse

---

[1] He was Talman of the Estate of Clergy on this occasion, the Archbishop, who had some inkling of the King's plans, having absented himself on the plea of illness.

Estates. "It was," says Wallqvist, "an unusual but by no means an unpleasant sight."[1]

When the first Estate had withdrawn, the King thanked the Ofrälse Orders in the most touching terms for their devotion, which was, he said, "his sweetest reward" and his "surest comfort," and then invited them to appoint delegates to consult with him as to the granting of those privileges "which it was only right and proper that all citizens should equally enjoy." He then retired amidst loud cries of "Long live the King."

Meanwhile, the Nobility proceeded from the Rikssaal to the Riddarhus, where Count Brahe, as premier peer, took the chair. The excitement of the gentry was terrible. An incoherent and uninterrupted murmur of half-broken words filled the House, and the gestures and faces of the majority expressed mingled rage, grief, and terror.[2] Fersen felt it to be his duty to implore the House to be calm, and the impressive dignity of the aged party leader does seem to have had a salutary effect. Yet the nobles were as far from yielding as ever, for Fersen's subsequent motion, that the President should inform the King in writing that the Nobility found it impossible to obey his Majesty's gracious command to apologise to the Landmarshal, was adopted almost unanimously, and Count Brahe placed the document in the King's hands the same day.

The same afternoon the Ofrälse Estates elected their delegates to the Privilege Committee, which held its first meeting in the Velvet Chamber at the palace, the King himself being in the chair. After the Archbishop had imposed an oath of secrecy on all present, Gustavus produced and read to the meeting a so-called "Act of Unity and

---

[1] The noble Adlerbeth naturally thought differently. "It was a remarkable sight," he says, "to see this Prince, with all his prejudices in favour of birth, now surrounded by nothing but commoners."

[2] Adlerbeth, *Anteckningar.*

Security," the object of which was to substitute for the existing Constitution an almost monarchical form of government—not, indeed, an absolute despotism, for the power of the purse was expressly reserved to the Estates ; but certainly the nearest approach to it compatible with an ostensibly free Parliament.   It abolished the old constitutional partnership between the King and the Estates, and vested both the executive and legislative functions in the former absolutely.   He alone had the power to declare war, conclude peace, and contract alliances.   He alone could appoint and dismiss all public functionaries.   He could summon a Riksdag when and how he chose, and the Riksdag could only consider such matters as he chose to lay before it. At the same time, Gustavus bid high for the support of the Ofrälse Estates.   Paragraphs 2 to 4 of the Act of Security broke down the invidious distinction between. noble and non-noble, which had so long been the standing grievance of the Ofrälse Estates.   Henceforth commoners were declared eligible to nearly all the offices and dignities of the State ; the privilege of acquiring and possessing land was now, for the first time, extended to every Swede, and many of the most vexatious exemptions of the Nobility from public burdens were at the same time abolished.   But, dazzling as these bribes were, they could not shut the eyes of the delegates to the fact that they were altogether disproportionate to the concessions demanded from them in return ; and when the King had finished reading the Act of Security, every one was absolutely speechless, and the meeting separated without the delegates coming to any decision.   At a private conference on the following day, the Archbishop told the King that he dare not present such a document as the Act of Security to his Estate. All that he could do for the King was to hold his tongue, and fall ill, so as to keep out of the way.   So the Primate went home and put a thick stocking on his foot to persuade all the world that he had the gout, and his presidential mace was intrusted to Lindholm, Bishop of Linköping. The timidity of the Archbishop proved contagious. At the next meeting òf the delegates, the Talman of the Burgesses also declared that he saw no chance of getting his Estate to accept the Act of Security. Then Gustavus resolved to submit the new Constitution to the Estates in Congress, first preparing the way for it by an act of authority sufficient to overawe the refractory and persuade the lukewarm. Now, with the Nobility mutinous, the Clergy wavering, and the Burgesses and Peasants doubtful, it was the last degree of audacity to attempt to force such a Constitution upon the Riksdag; but, fortunately, at the last moment, the three lower Estates themselves suggested a way out of the difficulty, by sending a joint deputation to the King humbly petitioning him to use his royal authority and power to " set the Riksdag going again." Gustavus assured the deputation that he deplored the existing deadlock quite as much as they did, and would strive as far as in him lay " to quell the headstrong, and chastise frowardness." No sooner had the deputation quitted the palace than the King gave orders to the Burgess Guard to arrest Counts Brahe, Fersen, Horn, Barons De Geer, Pechlin, and Sterngeld, Messrs. Frietzsky and Engeström, and the other prominent leaders of the Opposition—twenty-one in all—and within a couple of hours all these persons were safely under lock and key. There was no show of resistance, no attempt at a rescue. Half Stockholm knew nothing of what was going on. The streets were almost deserted ; an ominous silence prevailed. At six o'clock in the evening, the Duke of Sudermania, who, up to the last moment, had professed himself the champion of the patriots, but now suddenly went over to the winning side, was proclaimed

military governor of Stockholm, with plenipotentiary power.
The reign of absolutism had begun.

No doubt, however expedient, however necessary, this
*coup de main* was an act of tyranny, but it is quite certain
that "the tyrant" suffered far more than the tyrannised.
If Gustavus's most bitter enemies had seen him in private
that same evening they must have pitied him.   Wallqvist,
who was summoned to the Velvet Chamber at ten o'clock
at night, found the King alone at his desk with an erased
and blotted MS. before him.   " His face was so full of
anxiety," says the Bishop, "that it excited my compassion."
The King asked him what he thought of the arrests, and
Wallqvist replied that he deeply deplored them.   Then there
was a long pause.   Presently the King spoke again, and
said that he meant to make the Estates accept the Act of
Security on the morrow.   Wallqvist emphatically declared
that it was impossible.   " I'll try, all the same," replied the
King.—" All this while," continues the Bishop, " the King
appeared so distressed . . . that I ventured to ask him what
made him so sad.   'To-morrow I must introduce my proposition with a speech,' he replied, 'and I've been trying to
jot down the heads of it, but somehow it won't come right.'
Then he bade me suggest something."   Wallqvist did so, and
the King then made a few notes, which he used next day.

Of these inward qualms and secret misgivings, however, the world knew nothing, and when Gustavus met
the Estates in Congress in the Rikssaal, on the following
morning, he was apparently as serene and self-confident as
ever.   The King's first act was to assure the 850 gentlemen who stood in a solid phalanx on the right hand of
the throne that he would be the last to hold them responsible for the misconduct of a few of their number.   He
then solemnly reinstated the Landmarshal, but immediately
afterwards accepted the timid old man's resignation, and

appointed a Vice-Landmarshal in his stead. This done, Gustavus, without more ado, introduced to the Congress the Act of Unity and Security, which he described as a measure absolutely indispensable to their common welfare, and, after making Secretary Schröderheim read it aloud, solemnly asked each of the four Estates in order whether they accepted it or not? An energetic and unanimous shout of "Yes," from the Burgesses and Peasants, completely drowning the mingled "Yes's" and "No's" of the Clergy and the dissent of a portion of the Nobility, was the immediate response. Thrice the King put the question, and thrice the Estates responded in the same way. It was all done so quickly that no one had time to protest, but, at the first pause, Count Hamilton rose with the Constitution of 1772 in his hand, and, after pointing out that paragraph 42 thereof prescribed that no new law could be adopted unless the Estates had previously discussed it, begged leave for the Nobility to deliberate upon it in their own chamber. Gustavus, however, dexterously turning against the Nobility the very weapon which they themselves had forged for his confusion during the last Riksdag, at once declared that as the Act of Security had already been adopted by three Estates out of four, no further discussion was admissible. But now a strange and touching scene occurred. The poet Adlerbeth, equally well known as a lover of freedom and as a devoted friend of the King, cut to the heart by the humiliation of his order, burst impetuously from the ranks of the Nobility, and throwing himself at the King's feet, thus addressed him :—

"A subject, sir, who has had the most precious proofs of your Majesty's favour, and acknowledges them from the bottom of a grateful heart, now ventures to raise a faltering and unpractised voice before your Majesty's throne. Most gracious King! this is neither the time nor the occasion for

me to recite my personal obligations to you, my benefactor.
The only thing that moves me now is my zeal for you as
my King and for Sweden as my country. Bear with me,
sir, if my emotion prevents me from restraining my tears!
I see before me my compeers, the nobility and gentry of
this realm, agitated by the same emotions as myself. All
of them, sir, I am sure, burn with equal zeal for your
Majesty and their country, but they are as little able as
myself to fix their thoughts at this moment upon a matter
which is to settle the fate of a whole realm, the fate of millions of men yet unborn. So weighty a matter demands the
most careful consideration. It is therefore with the deepest
reverence of a subject, it is with the warmest affection for
all my fellow-citizens of the other Estates, that I implore
your Majesty, by your goodness of heart, by your high-
mindedness, in the name of posterity, in the name of God
Himself, to vouchsafe us some little time for deliberation."[1]

Gustavus had set his face steadily against the least concession, but this sudden appeal to his affections was too
much for him. He was deeply moved, and when he had
sufficiently recovered himself to find his voice, he granted
the Nobility leave to retire to their own chamber and deliberate as they desired to do. That he considered their
assent as a mere work of supererogation, however, was
evident from the fact that, two days later, the Talmen of
the three lower Estates, without waiting for the decision
of the first Estate, signed and sealed the Act of Unity and
Security in the King's presence, thus giving their solemn
and express sanction to the new revolution.[2]

Strong in the unanimous support of the three lower

---

[1] That same evening, when Adlerbeth went up to the palace as usual, the
King warmly embraced him, and said, "Vous avez fait la plus belle perorai-
son que j'ai jamais entendu." "Eh bien!" he added, "vous voyez si je sais
rendre justice!"—*Adlerbeth*, "*Anteckningar.*"

[2] The best account of this by far is in Tham; compare also Adlerbeth,
Wallqvist, and Schröderheim.

Estates, Gustavus was now able to deal with the Nobility as he chose. It revolted his naturally gentle nature to use violence of any kind, but his rare political instinct told him that here there was no room for compromise; concession on his part would inevitably be followed by fresh encroachments on theirs. "What could I do?" he said to Adlerbeth, who, in frequent private interviews, protested, with all the warmth and frankness of an intimate friend, against the recent revolutionary acts. "What could I do? I was obliged to save myself and my family. . . . Perhaps I have committed a fault, but it is too late to alter it; I can't go back now. Perhaps, had I not done it, a time would have come for me to shed torrents of blood." Adlerbeth protested that he disapproved of all violence in politics, to which the King at once rejoined that without some violence a revolution was impossible. "And," continued he, "I shall be obliged to draw still more closely to the Ofrälse Estates if the Nobility will not give way."

But the Nobility was in no yielding mood, and their repeated humiliations had only exasperated them. They knew now that they were playing a losing game, but their combativeness was inexhaustible, and they vigorously followed up their obstructive tactics. The debates in the Upper House on the Act of Union and Security, which was peculiarly offensive to the aristocracy because of the privileges it conferred on the lower Estates, were protracted over three weeks, and the only effect of a royal message sharply commanding the gentry to pass the Act at once was to make them instantly reject it. The King, not to be beaten, then sent for the Marshal of the Diet, and, placing a pen in his hand, made him add his signature to the signatures of the three Talmen at the bottom of the Act. The Nobility retaliated by passing a special resolution that the portrait of the Marshal should not, as usual, be added to the portraits of his predecessors in office which adorned the walls of the Riddarhus.[1]

But it was on the financial questions which the Riksdag had been specially summoned to settle that the Nobility found their great opportunity.

The Secret Committee of ways and means, after a thorough investigation of the state of the national finances, ultimately adopted a project of readjustment which Wallqvist, at the King's request, had drafted and laid before it. Wallqvist proposed that the Estates should guarantee the amount of the National Debt as it stood ; that, in return for this guarantee, the collection and administration of the public revenue should be transferred from the Crown to a *Riksgäldskontor* or *Board of Liquidation*, under the absolute and exclusive control of the Estates ; and that while the Estates voted subsidies sufficient to cover all current expenses, including the cost of the war (which was to be regarded as defensive), the King should engage to contract no more debts, and never allow his expenses to exceed his revenues. Wallqvist's proposition was substantially adopted by the Secret Committee, and recommended by it to the Estates. The Ofrälse Estates were, on the whole, dutiful and obliging. The guarantee question, which came on first for consideration, was adopted unanimously by the Burgesses and Peasants, but the opposition to it in the Estate of Priests was at first obstinate, till Wallqvist, adroitly seizing upon a disloyal expression which inadvertently fell from their most skilful debater, so worked upon the fears of his reverend brethren that he got the measure passed without a division. The subsidy question also passed successfully through the three lower Estates, but not at once, and only after a good deal of friction. The proposition, as it came before the Houses,

---

[1] The King thereupon retaliated by having it painted at his own expense and hung up in the Palace.

was that the necessary subsidies should be granted till
the following Riksdag, or, in other words, indefinitely.
After much debate, the Clergy and the Burgesses accepted
the proposition, but the Peasantry proved much more
difficult to deal with.    Most of their speakers laid great
stress upon the want and misery of their brethren in the
country, and declared that the gentry, who had all the
best land, and the clergy, who had their glebe to fall back
upon, ought to pay much more than they did, the long-
suffering peasantry much less.    At last, when the debates
in the fourth Estate had lasted a whole week without any
decision being come to, a royal message summoned the
whole of the Peasantry up to the palace, where the King
tried the effect of his eloquence upon them.    After promising to do all in his power to relieve their burdens,
emphasising the dangers of delay, and pointing out that
to limit the grant to any set time would be encroaching
on his prerogatives, he urged "the faithful Estate, which
nourishes and defends the soil," to now give him a fresh
proof of its traditional loyalty and devotion by accepting
the proposition in its entirety.    Hereupon Deputy Jan
Bengtson, a peasant Riksdagman of great experience, asked
leave to speak, and with much force and courage argued
in favour of a two years' grant only.    The arguments of
the shrewd and rugged yeoman were wonderfully clear and
cogent, but such was the glamour of the King's speech
that the Peasant deputies adopted his proposition on the
spot, and returned to their own House, "touched to the
heart by the way in which his Majesty had taken them
into his confidence." [1]

The guarantee question was sanctioned by the first
Estate after much grumbling, and solely on account of a
sinister rumour that the King meditated another *coup de*

[1] Report of an eye-witness, cited by Tham.

*main,* but against the subsidy propositions the gentry
made a most obstinate stand.   We have seen that the
three Ofrälse Estates had granted the subsidies for an
indefinite period ; the utmost the Riddarhus would do was
to grant them for two years.   Now, as the unanimity of
the four Estates on all subsidy questions was absolutely
indispensable, the opposition of the Nobles had to be
overcome somehow, and the King hit at once upon the
daring expedient of presiding personally in the Riddarhus,
and compelling the peers to follow the example of the
lower Estates.   The 27th of April was fixed for this last
exhibition of authority, and, after officially informing the
other Estates of his intention, and requesting them to
abide the issue of it in their respective chambers, Gustavus proceeded to the Riddarhus alone and unattended, and
arrived there in the middle of a debate.   The only notification of his coming that the gentry had was the cheering
of a mob in the square outside, whom the unusual spectacle
of his Majesty on foot and abroad at that early hour had
speedily attracted to the spot in large numbers.   On entering the house, the King stood at first by the side of
the Landmarshal's table,[1] and in "a mild but most solemn
voice"[2] reminded the gentry that the session of the Riksdag had already exceeded its legal limits, and that the
defence of the State demanded his presence elsewhere.
"I have come hither to-day," he concluded, "to prevent
you from breaking the bonds which still unite us . . . to
take my seat among you, simply as the first nobleman in
the land, beneath the shield of Gustavus Vasa."[3]   He
then sat down in the Landmarshal's chair and beckoned
to Vice-Landmarshal Liljehorn to sit down beside him,

---

[1] *Tham.*          [2] *Adlerbeth,* who seems to have been present.
[3] The walls of the Riddarhus were hung round with the armorial bearings
of the Swedish nobility.   The shield of Gustavus Vasa hung above the presidential chair.

while the secretary of the House recorded the proceedings. His enemies, he resumed, might perhaps accuse him of degrading the whole of the first Estate in the Rikssaal on February 17; but what he then had done, and necessity had alone forced him to do it, concerned those only whose conduct had brought the kingdom to the very verge of destruction. He had come to them now simply to strengthen the right-minded, enlighten the perplexed, and persuade the wavering; and he was certain that when he had explained to them why any limitation of the subsidies would be dangerous to the State, "those noble sentiments which should inspire noblemen really worthy of the name" would induce them to accept unanimously what they had hitherto been minded to reject. He then pointed out to them the danger of resisting any longer what was the manifest will of the nation at large; warned them against the possible vengeance of the lower orders, if, by their own negligence or vindictiveness, the country was disabled from defending itself against Russia, and finally declared that if they still persisted in refusing to grant him the new war-tax and subsidy till the next Riksdag, he would not answer for the consequences. Count Wachtmeister thereupon rose, and, after assuring the King of his own and his Estate's loyalty and devotion, declared that those who had the right to grant subsidies had also the right to fix their amount and period. Gustavus admitted as much, but added that he had not come there to dispute the rights of the Nobility, but simply to desire them to acquiesce on this single occasion with the other Estates for their country's welfare. He then formally put the question to the House, "Do the Nobility and Gentry grant the subsidy till the next Riksdag?" There were loud shouts of "Yes!" "No!"—the "No's" greatly preponderating, and many members attempted, but in vain, to speak. Gustavus then put the question again.    There were renewed cries of "Yes, yes!"    "No, no!" and a loud and prolonged uproar. When order had been restored, the King thanked the House "in the most touching terms"[1] for its kind consent; but was at once interrupted by cries of "We do not consent! Vote, vote! Yes, yes! No, no!" Ignoring the "No's" altogether, Gustavus directed the secretary of the House to record the consent of the majority in the protocols.    At this there was a perfect Babel of discordant voices.    The "No's" resounded from every part of the House.    Baron Duval protested that the prevailing turmoil was proof positive that no resolution had been come to; Count Wachtmeister shouted that force might deprive him of his liberties, but never of his convictions; but the King, with imperturbable composure, declared that the "Yes's" had it, and that the resolution was therefore adopted.    He then most cordially thanked the Nobility for a consent they had never given, and sent off a deputation to the three Ofrälse Estates to inform them of the result.

Thus the King had triumphed, and it may excite some surprise that he triumphed so easily.    But it should be remembered that, in the first place, he took the Nobles by surprise; that, in the second place, his presence greatly increased the number and the boldness of his adherents in the Riddarhus; and that, in the third place, the Nobility was much disturbed by the conduct of the populace outside.  From a very early hour in the morning the streets of Stockholm had been thronged with ragged royalists, who howled and hissed whenever they espied an imagined aristocrat.[2]    All the time the King was in the Riddarhus these defenders

---

[1] *Adlerbeth.*

[2] The Nobility afterwards accused the King of having secretly organised these popular demonstrations, through the agency of the terrible Minister of Police, Baron Liljensparre. This is not absolutely impossible, but by no means demonstrable.

of the throne assembled round the building in thousands, and were only prevented from penetrating into the Hall of Assembly by a few gentlemen who guarded the entrance with drawn swords.   Yet, all this time, it was not the Nobility, but the King who was in the greatest danger. During the last few days of the session he had, so to speak, held his life in his hands.   He had no material force behind him upon which he could rely in case of need.   The Burgess Guard was a mere decoration, while the Dalesmen had become so truculently insubordinate that both the King and Armfelt trembled at the thought of what might happen if they took it into their heads to visit the capital.[1] The King's friends expected every moment to hear of his assassination, and many of them went to bed in the evening uncertain whether they should see another morning.   It was, therefore, with a feeling of the most intense relief that they heard the trumpet-blast which blew out the Riksdag.   The parting speech from the throne was unusually brief, and full of gratitude and reassuring promises.   On the 11th May following a royal decree abolished the historic Raad or Senate, which, for the last six hundred years, had alternately ministered to and dominated the Crown.   There was, indeed, no room for it under the new system, and for the last sixteen years it had been little more than a State decoration.

The Revolution of 1789 converted Sweden from a limited into a despotic monarchy.[2]   The change was

---

[1] "Ce que vous me dites de vos Dalecarliens m'inquiete.  Je crois qu'il sera nécessaire de les renvoyer au plustôt, mais, en même temps, d'être très prudent quand ils retournerent pour qu'ils n'employent pas contre nous les armes que nous leur avons donnés."—*Bref till Armfelt.*

[2] Beskow (*Gustaf III. som Konung och Menniska*) and other Gustavan apologists argue that the Constitution of 1789 left the government of Sweden pretty much what it found it, and that as the Estates still retained the power of the purse, the monarchy could not fairly be called absolute.  It is hard to know what other name to give to a government where the Parliament is

abrupt and violent, but no impartial observer can deny
that it was absolutely necessary. But for this fiercely
debated act of authority, Sweden must have become a
mere dependency of Russia. The Confederation of Anjala
was as criminal, and might easily have become as fatal to
Sweden, as the exactly similar Confederation of Targowicz
was to prove to Poland three years later. The King had
for ever put a stop to the possible recurrence of any
such treason in the future, and Catherine II., who at the
opening of the Riksdag had talked loudly[1] of bombarding
Stockholm, and never abandoning the patriot cause so
long as a single nobleman belonged to it, now left the
Finnish rebels to their fate and fell back on the defensive.
And indeed, both to his friends and his foes Gustavus's
success seemed little short of miraculous. " Men may
wonder," says Wallqvist, in his summing up[2] of the
results of this famous Riksdag, " how it was that the King,
who in September 1788 seemed absolutely at the mercy
of his many foes, was able before May 1789 to summon
the Estates, convert the majority to his views, enlarge his
power at their expense, obtain the largest subsidies the
nation had ever granted, and get the Riksdag to almost
implore him to continue the war. . . . But our amazement will cease when we call to mind King Gustavus's
talents, his prudence, his influence over the minds of men,
qualities in which he has never yet had his equal among
monarchs."

degraded to a mere consultative assembly, and where the Ministers are mere
clerks, selected by the monarch often from outside the Legislature. We must
call things by their right names. The government of Gustavus III. from
1789-1792 was certainly despotic, but, for all that, it was salutary, necessary,
and highly popular,

[1] "When the King of Sweden has had his say to his Diet, I will have my
say to him," said Catherine to her private secretary in December 1788.—
*Khrapovitsky, " Dnevnik."*

[2] *Anteckningar.*

# CHAPTER XX.

THE Swedish revolution came just at the moment when
Catherine II.'s ambitious dream of restoring the Greek
Orthodox Empire under Russian protection seemed about to
be realised. The Confederation of Anjala had been more
useful to her than the Austrian alliance, for by disembarrass-
ing her of her one formidable rival in the North, it enabled
her to throw all her forces on her southern antagonist with
crushing effect. At the end of 1788, Oczakov, after a six
months' siege, was stormed by the Russians, though not without fearful loss, and triumphant themselves on the Dnieper
they were able to hasten to the help of their hardly-pressed

allies on the Danube. In April Derfelden defeated the Turks at Maximini and captured Galatz, while still more signal were the victories of Suvarov at Fokshani and on the Ruimnik, which led to the fall of the fortresses of Belgrade, Bender, Akkerman, and Passowitz, and the success of Repnin at Isakhi, which was followed by the investment of Ismalia. This series of successes seriously alarmed the Anglo-Prussian league, which, since the collapse of France, represented the rest of Europe, and it was therefore with no small satisfaction that they saw the King of Sweden prepare to take the field again at the beginning of 1789, although they lent him no material aid whatever, a loan of 733,000 rix-dollars, being all that Gustavus could squeeze out of the Court of Berlin, though he skilfully dangled the bait of Swedish Pomerania before Frederick William II. and his Ministers.[1]

In Finland, meanwhile, order and discipline had been restored, and the army, after the arrest of all the leading conspirators, had ostensibly at least returned to its allegiance; but all through the winter of 1788 the state of affairs in the Grand Duchy had been very critical, especially after the final defection of the Savolax corps, and the unexampled treachery of its commander, General Hastfehr, who, fearing that Gustavus's cause was hopeless, readily listened to the insinuations of Göran Sprengtporten, and, in consideration of a large sum of money down, a position of trust in the Russian service, and a guarantee for his personal security in case of failure, engaged to summon a Finnish Riksdag at St. Michel, the capital of the province of Savolax, when the Grand Duchy of Finland was to be separated from Sweden and placed under Russian protection. By way of demonstrating his *bona fides*, moreover, Hastfehr handed over to

---

[1] For an account of the vacillating policy of Prussia from 1786–1792, and its mischievous effects upon Europe generally, see R. Nisbet Bain's article in the *English Historical Review* for April 1891, " The Second Partition of Poland."

Sprengtporten four private documents, which had been in-
trusted to him by the King in the strictest confidence, and
which detailed Gustavus' most secret plans, and these documents Sprengtporten gleefully sent on to St. Petersburg.[1]
Catherine, during her long reign, had had many proofs of
human baseness, and had made capital out of them all;
but Hastfehr's conduct on this occasion was a little too
much for even her easy-going morality.   The surrender of
the King's letters by an intimate friend, who owed every--
thing to his past kindness, especially shocked her.[2]  "What
a precious traitor!" she exclaimed.  "If the King were not
what he is, he would deserve compassion.   But what's to be
done?  One cannot spare one's enemies!"  So she resolved
to use Hastfehr, and instructed him, through Sprengtporten, to perform his promises.  This he set about doing,
but soon found that, disaffected as the Finnish regiments
were, they were still not prepared to go the length of
severing the Grand Duchy from Sweden.   Then, too, his
offer to enter the Russian service had been coldly received;
subsequent interviews with Sprengtporten were not quite
satisfactory, and he had not yet received a penny of his
money.   Hastfehr grew uneasy, and reports reaching him
from Sweden that the King was likely to triumph there after
all, he repented him of his hastiness, suddenly recollected
that Gustavus III. had always been his benefactor, and
began to think that gratitude in this case would be a paying
virtue.   So he broke off his intercourse with Sprengtporten,
and resuming his correspondence with Gustavus, tried to
persuade him that his dealings with the Russians had been
nothing more than masterly finessing.   But it was too late.
The suspicions of Hastfehr's own officers had been aroused

---

[1] The most lucid and exhaustive account of Hastfehr's treason will be found
in chap. xi. of Tigerstedt's monograph, *Göran Magnus Sprengtporten* (*Finska
Tidskrift*, vol. xi.).          [2] Khrapovitsky, *Dnevnik.*

by his frequent and mysterious hobnobbing with the Russians. They opened his letters, therefore, during one of his protracted absences, communicated with the King, and on January 10, 1789, Hastfehr was arrested and sent to Stockholm. His apprehension gave the *coup-de-grâce* to the whole conspiracy. All the confederates of Anjala were now seized and sent in batches to Sweden to be tried by court-martial, and Stedingk and Meijerfelt, almost the only superior officers whose loyalty had never wavered for an instant, were appointed commanders of the Northern and Southern Finnish armies respectively.

The Hastfehr episode was little calculated to restore the confidence of Gustavus III. in his army. All through the ensuing campaign he was haunted by the fear of fresh treachery, and this doubtless was the cause of his otherwise inexplicably timid and wavering strategy. He seems to have been never quite sure how far his officers would follow him,[1] and therefore never dared his utmost. It was at the beginning of June 1789 that he arrived at the seat of war, but it was not till the end of the same month that the main army was able to take the field. The causes of this delay were the want of ready money, the consequent break-down of the commissariat,[2] and, above all, the significant inertia of the Board of Admiralty at Carlscrona.

It was upon his really magnificent fleet that Gustavus mainly depended, but, so far from seconding his operations during this campaign, it was throughout the year a perpetual source of vexation and anxiety to him. The army, on the whole, did its duty, and the zeal and energy with which the Secret Board of War at Stockholm, aided by Toll in Scania, grappled with the truly herculean task of provision-

---

[1] *Bref.* See also *Bref till Armfelt.*

[2] *Ibid.* The King's private correspondence reveals a terrible state of things. There was a lack of everything, and the officers often had to live on nettle-soup.

ing the army, collecting and transporting fresh.troops, and
mobilising the forces generally was beyond all praise.  But the
fleet, as Armfelt put it, was " the Moloch which devoured
everything and gave nothing in return."    At last the state
of things at Carlscrona reached such a pitch that Equerry
Munck, who, together with Armfelt, was a member of the
Board of War, was sent down thither to investigate matters.
He returned in a fortnight and reported " incredible horrors."
Carlscrona, he said, was a chaotic pesthouse.  The hospitals
were crammed full of patients suffering from a score of
different complaints.   Soldiers and sailors with fractured
limbs were huddled into the same beds with persons suffering from contagious diseases.   Medical care and attendance
there was next to none.   There were not even bandages for
binding up wounds.   Hundreds of corpses were stacked up
in the hospital gardens awaiting burial, and the coffins of
those that were buried were interred so carelessly that the
ends of them stuck up above the ground.   There was no
order, no management, no discipline.   Nobody was able to
command or willing to obey.   It was only too evident to
Munck and Armfelt that the cause of this chaotic state of
things was a deliberate design on the part of the subaltern
officers to wreck the whole campaign in revenge for the
humiliation of their order at the last Riksdag.  Armfelt,
who was mainly responsible for the mobilisation of the
army, was at his wit's end.   The loyalty of the young
colonel was absolute, his energy was splendid ; but he felt
that a firmer and stronger hand than his own was wanted
here to crush the hydra of intrigue and treason, and he had
the courage and honesty to recommend that his detested
and now disgraced rival, Toll, should be sent down at once
to Carlscrona as Intendant-General of the fleet with plenipotentiary power.   The King, whose unjust antipathy to
Toll was invincible, long hesitated ; but matters at Carls-

crona going rapidly from bad to worse, he at length gave
way, and Toll received the post. The very rumour of his
coming roused the Admiralty from its inertia, and on his
arrival he crushed every symptoms of disaffection with an
iron hand, speedily made the Admiralty the model branch
of the service, and contributed not a little by his masterly
management to the ultimate successes of the war.

It was only on July 6, 1789, that the Duke of Sudermania,
as High Admiral, quitted Carlscrona to go in search of
the enemy's fleet, and fell in with it on July 26 off the
southernmost point of the Isle of Öland under the command of Admiral Chichagov. The Duke at once gave orders
to engage, and a battle began which lasted from two o'clock
in the afternoon till eight o'clock in the evening.[1] The
Swedish centre, under the Duke's own command, and the
rear, under Admiral Modée, were soon hotly engaged ; but
the reserve, under Vice-Admiral Lilliehorn, stood aloof, and
gradually dropped more and more behind, despite repeated
signals to advance. The rest of the fleet sustained the
unequal contest with spirit, and even success, for four of the
enemy's ships were disabled and dropped out of line, while
the whole Russian fleet began to retire. But all attempts
to make Lilliehorn move proved fruitless, thus leaving the
Swedish fleet so inferior to that of the enemy that the Duke
dared not continue the combat, but drew off for repairs to
Carlscrona, where he was practically blockaded for the rest
of the year by Chichagov, who had in the meantime received large reinforcements. Fortunately the Russian fleet,
despite its superiority, vied with the Swedish in inactivity,
and towards the end of November both fleets went into
winter quarters.[1]

---

[1] The best Swedish account of the battle of Öland will be found in Bäck-
ström's *Svenska Flottans Historia*, p. 253. The best Russian account is
Chichagov's report to the Empress (Khrapovitsky, p. 302). Another good
Russian account is in Ordin, *Pokorenie Finlyandia*, vol. i.

The Duke's first act on arriving at Carlscrona was to court-martial Lilliehorn, whose extraordinary conduct had balked the Swedish fleet of an almost certain triumph. He was tried accordingly and condemned to be shot, but the King commuted the sentence to banishment. The whole affair remains to this day an inexplicable mystery ; but there is good reason to believe that Lilliehorn's scandalous inaction was entirely due to a deeply-laid plot of his subordinate officers to thus avenge themselves upon their unfortunate Vice-Landmarshal,[1] who had served his King only too well during the last Riksdag. This seems to have been Gustavus's own opinion,[2] and explains his leniency to Lilliehorn, who, however, was never employed again.

Equally indecisive, but far more honourable, were the operations of the army and the auxiliary *Skärgardsflotta*, or skerry flotilla.

Hostilities were begun in the northern province of Savolax by the Russians, who, taking advantage of their possession of the inner line of communication, rapidly concentrated their forces before the Swedes were well aware of their tactics, and falling with 5000 men on 800 men of Brigadier Stedingk's[3] army near the village of Kyrö, defeated them after five hours' hard fighting, and drove them back upon St. Michel, the capital of Savolax, Stedingk's headquarters. Thither the Russians advanced in force on the following day, and found Stedingk strongly entrenched in the pass of Parosalmi ; but being greatly superior in numbers, attacked him forthwith,

---

[1] Lilliehorn had been Lewenhaupt's substitute, and sternly put down all obstruction.

[2] *Bref till Armfelt.*

[3] Stedingk, by far the ablest of the Gustavan generals, had served with great distinction under the French flag in America and the Antilles. His conduct at the capture of Grenada was heroic, and won him the cross of St. Louis and the praise of Louis XVI. before the whole Court. At a later day he was to command the Swedish contingent at the great battle of Leipsic. He was always devoted to Gustavus III.

and a battle began which lasted all day. Sprengtporten led the attack in person, and, supported by the heavy fire of the Russian batteries on the neighbouring hills, took the bridge leading through the pass, and made a dash at the Swedish batteries on the slope beyond ; but Stedingk gallantly rallying his forces, hurled the foe down the slope again with great loss, Sprengtporten, moreover, being dangerously wounded. The Russians then resumed firing at long distances all the afternoon, till the Swedes received reinforcements and forced them to retire at all points with the loss of 900 men, the Swedes losing only 174 men.

Parosalmi was not a very big battle, but it greatly dejected Catherine II., who privately declared that it was the worst news which had reached the Russian capital for a hundred years ; while Gustavus III. was proportionately delighted. But this victory, such as it was, was speedily followed by a reverse. The Russians, reinforced in their turn, attacked Stedingk a second time at Parosalmi, drove him out of his entrenchments with a loss of 400 men, and pursued him to the very borders of Lapland. Not till the end of July was Stedingk able to recover from this blow; but then he again marched southwards, defeated the Russians after a fierce three hours' combat at Parksumäki with the loss of 600 men, and brilliantly repulsed a counter-attack of theirs at Laitasilta in October.

Nor was the southern army idle. The King's plan was to relieve the Savolax brigade, which had hitherto borne the brunt of the contest, by attacking the Russian fortress of Willamstrand with the main army, while Ehrensvärd and Meijerfelt, with the right wing and the coast flotilla, made a diversion against the fortress of Fredrikshamn, and Kaulbars covered the left flank of the army on land. The first operations were decidedly encouraging. In less than a week after crossing the border, the King, with only 1600

men, attacked 4000 Russians at Uttismalm, and drove them
back after several hours' combat ; but instead of following
up his advantage, the fear of a flank attack made him fall
back the same day. Five days later he made a similar
mistake, for, after attacking and defeating another Russian
division at Liikala, a victory which opened up the way to
the fortress of Fredrikshamn, he remained inactive on the
spot for three weeks, till the defeat of Kaulbars at Kaippais
compelled the whole army to retreat.

The event of the campaign, however, was the naval battle
of Svenksund between the rival flotillas, a battle brought
about by the attempt of the Russian Admiral, Kruse, to
drive the Swedish Admiral, Ehrensvärd, from the Firth of
Svenksund, which he had occupied at the beginning of the
campaign.    Numerically the Swedes were much weaker
than the Russians, but their position was strong, for the
Russians had to force their way through a narrow channel
full of sunken stakes and other obstructions.    Early on
August 24, Kruse gallantly attacked the Swedish positions,
but, after five hours' hard fighting, was compelled to fall
back in disorder (leaving five large vessels in the hands
of the enemy), hotly pursued by the victorious Swedes.
Meanwhile, however, Kruse's colleague, the Prince of
Nassau, arrived on the scene with large reinforcements,
and Ehrensvärd, whose ammunition was well-nigh spent,
and whose men were exhausted by a seven hours' contest,
would have retired.    But the King, who had been watching
the action from shore, and was quite carried away by the
excitement of the moment, ordered his Admiral to attack
the twofold odds, with the result that might have been
anticipated.    After a further five hours' combat, the over-
matched and wearied Swedes were compelled to take refuge
beneath the walls of the fortress of Svartsholm, leaving
thirty-three of their vessels in the enemy's hands.    " I have

the honour of informing your Majesty that you have no longer a coast flotilla," were the memorable words with which the discomfited Admiral announced a defeat which was no fault of his own, for it was Gustavus's trick of staking everything on a single cast which had converted an actual victory into a ruinous defeat. To do the King justice, however, he at once admitted his mistake by decorating Ehrensvärd on the spot with the grand cross of the Order of the Sword, a decoration only conferred on successful commanders. Ehrensvärd was so mortified, however, by his unmerited defeat that he retired from the service. He was succeeded by Rajalin, a brave old sea-dog, who had seen much service under the French.

The victory of Svenksund enabled the Russians to land on Swedish soil, attack the King's army in the rear, and, after some hard fighting, capture the fortress of Hogbars, which defended the line of the Kymmene. The remainder of the Swedish flotilla was subsequently destroyed in Barö Sound. These reverses, however, were somewhat counterbalanced by the brilliant storming of the island of Elgsö (which the Russians had strongly fortified and made the centre of their operations) by young Armfelt and his Dalesmen, who had arrived in Finland shortly after the affair of Barö Sound. Elgsö was quite a little Gibraltar, and the Russians regarded it as impregnable; but Armfelt, at the head of his gallant Dalesmen, carried the position at the point of the bayonet in the face of a murderous fire, and, though badly wounded, was the first to scale the hostile entrenchments. His valour on this occasion made a deep impression on the enemy. The Russian general desired to make the acquaintance of so gallant an officer, and Gustavus was enchanted to see the Dalesmen sustaining the reputation of their ancestors. Elgsö was the last important engagement of the campaign. Early in November both armies went into winter quarters, and the King, after a tour of inspection through Finland, returned to Stockholm.

The result of the campaign of 1789 is best summed up in the King's own words : " After fighting like madmen about every other day for two months, here we are at the same point at which we started ! "  Nor, considering Gustavus's many disadvantages, can we much wonder at it.  On the other hand, if there had been no great triumph, there had also been no great disaster, and excepting the inexplicable affair at Oland, the honour of the Swedish arms had everywhere been nobly maintained.  The King also had acquitted himself well. That he was no born general, like his uncle, the great Frederick, was now pretty plain, but he had displayed all the qualities of an intrepid soldier, and his daring impetuosity in action had frequently endangered his life.  Yet all his exertions had led to nothing, and though he had already grown tired of a war which promised him but scant laurels, he was too clear-sighted a politician not to perceive that a decisively successful campaign could now be the only guarantee of an honourable peace.  He therefore resolved to make unheard-of efforts to terminate the war in the ensuing campaign, and to rely mainly, if not entirely, on the fleet and the coast flotilla, the latter of which he meant to lead in person.

Throughout the winter, therefore, the equipment of the fleet proceeded with the greatest energy, thanks to the sleepless vigilance and vigorous initiative of Toll.  There was scarcely a port of any consequence in the kingdom which did not turn out its contingent of galleys or gunboats, to say nothing of the new frigates and liners which were launched from Stockholm and Carlscrona.  It is calculated that during the winter of 1789–90 the coast flotilla alone was increased by 150 large and small craft, so that by the beginning of May it numbered 349 sail, with 3055 guns

and 22,500 men, whilst the effective strength of the fleet
was raised to 25 liners, 15 frigates, and 14 smaller vessels,
carrying 17,000 men, and 2104 guns.   Never before had
Sweden possessed such imposing and well-appointed naval
armaments.   It was proposed to commence operations immediately the ice broke, so as to surprise the Russian squadrons
in their respective harbours, while the land forces made a
diversion in the remote inland provinces of Carelia and
Savolax.   The campaign on land commenced auspiciously
by a brilliantly successful attack by Armfelt and his Dalesmen on the Russian positions in the strongly fortified pass
of Kärnakoski, the key of Russian Finland, which was carried
at the point of the bayonet.   In South Finland, meanwhile,
Gustavus, with a swiftness and daring which the Russians
themselves could not sufficiently admire, threw himself upon
General Denisov at Valkiala, defeated him after an engagement which was the sharpest that had yet been fought,
captured his artillery and magazines, and opened up communications with Armfelt and the northern army.   The
plan of a combined attack, however, was frustrated by the
energy with which the Russians now assumed the offensive,
and Gustavus, outnumbered, was forced to retire again behind the line of the boundary river Kymmene, which, for
the next six weeks, was the theatre of a series of obstinately
contested but indecisive combats.   Encouraged by their successes in the south, the Russians now made a determined
attempt to dislodge Armfelt and his Dalesmen from their
lately won positions at Kärnakoski and Pardakoski, in
Northern Finland, by suddenly attacking the Swedes, who
numbered no more than 1500, with 6000 men from three
sides simultaneously at midnight.   Success was regarded
as a foregone conclusion, and the result was impatiently
awaited at St. Petersburg, where it was erroneously supposed that Gustavus was present with Armfelt's brigade.

The threefold assault failed utterly, however.  The Russian General Bagkov was defeated and slain at Pardokoski by Major Jägerhorn, while Armfelt and his Dalesmen repulsed the Prince of Anhalt, who was mortally wounded on the field, from Kärnakoski, and drove his forces back on Svataipol.  The third Russian column only arrived when all was over, and thought it prudent to retire by the way it came.  The losses on both sides were proportionately very heavy, the Swedes losing 222, the Russians 700 men.  Kärnakoski was, however, to be the last victory the Swedes were to gain on land, for Armfelt's subsequent attack on the impregnable Russian positions at Svataipol, after a display of heroism worthy of the days of Charles XII., was beaten back, and almost cost the gallant young Swede his life.  In the midst of "an infernal hail of bullets, bombs, and grenades," Armfelt, at the head of a battalion of the Guards, had charged the enemy's position with the bayonet, but was struck senseless to the ground, and only rescued with the utmost difficulty.  With a loss of one-third of its effective strength the attacking column then fell back upon Pardakoski.  The King consoled the wounded hero with the grand cross of the Order of the Sword and the rank of a major-general.

But the operations on land were, after all, mere demonstrations; it was on the sea that the fortune of the war was to be decided.

On April 30, the grand fleet, consisting of 22 liners, 12 frigates, and 13 smaller vessels, put to sea under the command of the Duke of Sudermania, and made for Revel Roads, to destroy, if possible, the Russian squadron of 11 liners and 5 frigates lying there.  Delayed by contrary winds, it was not till May 11 that the Duke cast anchor in Revel Roads, where he found the Russian fleet lying in such a strong position, beneath the protection of a formidable line of forts and batteries on shore, that even in the opinion of

such an audacious seaman as Sydney Smith,[1] it was almost
foolhardy to tackle it.   Nevertheless the Duke persisted in
sailing into Revel harbour and taking up a position alongside the Russians ; but the wind was so strong, and the sea
so rough, that the Swedes could neither form line properly
nor fire steadily, so that after a useless six hours' cannonade,
the Duke retired with the loss of 150 men and two liners,
which ran aground.

Meanwhile the King had been much more successful with
the coasting flotilla than the Duke had been with the fleet.
It was Gustavus's intention to penetrate through the rocks
and shoals of the Gulf of Finland to St. Petersburg and
extort a peace from the Empress by bombarding her in her
own capital.   But before this could be safely attempted, it
was necessary to first destroy that part of the Russian
coast flotilla which lay in the Swedish rear within the
harbour of Fredrikshamn ; and, secondly, to recall the fleet
from Revel, that it might protect the coast flotilla from
the possible attack of the Cronstadt squadron, and cover
its retreat in case of accident.   On May 14 the Swedish
flotilla appeared before Fredrikshamn.   In the roads lay
the Russian flotilla, consisting of 20 galleys and 70 common
sloops, with a crew of about 1000 men.   Batteries had
been erected on the more prominent headlands, but most
of the guns in them had not yet been mounted, and everything there pointed to surprise and confusion.   At four
o'clock on the morning of the 15th, the Swedes began the
action.   Their superior artillery and skilful manœuvres
speedily compelled the enemy to retire at all points, and
their sloops and gunboats dashing into the narrow fiord,
captured or destroyed 26 Russian sloops and gunboats,
and dismantled three unfinished batteries.   But for an un-

---

[1] Sir J. Barrow, Life and Correspondence of Sir W. S. Smith, vol. i. p. 48
et seq.

fortunate six hours' rest which Gustavus allowed his forces in the very middle of the battle, there can be little doubt that the hostile flotilla might have been annihilated, and the fortress of Fredrikshamn (which the Russians themselves had given up for lost)[1] easily captured.

It was immediately after the battle of Fredrikshamn that Gustavus was joined by a young English officer with a turn for adventure somewhat similar to his own, and who was to render him substantial service during the remainder of the campaign. This was no other than Captain William Sydney Smith, the future hero of St. Jean d'Acre. In January 1790 Smith had received a most flattering invitation from Gustavus, whose acquaintance he had made in the autumn of 1789, offering him the rank of post-captain in the Swedish navy. Smith eagerly jumped at the opportunity; but not being able to obtain his Government's consent, yet determined to see some fighting somehow, hastened all the way back from London to Finland for the purpose, and rejoined his royal friend (who received him with open arms) at Svenksund[2] just as the whole flotilla was on the point of setting out for the Gulf of Viborg to attack the Russian flotilla lying there. By Smith's advice, the grand fleet, which, since the affair of Revel, had been lying idle at Hogland, was ordered to co-operate with the flotilla by advancing and attacking the Russian Cronstadt fleet in front of them before the Revel fleet behind them had had time to come up; but it cost the gallant Englishman no end of trouble and a great many journeys to and fro between the King and

---

[1] Khrapovitsky's Diary.

[2] Smith's account of the campaign of Svenksund, though unfortunately very fragmentary, is invaluable as the description of an unbiassed eye-witness. The Brit. Mus. MS., Add. 28,066, which contains Smith's correspondence with Liston, the English Minister at Stockholm, is a preferable authority to Barrow's scrappy excerpts from Smith's letters. Compare also *Gustaf III. Bref till Armfelt*, which show how very highly the Swedish monarch thought of Smith, and what unlimited confidence he had in him.

the Duke of Sudermania before he could convince the latter of the expediency of hazarding an engagement so near to the Russian capital. Even when the Swedish fleet did sight the Cronstadt squadron, which was far inferior in strength, and might easily have been beaten if promptly attacked, the fatal backwardness 'of the Swedish officers, who would do nothing but keep up a cannonade at disgracefully long distances, threw away the opportunity, and the situation of the Swedes became downright embarrassing, when, at last, the Revel squadron also hove in sight and began to bear down upon them. As it was now impracticable to prevent the junction of the two Russian squadrons, the Swedish fleet was obliged to anchor in line across the entrance of the Gulf of Viborg, supporting its flanks by shoals and the mainland. For the next three weeks a strong sou'-wester kept the Swedish fleet in the same position, and then the position of Gustavus became well-nigh desperate. Food and water ran short. His sailors were put upon rations of black bread, and had to drink the brackish water of the Gulf of Viborg. Cabbage and salt fish were the only dishes to be seen on the royal table. The Russians, who received reinforcements daily, had now completely blockaded the Swedish fleet, and so certain of success were they, that they had already provided a state cabin on board their flagship for the King of Sweden's reception. On the 21st, 22nd, and 23rd June councils of war were held on board Gustavus's yacht, and a plan of Lieutenant Klints and Sydney Smith for attempting to break through the Russian lines at the point nearest the shore as soon as the wind veered was finally adopted. For another week the wind continued contrary, by which time the Swedes were reduced to the last extremity; but on July 2 it shifted, and at half-past five in the morning the King, whose coolness and good-humour seemed to grow proportionately with the peril of his situation, went on board the flagship to take leave of his brother, and exhort all his officers to do their duty.   At six o'clock the Swedish fleet raised anchor, and the van, "in a most able and gallant manner," bore down upon the left wing of the enemy, whose attention had already been distracted by a successful false attack upon their right at early dawn by Lieutenant Törning and Sydney Smith.    The strait through which the Swedish three-deckers and frigates had to pass in single file, with the smaller vessels of the flotilla alongside, lay between a sandbank and Cape Krosswort. Across the narrow passage lay five Russian liners ready to receive the Swedish vessels as they came up, and behind the three-deckers lay a second line of frigates.    Sydney Smith has left us a vivid picture of the beginning of the desperate venture.    "The concentric fire of the Russian ships which opposed our passage by Cape Krosswort," he writes,[1] "was really the most formidable I ever saw ; and considering that every ship, galley, and boat we had was obliged to pass under it, it is a wonder we are come off as well as we are. . . . I left the King just as we were about to enter the shower of bullets and cannon-balls, which made the water froth before us.    He was perfectly calm, reasoned with me with clearness, and gave orders for the execution of such things as I proposed, distinctly and coolly."   Puke, in the *Valorous*, at 7.30, was the first to pass through the murderous fire of the Russian lines, raking the ships on each side of him fore and aft, the other Swedish liners following his example.    By nine o'clock almost the whole of the Swedish fleet and the greater part of the flotilla had run the gauntlet.    The Russian left wing suffered terribly.    The officers of the Swedish flagship, as they passed through the lines, saw the scupper-holes of the Russian vessels literally running with blood.    The five

---

[1] Brit. Mus. MS.

hostile ships which barred the passage had nine-tenths of their crews put *hors de combat,* and at last two of them struck their flags, while the rest ceased firing. But neither did the Swedes escape scot free, and throughout the terrible passage both the King and the Duke carried their lives in their hands. As the flagship was running the gauntlet a bullet grazed the Duke's arm and pierced the heart of an officer by his side; while one cannon-ball shot away the standard of the royal sloop, and another tore off both arms of one of the rowers, who fell bathed in blood on the deck, whereupon the King instantly slipped off his scarf and helped to bind up the poor fellow's wounds with it. A few minutes later the royal sloop was so riddled by shot that she began to sink, and the King had to take to his yacht, the *Amphion,* in which he passed through the second line of obstructing frigates. On the whole, however, the dangerous manœuvre had hitherto been successful, and only the Swedish rearguard had still to run the gauntlet, when a mishap occurred which had the most disastrous consequences. An unskilfully handled fire-ship ran foul of and blew up a Swedish liner and a frigate, and in the darkness caused by this explosion the Swedish rearguard lost its bearings, and three liners, two frigates, and some smaller vessels were captured by the enemy; while a squadron of Russian frigates under Captain Crown, an Englishman, came suddenly out from behind the islands, and "laid about them with broadsides among the gunboats," "running over those they could not sink otherwise."[1] Fortunately for Gustavus, the Russians were so inexplicably remiss in pursuing their advantage that the Swedish fleet and flotilla got an hour's start of them, and were able to escape without much further loss. The Duke never stopped till he was safe beneath the cannon of Sveaborg; while the King, with the remains of the flotilla, took refuge in the

[1] Brit. Mus. MS.

fiord of Svenksund, the heavy sea preventing him from following the fleet.

"The King of Sweden will, no doubt, be accused of imprudence in getting himself into the situation in which he now is," wrote Sydney Smith[1] to Liston immediately after the battle. And Smith was right. All the Swedish military historians, without exception, unite in denouncing and deploring the rashness with which Gustavus again and again exposed his fleet to almost certain ruin. Smith, however, thought differently, and, as an impartial eye-witness, he speaks with some authority. In his opinion it was "the prudent gentlemen among us whose humble remonstrances were absolute refusals, and who opposed the word *impossible* to every plan of enterprise opposed to them," who were really responsible for the defeat for which Gustavus has so often and so unjustly been blamed. "It is in vain," writes the bluff Englishman,[2] "that the King and the Duke are firm in their resolves, calm in danger, and clear in their orders, if those who are to obey them employ themselves in weighing the probability of success . . . caballing together and reviving the question whether they should not be responsible to the States if any accident should happen to the King." "The Swedes of to-day," he adds, "are not the Swedes of Charles XII.'s days. . . . They are spoilt for enterprise, which every attack is more or less. Those of them who are brave are as thoroughly so as were their ancestors in the field, but the greater number of them are always looking behind them to see that their retreat to their own frontier is secured, which, to my mind, is neither more nor less than a previous resolve to give way."

The battle of the Viborg Gauntlet made a profound impression on the rest of Europe. Immediately on the news

[1] Brit. Mus. MS.

[2] Brit. Mus. MS.   Compare also Barrow's Life of Smith.

reaching London, a cabinet council was held, at which the advisability of vigorously mediating between the belligerents was anxiously discussed. Friends and foes alike gave Gustavus up for lost. Even the gallant Sydney Smith began to lose heart. "His Swedish Majesty," wrote he to Liston, "with a disaffected army and fleet, is now in a worse hobble than ever." The only thing in his opinion that could save the remainder of the Swedish flotilla from destruction was the speedy appearance of a British fleet in the Baltic.

The Russians had now closed in upon the Swedes from all sides, and the Russian commander, the famous Prince of Nassau, had fixed the anniversary of the Empress's coronation, July 9, for his easy and insulting triumph. The Swedish officers, sensible of the peril of their position, besought the King to retire among the rocks while there was still time and take refuge behind the cannon of Svartholm; but Gustavus, reinforced at the last moment by the Pomeranian squadron of thirty cannon-sloops and eighteen gunboats, and stimulated by the energetic counsels of Sydney Smith,[1] peremptorily silenced all objections by declaring that he meant to remain where he was and fight. The position of the Swedes among the rocky islets of Svenksund was naturally strong, and they well employed their week's respite by making it still stronger. Batteries were erected on every vantage-point, and lighters and other obstructions were sunk in the narrowest parts of the narrow sounds. Gustavus had a numerical superiority in vessels, opposing 195 sail to the Russians' 151; but Nassau's ships were far larger, carried more guns, and were manned by 18,500 men, while the whole of the Swedish forces only amounted to 14,000. The Swedish line of battle, which was crescent-shaped, extended for 8000 yards along the coast. The

---

[1] Brit. Mus. MS.

Russians advanced in three columns, which occupied the whole width of the channel, but the size and number of their ships prevented them from properly deploying their line or making full use of their superiority in artillery, while the Swedes had the further advantages of a fixed position and a concentric fire. At 9.30 the first shot was fired, and a quarter of an hour later the action was general along the whole line. Gustavus himself opened the attack on the Swedish side from the yacht *Amadis*, which stood in the centre of the line. The Russians had concentrated their forces on their left wing, and vigorously attacked the Swedish right, but here they met with a most stubborn resistance, and after two hours' desperate fighting were driven back. A second attack with fresh ships was repulsed in equally gallant style, and towards four o'clock the battle began to go at all points against the Russians, who lost heavily. The firing was kept up, however, till ten o'clock at night, when darkness put an end to that day's fighting. The Russians had suffered so severely that they had now little hope of success, but to retire had become impossible, as the south-west wind, which had been blowing stiffly all day, now gradually swelled to a gale, and thus compelled the Russian flotilla to remain all night on the battlefield. At early dawn on the 10th, however, they made a desperate attempt to escape, but were immediately attacked on all sides by the Swedish sloops and gunboats, which drove them into the open sea in the utmost disorder, and captured a multitude of prizes. At ten o'clock the firing on both sides finally ceased. The Russian loss during the battle had been terrible, but the real magnitude of their defeat was not known till several days afterwards. Hundreds of Russians had taken refuge on the rocky islets along the coast, where they were cut off from all assistance and obliged to surrender to escape starvation. Thus in a week

the number of prisoners rose to 6000 men, 800 of whom
were officers, so that, including the killed and wounded,
the total loss of the Russians amounted to 9500 men, to say
nothing of the fifty-three vessels which had been destroyed
or captured by the victors.   The Swedes only lost 300 men
and four small vessels.

The moral effect of this great victory, the most signal
triumph ever won by the Swedish arms, was naturally extraordinary.   On Catherine II. its effect was crushing.   The
pages of her private secretary show us very plainly that,
from the very commencement of the campaign, the haughty
dame had had nothing but anxious days and sleepless nights.
The early appearance of the Swedish fleet in Russian waters
had greatly disquieted her.   " It is God's miracle," she cried,
with a sudden access of religious fervour, when the news
of Chichagov's victory at Revel reached her.   But when,
at the end of June, Gustavus threatened Cronstadt itself,
there was a perfect panic in the Russian capital.   On June 4
a frightful cannonade, which lasted from dawn to evening, was distinctly audible at Tsarkoe-Selo, and a courier
aroused the Empress at midnight with the intelligence that
her admirals had been defeated in the Gulf of Viborg.   It
proved a false alarm, for, on the anniversary of Pultava,
young Chichagov arrived at St. Petersburg with the news
of his father's great victory.   Catherine was transported
with joy.   Chichagov was loaded with gifts, a solemn *Te
Deum* was sung in the cathedral, and Catherine, in a jubi-
lant letter to Grimm, informed him that she was about to
administer the *coup-de-grâce* to the King of Sweden.   But her
exultation was a little premature.   Only a week later another
courier awoke Secretary Bezborodko with the tidings of the
catastrophe of Svenksund.   The Empress, though deeply
shaken, set her Ministers a splendid example of fortitude.
She bade the tearful Bezborodko imitate Frederick the Great,

who never lost his head even amidst the most terrible disasters.  To Nassau, who, full of shame and confusion, had returned all his decorations and begged for his discharge, she sent a letter full of consolation and encouragement.  In a letter to Grimm,[1] indeed, she pooh-poohed the whole affair as trumpery; but her real sentiments will be found in a private letter to Potemkin, in which she assures the sympathetic favourite that the defeat of Svenksund had well-nigh broken her heart.  Catherine's difficulties were now multiplying.  In the spring of 1790 her solitary ally, the Emperor Joseph, died of grief at the collapse of all his military and political plans, and his successor, Leopold, made peace with Turkey on a *status quo ante bellum* basis.  Prussia, almost simultaneously, guaranteed the possession of the Crimea to the Porte by a special treaty, and, on March 29, 1790, took the extreme step of concluding a definite offensive and defensive alliance with Poland, which was evidently directed against Russia.  Under these adverse circumstances Catherine was inclined to listen to the pacific overtures which the King of Sweden was now willing to make.  Despite his brilliant victory, Gustavus's situation was most insecure, and he had little prospect of continuing the war with success.  He was nearly at the end of his resources, and his professed allies, England and Prussia, showed no disposition to assist him.  An honourable peace, moreover, was now within his grasp, for it was not beneath the dignity of the victor of Svenksund to extend the hand of clemency to his defeated rival.  Negotiations were accordingly opened near the ruins of the little town of Värälä, on neutral territory between the two camps, Armfelt being the Swedish commissioner, and on August 15, 1790, the treaty was signed in

---

[1] *Sbornik* of the Russ. Imp. Society, tom. xxxiii.  Perhaps the reader should here be reminded that, as historical documents, Catherine's letters to Grimm are almost worthless.  Grimm was Catherine's private advertising agent, so to speak.

his tent. The Peace of Värälä, though it left the boundaries of the two States exactly as they were, was nevertheless both honourable and beneficial to Sweden. Russia tacitly renounced her right of intervention in Swedish affairs, and Igelström, the Russian commissioner, expressed the hope that the treaty would speedily be followed by a still closer alliance between the two Powers, in which case Russia might be willing to indemnify Sweden for the expenses of the war. Thus Gustavus had gained his main object, the emancipation of Sweden from her humiliating dependence upon Russia, which had crippled her for the last half century, and for such a gain even 50,000 men, fifteen line of battle ships, and 24,000,000 rixdollars was, in the eyes of every patriotic Swede, not too heavy a price to pay. Nor should we forget, as the present King of Sweden has so well pointed out,[1] that this was the only war since the beginning of the century from which the country had emerged without loss of territory. This healthy and stimulating experience Sweden owed entirely to the determined courage with which Gustavus had carried on the war, and to the tact with which he had seized upon the right moment for offering peace.

[1] In his article on Charles XII. in the *Nineteenth Century* for June 1890.

# CHAPTER XXI.

## GUSTAVUS III. AND THE FRENCH REVOLUTION TILL SEPTEMBER 1791.

Gustavus's hostility to the French Revolution—Refuses to receive an ambassador from the French Assembly—Repudiates the tricolour—Staël and Fersen—Gustavus's plan for the restoration of the French monarchy—State of Europe at the beginning of 1791 —Gustavus's first project for the invasion of France—Desperate situation of the French royal family—Preparations for their flight —The Marquis de Bouillé—Fersen's energetic preparations— Gustavus at Aix-la-Chapelle—The flight to Varennes—Aix the centre of the anti-revolutionary movement—The Regency plan— Return of Gustavus to Sweden—The Russo-Swedish alliance— Dishonest tactics of Catherine—Gustavus presents the first plan of a general coalition against France—Practicability of Gustavus's scheme if promptly carried out—Hostility of the Emperor to it— Fersen's mission to Vienna—Russia draws back—Gustavus's Normandy invasion project — Foreign policy of England in 1791— Gustavus's extra-official negotiations with her—Treaty of Drottningholm between Russia and Sweden.

WITH the Peace of Värälä we enter upon the last, and, in many respects, the most interesting stadium of Gustavus's adventurous career, his *combat à l'outrance* with the French Revolution. Gustavus not unnaturally regarded himself as the natural champion of the French monarchy, which had been Sweden's faithful ally for more than 250 years, and to whom he himself owed so much.[1] He was, moreover, opposed to the Revolution on principle. His philosophical scepticism did not prevent him from believing in the divine right of kings, and a bitter political experience had

[1] The total amount of subsidies paid to Sweden by France between 1772 and 1788 was 38,200,000 livres.—Akeson, *Gustaf III.'s Förhallanden, etc.*

familiarised him with the uglier aspects of democracy. Rebellion in his eyes was little short of sacrilege. It might be forgiven, but could never be excused. From the very first, his unerring political instinct had recognised in the French Revolution the enemy of all authority with whom there could be no question of compromise. " The King of France has lost his throne—perhaps his life ! " he exclaimed, when the news reached him that Louis XVI. had convoked the States-General. Unlike his contemporary sovereigns, he never had the least delusion that things in France would right themselves if only left alone. It was his fate to be a political Cassandra, vainly warning the other European Powers what they had to expect unless they united all their forces to crush the Jacobin hydra in its infancy, and he was to be the life and soul of the anti-revolutionary league which collapsed so miserably after his death.

So long as he himself was embroiled with Russia, Gustavus could not, of course, lend a helping hand to his ancient ally ; but his whole correspondence shows that he was so engrossed by her misfortunes as almost to forget his own. Not without reason did those about him complain that the French Revolution had killed every other topic of conversation. In his despatches he frequently interrupts the recital of a victory or a defeat to bewail the condition of " *cette pauvre France,*" and his slumbers were disturbed by visions of the *sans-culottes* of Paris worrying the unhappy Delaunay to death, in the Place de la Grêve. At the same time his strong common-sense told him that the feebleness of the King of France and the imbecility of his counsellors were responsible, at least in the first instance, for the " horrible confusion " into which " delicious France " was falling, and his indignation was loud and vehement. The much-belauded Necker he regarded from the first as a vainglorious charlatan. Commenting on the failure of that

Minister's schemes he says: "There you have the result of the counsels of a democratic Minister, a citizen of a tiny Republic, who fancies that the realm of France can be governed on the same principles as the town of Geneva!" Louis XVI. he looked upon with half-wondering, half-contemptuous pity. "Poor prince!" he exclaims, "he is really the living image of a Bedlam king, with whom one does exactly as one likes. . . . He has delivered himself bound hand and foot into the hands of M. De la Fayette . . . who is really the Mayor of the Palace. . . . 'Tis a poor king in the fullest sense of the word. . . . In such desperate circumstances the worst possible policy is to sit still and do nothing, and this, it seems, is just what the King of France means to do."

When the emigration began, Gustavus offered an asylum in his camp to the French Princes, and took up an unmistakably hostile attitude towards the new French Government, although the National Assembly for long persisted in regarding him as a well-wisher, and the very Jacobins distinguished at first between him and the other sovereigns.[1] But a rupture sooner or later was inevitable, and when it did come, Gustavus took good care that it should be final.

In the course of the summer of 1789, the National Assembly determined to make a clean sweep of the diplomatic service of France, and accredit the new Ministers to the "King of the French," instead of to the "King of France," as heretofore. Gustavus at once notified to Staël that he would never recognise any envoy coming from Paris with such credentials. "I know very well," he adds,[2] "that the expression 'King of the French' is, in itself, quite indifferent, and that at Gripsholm [3] there is even a portrait of Francis I. with the inscription 'Francorum Rex.' The title 'King of the French,' therefore, is no novelty; but the importance

---

[1] Stael, *Correspondance Diplomatique.*    [2] Akeson, *Gustaf III.*, etc.
[3] A royal château famous for its splendid picture-galleries.

attached to it by the *soi-disant* National Assembly is sufficient to make even a trifle of this sort a serious matter, and
neither directly nor indirectly do I mean to sanction it. . . .
I make no secret of my sentiments, and proclaim to all the
world that it is just because I do cherish genuine popular
liberty (which I take to be security of life and property),
that I am so incensed at this spirit of insubordination, which
would utterly destroy the welfare, nay, the very existence
of every State." In a subsequent despatch to Staël he adds,
" I regard all who come from this Assembly as so many
conspirators leagued together to kindle the flames of civil
war in the very States of Europe, and . . . let me add that
I shall hold you personally responsible if this Minister of
theirs arrives."[1]

It was the same anxiety to guard his domains against the
contagion of Jacobinism which made Gustavus attempt to
exclude from the Baltic the new French tricolour, which the
National Assembly, in October 1790, had substituted for the
historical white flag. In the beginning of January 1791,
Gaussen, the French *chargé d'affaires* at Stockholm, delivered
to Secretary Franc an official notification of the change of
flag, with a coloured diagram annexed, so that the Swedish
Admiralty might take cognisance of the change. Gustavus,
however, did not even deign to receive the despatch, and the
more to impress the demagogues "who had so impudently
derided sovereignty in the person of the King of France,"
proposed that Russia, Sweden, and Denmark should simultaneously repudiate the tricolour. " To permit the national
flag in our harbours," he wrote to Stedingk, now his Ambassador at St. Petersburg, " would be tantamount to recognising the symbol of rampant demagogism in its most
outrageous form. We should thus be tacitly acknowledging the legality of this usurping Assembly's presumptuous

[1] Akeson, *Gustaf III., etc.*

measures, and thereby sanction and promote the mischievous Jacobin propaganda which is bent upon overthrowing law and order in every European State." This proposed joint action of the three Northern Powers came to nothing through the disinclination of Russia to make an enemy of France ; but during Gustavus's lifetime it was not safe for a French ship to show the tricolour in the Baltic.

But it was not till after the Peace of Värälä that Gustavus was able to proceed from words to deeds. It was necessary, first of all, however, that he should have at Paris an agent thoroughly in the confidence of the French royal family, and at the same time sufficiently able and audacious to help them in their desperate straits. He had lost all confidence in Staël, his accredited Minister, whose own despatches certainly stamp him as a diplomatist of little tact and less judgment, always admiring the wrong persons, mistaking the real bearing of events, and frequently dabbling in disreputable intrigues. Moreover, Staël's meddlesome spouse, piqued at the cold contempt of the French Court, began to openly coquet with the revolutionary leaders and compromise her husband by the indecent frivolity of her proceedings.[1] After fruitless warnings and rebukes, Gustavus was forced to recall Staël, and though he still retained a *chargé d'affaires* at Paris, it was through his secret agent, Count Hans Axel von Fersen, whom we have already [2] learned to know as the romantic friend of Marie Antoinette, that he negotiated directly with the French royal family.

Fersen [3] arrived at Paris early in 1790, full of confidence and hope, but before the end of the year he was forced to admit that the cause of the French monarchy was hopeless,

[1] Compare Feuillet de Conches, *Louis XVI.;* Geffroy, *Gustave III.;* Klinckowström, *Le Comte de Fersen.*

[2] Chapter XV.

[3] His correspondence, edited by Klinckowström, is one of the principal documents on the earlier stages of the French Revolution.

while the subsequent refusal of the populace, on April 18, 1791, to allow Louis XVI. to leave the Tuileries in order to spend Holy Week at Saint-Cloud, proved to demonstration that the King and Queen of France were nothing but captives in their own capital, and absolutely at the mercy of an excitable and irresponsible mob. It was immediately after this ominous event that Gustavus came forward as the champion and deliverer of the French royal family.

His plan was for their Majesties to escape from Paris, convoke a Congress of all the Provincial Parliaments, which should declare the National Assembly illegal and all its members rebels and traitors; invite the provinces to rise in defence of the monarchy against the capital; restore everything as it had been before the Revolution, but declare, at the same time, that all three Estates were equally liable to taxation; arrest, try, and execute the Duc d'Orléans, and set up the monarchy again in its absolute integrity. Finally, the Court was to remove for ever from Paris, and totally ignore the existence of that "den of assassins, for," added Gustavus significantly, "so long as there is a Paris, kings cannot exist in France; her history proves it only too well."

Such, then, was Gustavus's program, and utterly abominable as it may seem from the modern political standpoint, at the end of the eighteenth century it found many able and conscientious defenders. Even such a temperate and far-sighted politician as the younger Fersen regarded the Revolution as much too dangerous an example of rebellion to remain unpunished. "It should be," he writes, "the common interest of all sovereigns to nip in the bud an evil whose progress is alarming. It is not a simple question of policy, for here the cause of all kings is at stake. Without order, no society, no security, no property can exist. Kings are the born depositaries of order; they ought to preserve their authority for the welfare of their peoples. . . .

The remedy for such an evil is difficult perhaps, but not impossible."

Not impossible, perhaps, but most improbable, considering that the rehabilitation of the French monarchy was the question which hopelessly divided all the Courts of Europe. The Revolution, which was ultimately to give the dominion of Europe to France, had at first the diametrically opposite effect of reducing her to a mere geographical expression. Her place was provisionally taken by the Triple Alliance, recently formed at the Hague between England, Prussia, and Holland, whose policy was an attitude of watchful neutrality with an eye to ulterior advantage at the least possible risk and expense. The ultimate exhaustion of the belligerent Powers, Russia, Austria, and Sweden, was to be the opportunity of the neutral Powers, and therefore all the resources of diplomacy were employed to prolong and complicate the double war. Hence the direct intervention of England and Prussia in 1788 to prevent Denmark from assisting Russia by assailing Sweden. Hence the successful intrigues of the same Powers at Constantinople to encourage the Porte to prolong a hopeless struggle. Hence their efforts, too, to draw Poland over to the alliance at the expense of Austria. But so long as rival national interests are supported by standing armies, a peace-at-any-price policy must recoil upon its promoters. So now, too, the Triple Alliance overreached itself. Again and again it was in a position to dictate to the rest of Europe, and again and again it let the opportunity slip. Russia was the Power against which the Alliance was primarily directed, and twice within two years Russia had been absolutely at its mercy. If England had only provided Gustavus III. with the sinews of war in the shape of subsidies, and if Prussia had at the same time co-operated by an invasion of Russia in concert with the Poles, who, beneath the vigorous impulse of the famous Quadrennial Diet (1788–1792), had already boldly shaken off the galling Muscovite yoke, Catherine II. must have submitted to the dictation of an irresistible league, and, with a strong Sweden at the very gates of her capital, and an independent Poland on her flank, must have ceased for a long time to trouble the peace of Europe. But the Triple Alliance was incapable of an imperial policy, and so the control of Europe slipped from its grasp. Gustavus, seeing that no help was to be looked for from the West, prudently came to terms with his formidable rival. Austria gladly accepted the mediation of the Allies at the Congress of Reichenbach to make peace with the Porte on a *statu quo ante* basis, and, beneath the sceptre of the prudent Leopold II., she speedily recovered from the dilapidation into which Joseph II. had plunged her, and was soon strong enough to counterpoise Prussia. But Sweden also had now to be reckoned with. The Peace of Värälä, by relieving Gustavus from his embarrassments, had introduced a new and disturbing element into European politics. We have seen how his interests imperatively demanded the restoration of the French monarchy; but this would, of course, have clashed with the interests of the Triple Alliance, and, as necessarily leading to a fresh war, was thoroughly distasteful to convalescent Austria. No one understood the situation better than Gustavus himself, and assuming from the outset the inertia of Austria and the antagonism of the Triple Alliance, he proposed to create a new and independent league between Russia, Sweden, and Spain, for the purpose of re-establishing the French monarchy. The cost of the expedition was to be defrayed provisionally by Spain, who was to be indemnified by the French Court as soon as the French King had got his own again. The neutrality of England, Gustavus's especial bugbear, was to be purchased by the cession of the French

West Indies; while Prussia, he hoped, would be held in check by the Emperor, who, as the brother of the Queen of France, was supposed to be more interested than any one else in the welfare of the French royal family. Every obstacle being thus removed, Gustavus proposed to land at Ostend, or one of the Norman ports, with 16,000 Swedes and 8000 Russians, marching from thence straight upon Paris; while the Marquis de Bouillé, aided by an auxiliary corps of 12,000 Austrians, was to co-operate from the north-east with the French troops who still remained loyal.

Now, gratifying as the fiery zeal of the King of Sweden must have been to the French royal family, it was, nevertheless, decidedly embarrassing. Want of money, the chronic complaint of the French Court, made the execution of such a plan at present a sheer impossibility; and the Baron de Breteuil, Louis XVI.'s confidential plenipotentiary, resident just then in Switzerland, was instructed to implore Gustavus to postpone his project till their Majesties were safely out of Paris. Fersen, who, as the intimate confidant of the French royal family, understood the whole situation better than anybody else, wrote in the same strain, and by his advice the contemplated invasion was put off till the flight from Paris had been accomplished, to which end he now devoted all his energies and resources.

But the French royal family was by this time in such evil case that even a flight had become a break-neck adventure. They were kept at the Tuileries under the strictest surveillance. Their every movement was watched. Their very food was provided by Jacobin caterers.[1] They were conducted to their respective bedchambers by a guard of honour consisting of secret spies, and National Guards slept all night on their door-mats. It was only after infinite precautions that they were able to correspond with their friends; and

---

[1] Fersen's Correspondence.

their private communications, written in cipher, with in-
visible ink, between the lines of newspapers, were surrepti-
tiously forwarded to their destination by Swedish or Russian
couriers.[1]   To endure such things very much longer was
beyond the power of human nature, so it was resolved to
risk everything on the offchance of an escape.   But even sup-
posing the royal family safely out of Paris, their difficulties
would only then begin.   There was only one place in France
whither they could safely venture, only one General upon
whom they could absolutely rely.   This was the gallant
and energetic Marquis de Bouillé, the hero of the Antilles, one of the few French officers who still dared to do
his duty, and who had lately received the thanks of the
National Assembly itself for the heroic firmness with which,
in August 1790, he had quelled the terrible mutiny at
Nancy at the peril of his life.   Yet Bouillé's own position
at that moment was most precarious.   He lay at Metz with
6000 men, most of whom, as he privately informed Fersen,
were eaten up by the revolutionary gangrene, and owed him
a mortal grudge besides for preventing them from plunder-
ing the military chest.   Nevertheless, he was ready to assist
the King's flight so far as he was able, but absolutely insisted on the co-operation of 12,000 of the Austrian frontier
troops, and the possession of a sufficiently large sum of
money to purchase the services of his own.   Most of the
requisite money was found, at the last moment, by Fersen
himself, who also persuaded the Emperor to have the frontier
troops in readiness.   And now, with unexampled energy
and devotion, the young Swede proceeded to carry out all
the details of the perilous scheme.   Six months beforehand
he had ordered the construction of a regally luxurious carriage for six, in the name of the Baroness von Korff, a rich
Russian lady, who was obliged to leave Paris suddenly on

[1] Fersen's Correspondence.

pressing business. This sumptuous equipage, when finished, at a cost of nearly 6000 livres,[1] was conveyed to Fersen's hotel, Rue Matignon, and kept in the courtyard there, so that all Paris might get accustomed to the sight of it. The flight had originally been fixed for June 5, but all sorts of unforeseen obstacles intervening, it was not until midnight on the 20th that it could be safely accomplished. By that time Bouillé, under the pretext of protecting a consignment of money from Paris, had pushed forward small detachments of his troops as far as Châlons. At the last moment Gustavus himself resolved to come to Aix-la-Chapelle, so as to be quite close to the scene of action, but it was justly feared by Fersen, Breteuil, and Bouillé, the only other persons in the secret, that his presence so near the frontier might diminish the chances of escape of the royal family by increasing the vigilance of their janitors.

On June 16 Gustavus arrived at Aix, where a perfect ovation awaited him. The *élite* of the French aristocracy there assembled hailed him as their hero and deliverer. Women and children fell down on their knees before him, and implored him to restore them to their country. Marie Antoinette had already sent him a sword in a gold sheath, with the inscription, "For the defence of the oppressed." No eulogy was too extravagant for him. He was to excel the exploits of all his great ancestors. Gustavus, on the other hand, treated the emigrants with romantic tenderness, and entertained them with magnificent hospitality. Three times a week he kept open table for them,[2] and it was with a very sensible pleasure that this mob of reduced noblemen, whose ordinary fare just then was milk and potatoes, banquetted in batches of a hundred at a time with the King of Sweden. But Gustavus was far too sharp-sighted not to see

---

[1] Bimbenet, *Relation fidèle de la Fuite du Roi Louis XVI.*
[2] Geffroy, *Gustave Trois et la Cour de France.*

that the *emigrés* deserved his sympathy rather than his confidence. "I find here," he writes [1] soon after his arrival, "all the illustrious exiles of the Court of France. 'Tis perhaps the best society of both sexes in the world, and misfortune has made them even more amiable than they were before. They are all possessed by a common loathing of the National Assembly, and you have no idea of their exaggerated notions on all subjects. 'Tis certainly curious to hear them, but it is melancholy too." He had been warned beforehand that, even at Aix, he would be surrounded by the spies of the National Assembly, and cautioned against confiding anything to the *emigrés* themselves, and he behaved throughout with exemplary tact and discretion.

Meanwhile the flight from Paris had already taken place. At a quarter past eleven on the night of June 20, the palace domestics left the King of France apparently asleep in bed; but he arose fully dressed the moment they had quitted him, and by half-past the King, the Queen, Madame Elizabeth, the Dauphin, and Madame, attended by Madame Tourzel, were safely outside the Tuileries. To avoid detection, they were to proceed separately to the Carrousel, whence they intended to drive together to the Porte Saint-Martin, where Madame de Korff's [2] carriage, with Fersen's swiftest horses harnessed to it, already awaited them. Fersen, disguised as a coachman, and followed by Madame de Tourzel with Madame, carried the Dauphin in his arms to the fiacre which he had hired for the purpose, and drove them to the Carrousel, where, for a terrible three-quarters of an hour, they awaited the rest of the royal family, during which time Lafayette and Bailly,[3] who were going their nightly rounds,

[1] Tegner, *Konung Gustaf III.'s bref till Armfelt.*

[2] That lady, with her suite, had quitted Paris a few days before.

[3] Madame de Tourzel tells us that she hid the Dauphin under her petticoats till they had passed.

came up and actually stopped to speak to Fersen, who played the part of coachman to admiration, taking snuff and cracking jokes with another coachman who also happened to stroll up. Madame Elizabeth was the first to arrive, and shortly afterwards the King appeared, and finally the Queen, who had lost her way in the dark. This unfortunate delay proved the ruin of the whole enterprise.

The carriage at the Porte Saint-Martin had now been waiting for the fugitives for more than two hours, and still there was not a sign of them. At last, just as the day was about to dawn, a fiacre dashed up at full gallop, drew up alongside the carriage, and its occupants immediately passed from it into the more commodious vehicle without alighting. Fersen then took his seat on the box beside the coachman, and they set off with such celerity that the first stage, Bondy, was reached in less than half-an-hour. Here the King, with characteristic unselfishness, insisted that the faithful Fersen should quit them. " If we should be stopped and you taken," said he, " it would be impossible for me to save you. . . . God bless you, Monsieur de Fersen ; " he added, " accept the offer of my friendship, and be assured that, happen what may, I shall never forget your zeal and your good services." [1] Unwillingly, and with many misgivings, Fersen at last obeyed, and set out for Mons, from whence he meant to make his way to Montmedy and there rejoin the fugitives. The end of that fateful flight is only too well known. How the young Duc de Choiseul, who should have escorted them from Pont de Sommevesle, after vainly waiting there for two hours beyond the appointed time, thought that the secret had been betrayed and returned by the nearest road to Montmedy ; how the royal family was recognised at Saint-Menehould, arrested at Varennes, and taken back in triumph

---

[1] Crawfurd's narrative, contained in the Bland-Burgess Papers, pp. 366 *et seq*. Crawfurd had this from his friend Fersen direct. Compare Bimbenet.

to Paris by the mob—all these things are matters of history. The horrors of that return journey no pen can describe, but two little anecdotes which Fersen had from the Queen's own lips [1] a few months later, we cannot omit. To pacify the mob, Marie Antoinette offered a piece of beef *à la mode* which they had with them in the carriage to one of the ragged wretches howling around them. He was about to greedily devour it when a voice cried out, " Don't eat it! Don't you see that it is poisoned!" Full of indignation, the Queen at once ate a portion of it herself, and gave some to the Dauphin; but the crowd after that remained invincibly suspicious. Pétion, one of the commissioners sent by the National Assembly to bring the royal family back, behaved most unbecomingly to the Queen. He said that he knew all about the preparations for the flight, and declared aloud to those around him that the King had hired a hackney-coach close to the château driven by a Swede. Then affecting to forget the name, he turned to the Queen and asked, with a covert sneer, who it was. [2] " Monsieur," replied Antoinette haughtily, " I am not in the habit of inquiring after the names of my hackney-coachmen."

Gustavus III. was the first to learn the news of the catastrophe. At Spa, whither he had gone to be still nearer the frontier, he patiently awaited, watch in hand, the arrival of a special courier with full details of the escape. But the day wore on, and still there was no sign of him. Early on the following morning, the King was awakened by his equerry, who brought him Fersen's note containing the terrible tidings of the arrest. Gustavus immediately arose, and had scarcely had time to throw on his dressing-gown when he was surrounded by a whole crowd of *emigrés* who pressed into his room. Their grief was heart-rending, and Gustavus

---

[1] Fersen's Diary for 1791, Klinckowström, vol. ii.
[2] Insinuating, of course, that he was her lover.

himself was so overcome that at first he could only mingle his tears with theirs.

The first sign of life given by the prisoners of the Tuileries was an almost illegible little note from Marie Antoinette to Fersen at Brussels, followed by a longer one concluding with these words: " We are guarded in our rooms day and night,[1] but don't worry, nothing evil will befall us. The Assembly means to treat us leniently.[2] . . . Farewell! Perhaps I shall never be able to write to you again." Fersen stayed a whole week at Brussels, whither Monsieur, Madame, the Count d'Artois, and a whole host of distinguished *emigrés* speedily arrived, "all like madmen," as Fersen contemptuously describes them, shrieking for vengeance but incapable of any coherent plan of action. Count Mercy d'Argenteau, Marie Antoinette's life-mentor, was also at Brussels, and took a very gloomy view of matters. On his advice, Fersen wrote to the Queen proposing that the royal family, during their captivity, should delegate their authority, and sending on approval a sort of power of attorney for appointing Monsieur Regent of France in the King's stead. Then he hastened back to his own master at Aix, whither Bouillé, now a full-pay general in the Swedish service,[3] had already preceded him.

So far from being daunted by the Varennes fiasco, Gustavus III. was now more than ever resolved to chastise the National Assembly, and restore the French monarchy in

---

[1] How strict this surveillance really was we best learn from the following extract from a letter from Gustavus III. to Armfelt, dated 7th July 1791 :— " Le roi et la reine sont tellement captifs qu'ils ne peuvent se voir que portes ouvertes. Le roi pour parler à la reine sans temoins a voulu couchez chez elle ; on le lui a refusé. Le Dauphin ne voit plus sa mère ; on l'a placé dans une chambre d'où la reine l'entend crier mais ne peut le voir."

[2] Because the Assembly feared an immediate invasion of France. See Miles' Correspondence, p. 302.

[3] Bouillé had intended at first to enter the Russian service, but, as he tells us in his Memoirs, " Subjugé par ses (Gustavus's) louanges flatteuses (on résiste difficilement à celles d'un héros) je me rendis."—*Memoirs*, p. 199.

its integrity. During the remainder of his stay at Aix he developed an almost feverish activity, scattering despatches broadcast, and sending couriers in every direction. He succeeded in sending a letter to Louis XVI. urging him to resist every encroachment upon his authority, and assuring him of the unfailing devotion of his friends.[1] Staël, not yet recalled, was warned against doing anything which might be interpreted as a recognition of the *soi-disant* French Government, and Bergstedt, the Secretary of Legation, was secretly instructed to spy upon Staël and see that he did his duty. He was also instructed to advise as to the practicability of a fresh fligh from Paris; but Bergstedt, who had little relish to make the closer acquaintance of the mob, reported that an escape from the Tuileries was impossible, and any one attempting it would inevitably be hanged on the nearest lamp-post.

Aix now became the centre of the anti-revolutionary movement. In the beginning of July the French Princes came thither from Treves. Gustavus received the illustrious exiles with the most demonstrative sympathy, and at a secret conference in his rooms at Aix read to them a memorandum of his own composition proposing that Monsieur should at once take the title of Regent, form a Ministry of his most uncompromising supporters, send special diplomatic agents to the various Courts of Europe, and officially invite all the well-wishers of France at home and abroad to rally round the white flag. Stimulated by the enthusiasm of the *emigrés*, his attitude towards the National Assembly became more and more menacing. So far from making any secret of his plans, he gloried in posing before all the world as the irreconcilable antagonist of the Parisian reactionaries. On being informed that his letter to Staël of June 27 had

---

[1] It concluded with these words : "Ne souffrez surtout qu'on avilisse dans votre personne la dignité royale, et les rois viendront a votre sécour."

been printed at Paris, and that the whole Jacobin press had been reviling him ever since, he expressed his satisfaction at the publicity given to his sentiments, and his utter indifference to the criticisms of " such pamphleteers as Messrs. Marat & Co."

Even amongst Gustavus's own supporters, however, there was a growing feeling that his anti-Jacobinism was carrying him too far. Warning voices reached him from every corner of Europe. Stedingk, his Ambassador at St. Petersburg, urged him not to build too much on the false representations of the *emigrés*. Armfelt, who detested his master's anti-Gallic policy because it gave too much influence to his rivals—Fersen and Taube—questioned the sincerity of the Emperor and the ability of the French Princes. Staël repeatedly represented the utter impossibility of restoring the ancient order of things in France, and even dared to hint at the great advantages which would accrue to Sweden from an alliance with constitutional France. Count Wrangel,[1] Gustavus's Minister at Florence, took the same view, significantly adding that Simonville, the new French Minister at Genoa, had confidentially informed him that the first Power which openly allied itself with France might expect large subsidies and important commercial concessions. Nay, Marie Antoinette herself was averse to violent measures. She was just then negotiating with the leaders of what Staël called " the Fourth party "—Barnave, Duport, the Lameths, and their friends—who were shrewd enough to see that a constitutional monarchy was very desirable, but not very easily realisable so long as France was in danger of an invasion and harassed by the intrigues of the *emigrés*. They therefore appealed to the Queen to write to her brother, the Emperor, and the other European potentates, earnestly dissuading an invasion, and this she accordingly

[1] Akeson, *Gustaf III.'s Förhallanden, etc.*

did.  Louis XVI., moreover, declined to invest his brother
with even a temporary regency, and both he and the Queen
agreed that, under the circumstances, an "armed conference" was the only practical form which external aid could
safely take.  Convinced as he was that "steel and cannon-
balls" was the only remedy for France in her present condition, Gustavus was not best pleased with Marie Antoinette's
preference for less drastic methods.  In painful uncertainty
as to the issue of his plans, dissatisfied with the French
Court, and disgusted with the general aimlessness of the
*emigrés*, he quitted Aix (July 27, 1791) for Stockholm,
whence he hoped to direct the intricate and complicated
diplomatic machinery which he had already set in motion
for the furtherance of his plans.  His chief hope now was in
his new ally and former antagonist, Catherine II.

The Peace of Värälä had opened the way to a Russo-
Swedish alliance by convincing Gustavus and Catherine that
it would be better for them both to live together in amity
for the future.  Although quite determined from the first
to avoid all direct interference in French affairs, Catherine
hated the French Revolution and all its works as energetically as Gustavus; but it was to her, at least primarily, a
heaven-sent opportunity for giving her dangerously restless
cousin something to do in the West, so that she herself
might have "free elbow-room"[1] in the East.  To prevent his
enthusiasm from cooling, she sent Baron Pahlen to Aix with
an autograph proposal for a league of princes to regenerate
France, in which she declared that Gustavus was the only
prince of sufficient ability and dignity to take the supreme
command of such a coalition; while, in a note to Stackelberg,
her new Minister at Stockholm, which, ostensibly private,
she knew, nevertheless, could not fail to be reported to the
King of Sweden, she declared it was her fondest wish to win

---

[1] Khrapovitsky, *Dnevnik.*

a trusty ally in her good cousin. "We must," she went on, "devote all our attention to French affairs, because our honour and our interest are equally concerned therein, and besides, the King will there find an opportunity of fully employing those talents which God has given him." She further declared her willingness to conclude with him a secret convention, not only to uphold the Peace of Westphalia, but to restore the old French monarchy also. This was all very well, but beyond a few vague phrases about a possible Russian contingent and a paltry half million of roubles, there was still nothing definite as to Russia's participation in this new crusade. Still, unsatisfactory as Gustavus knew it to be, the Tsarina's memorandum gave him something to go upon, and henceforth the Russian alliance was to be his trump-card in all his dealings with the Western Powers, and his reply to Catherine's memorandum is noteworthy as containing the first definite plan of a general coalition against Revolutionary France.

After a flattering preamble and a lucid exposition of the actual state of affairs, in which he laid special stress upon the proposed Regency of Monsieur pending the captivity of the King of France, he demanded the Empress's active co-operation in the following plan. He proposed to invade France from several points simultaneously, so as to d'stract the Jacobins as much as possible. While 30,000 to 35,000 Imperialists invaded Artois, 12,000 to 15,000 Swiss Franche-Comté, and 15,000 Sardinians Dauphiné, 20,000 Spanish troops were to cross the Pyrenees, the Princes of the Empire at the same time making a diversion in Alsace. The neutrality of England was almost certain, or, at any rate, could be purchased.[1] Once on French soil, an assembly of notables should proclaim Monsieur Regent till the King was released.

---

[1] By the cession of the French Antilles. In that age of partitions even *inaction*, it seems, had a claim to reward.

But the primary requisite of such a coalition was "a supreme chief of sufficient rank and disinterestedness" to make him superior to all petty jealousies, and of sufficient authority to silence all contradiction. This supreme chief was to have at his immediate disposal a powerful force, solely dependent upon the Empress and himself, or, in other words, was to be the writer. "Six thousand Swedes," he proceeds, "united to 6000 Russians, transported upon Russian and Swedish vessels to Ostend, and conveyed from thence to Liège, to form with the troops of Hesse and the Palatinate the centre of the grand army, whose right wing is assumed to rest upon Dunkirk and its left upon Strasburg, would thus give to the Northern Powers the necessary preponderance," and thus enable them to hold the balance between the selfishly divergent interests of the other Powers, who would like nothing better than a partition of France.[1] "Nothing," concluded Gustavus adroitly, "would give a grander or juster idea of the Empress's resources than the sight of her hastening, despite the entanglements of the costly Oriental war, from the distant North to the assistance of the King of France." Once on French soil, the maintenance of the troops would be easy, and at the expense of the inhabitants, who had made such a coalition necessary, and, marching straight upon Paris, the allies headed by the King of Sweden, with the Marquis de Bouillé as his chief of the staff, would destroy the evil in its very centre once and for all. This plan Gustavus also communicated to the King of Spain, and Ehrensvärd, the Swedish Minister at Madrid, was instructed to lay special stress on the danger of leaving France to the tender mercies of Austria and Prussia, and hint at the necessity of a closer alliance between Sweden and Spain.[2] Stedingk, at St. Peters-

---

[1] It was in this memorandum that Gustavus said it would even be better to take the part of the National Assembly itself than to remain indifferent spectators of the course of events.

[2] Akeson, *Gustaf III.'s Förhallanden, etc.*

burg, was also to energetically follow up his master's letter and insist on a categorical answer.

Venturesome as it was, Gustavus's plan of invasion had, after all, far more chances of success than any of the subsequent coalitions which succeeded it. To begin with, it foresaw and tried to guard against the obstacles on which the subsequent ill-starred Brunswick expedition so miserably foundered. The generalissimo of the league of princes was to be no subaltern potentate, bound down at the very outset by impossible conditions and perpetually overruled by the contradictory commands of many masters. No; he was to be an independent sovereign prince with forces behind him sufficient to impose obedience on his colleagues. The invading army, instead of anxiously lingering on the frontier (as Brunswick did) till it had secured all the fortresses likely to interrupt its communications or hamper its retreat, was to march straight upon Paris, and crush the Revolution in its cradle before the Jacobins had time to act on the defensive. Add to this that circumstances in France itself were far more favourable to the allies at the beginning of 1791 than they were at the end of 1792. Most of the provincials were still loyal. The majority of the National Assembly was actually anti-republican. As yet, no great political crime stood in the way of a compromise between the partisans of the old and the partisans of the new system, and Gustavus did not absolutely exclude from his calculations the possibility of negotiations with the Assembly.[1] Finally, the projected coalition of 1791 would have had a far more capable leader than the coalition of 1792. The Duke of Brunswick was the effete representative of a decrepit system of strategics. To pit such a man and such a system against the volcanic energy of the young Revolution was to court defeat. Gustavus, on the other hand, though no professional soldier, was possessed by a

[1] Akeson.

restless energy and a passion for adventure which stuck at nothing. In a prolonged and regular campaign with veterans for his opponents, he would, doubtless, have come off second best; but, as the leader of a swift and sudden *coup-de-main*, he would, most probably, have proved irresistible.[1] Moreover, in his proposed chief of the staff, the Marquis de Bouillé, he possessed a military adviser of energy and great experience. But this first proposed coalition was to come to nought. Without the co-operation of the Emperor, nothing could be done, and the "cursed Florentine," as Fersen and Taube indignantly called him, set his face against it from the first. Leopold disliked Gustavus, dreaded his mercurial restlessness, and regarded the intrusion of this Prince from *Ultima Thule* in French affairs as an impertinence. So far from desiring the help of Sweden, he would, if possible, have excluded her from the European concert altogether, and it was an ominously significant fact that the manifesto which the Emperor, immediately after the Varennes collapse, had addressed from Mantua to the European Powers, urging them to unite with him in defence of Louis XVI., had not been communicated to the Swedish Court at all. Hurt though he was by this deliberate slight, Gustavus, nevertheless, could not afford to quarrel with Leopold, and young Fersen was despatched forthwith to Vienna to inform the Emperor of the proposed coalition and obtain permission to make the port of Ostend the headquarters of the Northern fleets and forces during the course of the campaign. He was further to suggest to the Austrian Chancellor, Kaunitz, the formation of an alliance between Sweden, Austria, France, and Russia, and if possible get Gustavus recognised as the chief of the League of Princes.

---

[1] His exploits during the Russo-Swedish war justify this assumption. The relief of Gothenburg in 1788, the battle of Liikala in 1789, and the crowning victory of Svensksund in 1790 were all brilliant dashes, in which the royal knight-errant risked everything on a single bold cast and won every time.

Fersen arrived at Vienna on August 2, and two days afterwards had his first interview with the Emperor, with the result of which he was anything but satisfied. Leopold was evasive and discursive throughout, "talking much and listening little." Still less satisfactory were his interviews with the Austrian Ministers. Kaunitz was polite and obliging, but would pledge himself to nothing, and the Vice-Chancellor, Cobentzl, while admitting that the state of France was "frightful," felt quite sure that it could not be improved so long as the nation remained imbued with such ideas. "It seems to me that it will be a long job, and that they don't put much heart into it," wrote the baffled Swede in his laconic diary. His general impression was that the Emperor and his Ministers were pulling different ways, and were afraid of Prussia, to whom they attributed a self-seeking, *quid pro quo* sort of policy, and Cobentzl was inclined to adjust matters provisionally by holding an armed Congress at Aix-la-Chapelle, and postponing all active preparations till the following spring. At last, after following the Emperor to Prague, and waiting upon him there also, Fersen began to lose heart, and a final interview with Leopold confirmed his suspicions that the Austrian Court meant to do nothing at all at present. The Emperor agreed with everything he said, in order to get rid of him as speedily as possible. So Fersen informed his master that any further stay at Vienna would be sheer waste of time, and at his own request was transferred to Brussels, where he could be of more service to the Queen of France.

The Emperor's procrastination was the death-blow to Gustavus's first coalition project. As Fersen had all along predicted, the petty German courts with whom Sweden had been negotiating throughout the last two months looked to the Emperor alone for orders, and without him would do nothing. Even the French Princes, though they very readily ate Gustavus's dinners, were indisposed to submit to his dictation; and worst of all, the Tsarina also now began to throw cold water on the project.

The failure of the Varennes expedition had made a deep impression upon Catherine. She expressed her disapproval of the King's flight, and of the way in which it had been managed. She even thought it would have been better to have done nothing, but simply left the National Assembly "to simmer in its own gravy." Opinion at the Russian Court was, however, much divided on the subject. The Prince of Nassau and the Grand Duke Paul (the latter had conceived for Gustavus that sudden and violent admiration which he afterwards transferred to Napoleon) were enthusiastic for the good cause; but most of the Ministers were of quite the contrary opinion, and the still omnipotent Potemkin said, with a shrug, that Russia was too remote to meddle with such matters. The Empress herself declined to move a step in the matter till the sentiments of all the other Powers had been ascertained, and insisted on the neutrality of England and the co-operation of the Emperor as indispensable preliminaries. "These people are wearing out my patience, sir," wrote Stedingk to Gustavus, "and I find that it is a thousand times more difficult to negotiate with the Russians than to fight them." Presently the Empress began to say that she thought the projected invasion of the King of Sweden was on far too vast a scale; that the Emperor was the fittest chief for such a league; that Ostend was not a suitable place for disembarking troops, and that the season was far too advanced for any such expedition. Thus Gustavus, who, while still at Aix, had nourished the hope of invading France with 100,000 men in the course of the summer, saw all his expectations fall to the ground one after the other before the autumn was over. At this juncture, however, he received a new project of invasion from the French Princes, which spurred him on to fresh endeavours.

The opinion generally prevalent in France after the Varennes fiasco, that the foreign Powers were about to intervene, alarmed not only the Revolutionaries, but the King's friends likewise. The inhabitants of Normandy in particular, most of whom were devoted to the royal cause, feared that in case of an invasion they would be the first victims of the Jacobins' revengeful fury, and being too weak to defend themselves, appealed to Coblentz for help. The Princes, unable to promise anything definite, turned to the King of Sweden; suggested that he should make a descent upon the Norman coast with 8000 men, and indicated the ports most suitable for such a descent, as well as the safest anchorages for ships of war. The whole plan was discussed in council by the Counts of Provence and Artois at Schönbrunn in Taube's presence, and adopted in its entirety. The reflection that its execution might perhaps be attended with some little difficulty never seems to have occurred to the Princes. A Russo-Swedish fleet had only to blockade the mouth of the Seine, and cut off Paris from all communication with the sea, while the King of Sweden with his army marched straight upon the capital, and the thing was done. Gustavus's approval was taken for granted, and to stir up the Empress they despatched the Marquis de Bombelles to St. Petersburg, to invite the Tsarina to co-operate with the King of Sweden in the expedition. But the Empress did not take quite such a roseate view of matters. To show her " good-will," indeed, she sent the Princes 2,000,000 livres, but declared at the same time that a naval expedition so late in the season was out of the question. It was plain to her, she subsequently said in a private letter to the Prince of Nassau,[1] that the French

---

[1] Feuillet de Conches, *Louis XVI.*, ii. 247.

Princes were richer in expedients than resources, and that their paper army was in exactly the same condition as the 120,000 men of the King of Sweden. If they waited for the concert of the Powers, they would have to wait a pretty long time. Prussia's proceedings were, as usual, tricky and pettifogging; and Prussia's transmarine ally (*i.e.*, England) was not a bit better. She was quite at one with the King of Sweden in wishing to promote " the good cause," and, with the return of spring, would take her proper place in any coalition that might be agreed upon. Meanwhile she recommended Monsieur to assume the title of Regent of France, and sent Romanzov to Coblentz to represent her.

Gustavus, on the other hand, always averse to half measures, welcomed the idea of the Norman expedition with enthusiasm, especially as the attitude of England, hitherto his great obstacle, had now become more promising. Her mysterious silence on French affairs had so impressed Russia, Austria, and Prussia, that they had refused to move a step till Pitt's intentions were disclosed. England, indeed, was still pursuing a waiting policy, like the Empress. Throughout 1791 England had been sorely disquieted by the ambition of Catherine II.; Pitt, with the nation at his back, was ready to risk a rupture with " Russia's haughty dame," and in the spring of 1791 a war in defence of the Ottoman Empire seemed likely. But the Opposition succeeded at last in inspiring the country with doubts as to the expediency of a costly contest on behalf of the already badly-beaten Turk, and most of Pitt's own colleagues were dead against him.[1] Besides, circumstances were no longer favourable to such a war. Had England broken with Russia in the beginning of 1790, and sent a fleet to the Baltic to co-operate with Gustavus III. in his daring *coup-de-main* on St. Petersburg, peace might have been dictated to the Tsarina in her

[1] Bland-Burgess Papers, ed. Hutton, pp. 148–149, 154.

own capital. But Pitt had let this golden opportunity slip; Sweden had meanwhile made peace with Russia, and England suddenly found herself completely isolated, for the Conference of Pilnitz had tacitly dissolved the triple alliance between England, Prussia, and Holland. Henceforward the British cabinet was more than ever bent upon sitting still. The prevalent opinion was that it would suit England's interests best to simply let France alone. " We have felt too strongly," wrote Under-Secretary Burgess to Lord Auckland, " the immense advantage to be derived for this country from such a state of anarchy as France is plunged in, to be so mad as to interfere in any measure which may, even remotely, tend to put France into the situation where, as a long and terrible experience has taught, she had the power to injure us, and when she had the power . . . she never wanted the will." [1] The King of Sweden and his Ministers were well aware of England's sentiments on this point. Neutrality, they thought, was the utmost they could reasonably expect of her; the only question was what price they might have to pay for it ? " I fancy," Fersen had shrewdly observed to the Emperor,[2] " that Pitt wants to justify his costly armaments by obtaining something which he will put at a pretty high figure. That is the cause of his vague responses. We must offer to accept his terms. . . . That will decide the matter." Gustavus therefore resolved to sound the intentions of the English Government extra-officially, and at first, while still at Aix, seems to have been bent upon crossing the Channel and negotiating personally. But the English Ministers had no desire to meet, face to face, a monarch they had already twice deceived,[3] so Gustavus,

---

[1] Bland-Burgess Papers, ed. Hutton, pp. 148–149, 154.

[2] Klinckowström, *Le Comte de Fersen, etc.*

[3] First, by urging him on to war with Russia, with the assurance of aid that was never rendered ; and, secondly, by their ambiguous conduct to him during

at Fersen's suggestion, determined to employ Mr. Quentin Craufurd, whose intimacy with and devotion to the French Royal Family was second only to his friend Fersen's. Craufurd was accordingly presented to the King of Sweden at Aix, and received his final instructions from Gustavus personally on July 20, 1791. Gustavus told Craufurd [1] that his championship of the King of France, and his determination to deliver France from "the abominations which prevailed there," were founded on "principles of justice and good policy, and did not arise from a spirit of chivalry, as some of the late French orators were pleased to ascribe to him; for that, whatever might be his dispositions, it was sufficiently evident that neither the state of his country nor his finances admitted of his making campaigns by way of amusement or for the sake of being spoken of." Craufurd acquitted himself of his commission to the satisfaction of all concerned.[2] He failed, indeed, to procure a loan from the English Ministry, but he drew forth a letter [3] from the King of England to the King of Sweden, which, though somewhat ambiguous, was far more satisfactory than Gustavus had dared to expect. He saw in it a guarantee of England's complete neutrality, and that, he opined, was as much as could be looked for under the circumstances. He now, therefore, threw himself heart and soul into the Normandy invasion project. The idea of it had, indeed, occurred to him long before. In the beginning of June two Swedish officers, Fiandt and König, had been sent from Sweden to survey and map out the whole basin of the Seine from Paris to Havre, which task they actually succeeded in accomplishing despite the suspicious

the war. The news of Gustavus's projected visit to England, which most historians have overlooked, was communicated to Catherine II. by Voronzov, her Minister at London. *Khrapovitsky.*

[1] Bland-Burgess Papers. We know from Gustavus's own correspondence that he gave Craufurd a letter to Pitt.

[2] Klinckowström.     [3] Klinckowström gives a full copy of it, i. 173–174.

watchfulness of the French authorities.[1]  But it was not till the grand coalition project fell through that Gustavus occupied himself seriously with the Norman invasion alternative.  For this he considered 30,000 men amply sufficient, and he now used the assumed neutrality of England as the strongest argument for the Tsarina to declare herself in its favour But Catherine was even less satisfied with the Norman invasion project than she had been before with the plan for a general coalition.  The Russian Ministers regarded any such isolated attack as altogether impracticable, and Stedingk doubted very much whether the Empress would even find the money for it.  Nevertheless, though steadily rejecting every proposal for a direct and immediate invasion of France, the Russian Court continued to take a lively interest in French affairs, and the definite conclusion of the long-pending defensive treaty with Sweden, generally known as the Convention of Drottningholm (19th October 1791), seemed be a guarantee for future joint action in the matter.[2] At the same time Catherine expressed her joy that the views of her "good brother and cousin" upon French affairs corresponded so exactly with her own; declared she could not sufficiently admire the foresight with which he had so carefully pioneered the way, and regretted that the advanced season and the ice-bound seas made instant action impracticable.  She therefore advised him to abide the development of events, and lull the National Assembly into a false security by an affected indifference, employing the winter in bringing about an understanding between the various Powers, with the view of forming a general coalition in the spring of 1792.

[1] Akeson, *Gustaf III.'s Förhallanden.*
[2] By this treaty Russia undertook to pay to Sweden subsidies amounting to 300,000 roubles per annum.

# CHAPTER XXII.

## GUSTAVUS III. AND THE FRENCH REVOLUTION FROM SEPTEMBER 1791 TO MARCH 1792.

State of affairs in France—The flight beneficial to the King—The Barnave faction espouses the cause of Louis XVI.—The new Constitution—It is notified to the Powers—The Emperor acknowledges it—Indignation and hostility of Gustavus III.—His fresh proposal of a league between Russia, Sweden, and Spain—Fersen's scheme of an armed Congress—The Elector of Treves applies to Sweden for help—Collapse of the armed Congress project—Meeting of the Legislative Assembly at Paris—First appearance of the Girondists—Ultimatum to the Elector of Treves—Withdrawal of the Swedish Ambassador from Paris—Secret missions of Talleyrand to London and of Segur to Berlin—Both missions nullified by Fersen—Gustavus's plan for the escape of the Royal Family of France to England—Fersen succeeds in reaching the Tuileries to consult with Louis XVI.—Desperate position of the King and Queen—The National Assembly's ultimatum to the Emperor—Resignation of the French Ministry—The first Girondist Administration—War declared against the Emperor.

WE must now very briefly review the state of affairs in France itself. The attempted flight of the Royal Family has too often been regarded as a mistake, but its immediate sobering effect on the National Assembly seems to us to point to exactly the opposite conclusion. The popular leaders were shrewd enough to understand that a successful flight would pretty certainly have been followed by a foreign invasion, and we have unexceptionable testimony to the fact that just at this particular time—a few months later it was already too late—a well-concerted invasion (similar, for instance, to Gustavus's plan) would, in all probability, have proved irre-

132

sistible. "An army of 40,000 or 50,000 men invading Alsace at this moment," writes the acute and far-seeing W. A. Miles, "would ravage the kingdom and threaten all France with ruin, because the noblesse, the clergy, the lawyers, and other Royalists would join them, and these amount to some 300,000 men. Never was France so nearly being inevitably ruined as at this instant (March 1791). If she escapes, she will owe much to the folly or the generosity of Europe."[1] The reforming zealots of 1789, chastened and schooled by a two years' experience of affairs, and scared by the red spectre of anarchy already arising in their midst, suddenly awoke to the danger of their position and endeavoured to restrain the mob. A close alliance with the King henceforth became their chief aim, and the very men, Barnave and his colleagues, for instance, who had addressed the most fulsome flattery to the "refuse of all that is infamous,"[2] now did their best to bolster up the sinking monarchy, and thus it came about that, so far from being injurious to the King, as his friends abroad had anticipated, the attempted flight was, at least in the first instance, distinctly beneficial to him and his. The Barnave faction, with a decided majority in the Assembly, at once proceeded to make the cause of the King its own. At first, indeed, the King and Queen were treated as prisoners under arrest, but this was only to save appearances. On July 13, the Select Committee appointed to report to the Assembly on the matter of the flight to Varennes declared that there was no ground of complaint against his Majesty. A long and stormy debate immediately ensued on the question of the inviolability of the King, a political dogma which Robespierre furiously assailed and Barnave as hotly defended. A compromise was at last come to. The majority, while declaring the King absolutely innocent, consented, nevertheless, to sus-

---

[1] Miles, Correspondence.        [2] Ibid.

pend him from the exercise of his functions till he had
accepted the new Constitution, which had yet to be framed.
The absurdity of such a resolution is obvious. While declaring the King innocent, it at the same time treated him as
guilty, thus insinuating a doubt as to the honesty of the
monarch at the very moment when the rehabilitation of the
monarchy was essential to the success of the Barnave programme. Nevertheless, self-contradictory and inconclusive
as it might be, this resolution was still the first act of courage,
the first symptom of impatience at the domination of the
gutter which the Assembly had displayed since the death of
Mirabeau, and its effect upon the irreconcilables was prodigious. Robespierre, who had previously declaimed against
the Assembly as "a Parliament of traitors," now meekly
repudiated, in the midst of the Jacobins, the very idea of
being a republican, and declared that an honest man could
live as freely under a monarchy as under any other form
of government. Almost all the deputies who had hitherto
belonged to the Jacobin Club suddenly withdrew from it and
formed a club of their own at the old convent of the Feuillants,
to which they gave the name of "Society of the Friends of
the Constitution," and when the *sans-culottes* got up a monster
meeting, on July 17, in the Champs de Mars, for the purpose
of petitioning the Assembly to depose the King, the Government for once did its duty. Lafayette appeared at the head
of the National Guards, and a couple of salvoes dispersed
the mob. The triumph of the monarchists seemed complete ;
Barnave and his friends now had the game entirely in their
own hands, and, with a very moderate exercise of courage and
prudence, might easily have won the stake for which they
were playing. But they never went beyond good intentions.
They had not the courage to boldly carry out a counter-
revolution. Their antecedents, too, were against them, and
the extremists, White and Red, united to oppose them at

every step. Their first act was to try to win the Queen over to their side, and with the Queen the Emperor. With Barnave and the Lameths Marie Antoinette entered into "a sort of correspondence," which, as she told Fersen, "not a soul in the world, not even their own friends, suspect." But *her* confidence was all pretence. She naturally detested and distrusted the professions of men at whose hands she had hitherto suffered every imaginable insult and wrong, and whom fear alone had at last brought to her feet. She proposed to use them for her own purposes and then cast them aside, and she secretly warned her imperial brother against putting any trust in the envoys whom her new friends were diligently despatching to the various foreign Courts. In the Assembly itself, too, the Constitutionalists, as they now styled themselves, met with many obstacles. All their attempts to revise the Constitution in a monarchical sense failed utterly, and on September 3, 1791, that "tissue of impracticable absurdities," as Marie Antoinette not inaptly termed it, was presented for acceptance to the King. Louis XVI.'s mind was already made up. To lull the suspicions of the Assembly by inspiring it with a false confidence was the line that most honest of men had reluctantly decided to take. "In our position," wrote the Queen to Mercy,[1] "it is impossible for the King to refuse his sanction. Accept it he must, and when I say so you will believe it, for you know my character well enough to understand that it naturally prefers noble and courageous deeds. But I do not call it courage to run the risk of more than certain disaster. We have now no other resource but the Foreign Powers. Cost what it will, they must come to our assistance. . . . I assure you that things have now come to such a pass that it were better to be King of a single province than of a kingdom so vitiated and disordered as this one."

[1] Arneth, *Marie Antoinette, etc.*, pp. 205-206.

On September 13, 1791, the King formally accepted the Constitution, and, amidst enthusiastic applause, pledged himself to defend it against every attack.[1]  On September 18 he officially notified his sanction to the Empress, "in accordance with the wishes of the majority of the French nation," as he expressed it.  And now had come to pass what Chancellor Kaunitz had predicted a fortnight before to his colleague, Spielmann, who was becoming alarmed at the growing turbulence of the French Assembly, " Possibly the weakness and poltroonery of the worthy Louis XVI. will relieve us from all our embarrassment."  For Louis XVI.'s acceptation of the Constitution was eagerly seized upon by the Austrian Court as a complete justification of its *laissez-aller* policy.  In a memorandum of November 12, 1791, Kaunitz notified to the Courts of St. Petersburg, Madrid, Berlin, and Stockholm that the Emperor had given an audience to the Constitutional French Ambassador, and received from him the official notification of the King of the French's acceptation of the new Constitution.  In the opinion of his Imperial Majesty the whole situation was now entirely changed.  The dangers which had prompted him to issue the manifesto of Mantua could no longer be regarded as existing, and the favourable turn of events in France gave the best hopes for the future.  It was clear to him that the vast majority of the French nation was now animated by more moderate counsels.  Louis XVI.'s acceptance of the Constitution must be regarded as voluntary, and, for the present at any rate, his Imperial Majesty has no further

---

[1] It is only fair to add that he frankly told the Assembly that "truth compelled him to confess that the means of government thereby placed at the disposal of the executive" seemed to him altogether inadequate.  Nevertheless, as opinion seemed divided on the subject, he was content to "leave it to experience to decide upon its merits."  There can be little doubt that Taine is right when he says that : "En acceptant la Constitution, il (Louis XVI.) avait jugé que la pratique en devoilerait les defauts et en provoquait la reforme."—*Taine, " Les Origines, etc."*

need of any more "declarations" or "concerts," let alone
warlike demonstrations.   Not content with this manifesto,
Leopold now opened his harbours to the new French flag,
and his example was speedily followed by Prussia.   England
and Holland also responded favourably to Louis XVI.'s
notification.

Gustavus's indignation at the Emperor's sudden and complete change of front knew no bounds.   He himself remained
immovably firm in his reactionary policy.   Alone of all his
contemporary sovereigns he grasped the real meaning and
foresaw the inevitable tendency of the Revolution, and he
rightly assumed that between the new political dogmas and
the old monarchical principles there could be no possible
compromise.   It was only natural, therefore, that the pliancy
of Louis XVI. and the purblindness of Leopold should revolt this ardent and resolute champion of the divine right of
kings.   Experience had taught him, he said, that nothing but
weakness was to be expected from the King of France; but
certainly, on this occasion, Louis XVI. had transgressed the
ordinary bounds of cowardice and ignominy.   Even if circumstances had required an "illusory assent," there was
absolutely no need for him to degrade his royal person and
dignity by volunteering to defend what he had been forced
to accept.   The Emperor's shifty policy Gustavus rightly
put down to purely interested motives.   Leopold, doubtless,
meant to play the same part in France as Russia had played
in Sweden and Poland.   It was necessary to counteract the
baneful Austrian influence at once, and Gustavus proposed
to do so by bringing about a new alliance between Russia,
Sweden, and Spain.

Even of Spain Gustavus had for a moment been uncertain,
but he speedily received information which seemed to dispel
all doubt.   The Spanish Government not only refused to
recognise the King of France as free, but even submitted

to the other Powers a scheme of an armed intervention for the purpose of upsetting the new French Constitution. According to this plan, if the new or Legislative Assembly, which had met in the meantime, did not, within a given time, set the King of France at liberty, Spain was to break off all relations with France, and place the King of Sweden and the *emigrés* in a position to invade the country by way of Flanders in the course of the ensuing spring. The other Powers were to marshal corps of observation along the French frontier, but not cross it, lest the French should be driven to desperation by the fear of a partition.

Gustavus, however, was dissatisfied with this plan, which he regarded as quite inadequate. With wonderful foresight, he predicted that during the course of the winter the Revolution's power of resistance would increase so enormously that an isolated invasion by way of Flanders in the spring of 1792 would no longer be sufficient to overpower it. He proposed instead a convention between Russia, Spain, and Sweden on the following terms. The three allies were to jointly guarantee France all her European possessions, and the French King his full prerogatives, using force to that end, provided pacific representations had no effect within a certain time. They were to recall their Ministers from Paris, refuse to receive the so-called national flag into their harbours, and recognise Monsieur as Regent till the King had been set free. Secret articles of the same convention fixed the contingent in troops of each of the three Powers, the amount of subsidies to be advanced by Spain to Sweden, and the general plan of operations. The King of Spain, as " the first crowned head of the house of Bourbon, in view of the political non-existence of the King of France," was to be the official head of this triple alliance. The Emperor, Gustavus now reluctantly gave up altogether; Prussia, however, he did not quite despair of winning over; but to break down what he called "this boulevard against the coalition of the Powers," an absolutely irrefutable testimony of the *real* sentiments of the Royal Family of France was necessary, and this he succeeded in obtaining through the devoted and indefatigable Fersen.  There is something inexpressibly pathetic in Fersen's unwearied and unrequited devotion to Marie Antoinette at this period; and the infinite tact with which he not only defended the Queen against the insinuations of her numerous enemies, but also saved her from the consequences of her own impulsiveness; the inexhaustible patience with which he made the most complicated questions clear and plain to her, and the gentle firmness with which he guided her step by step along her ever-darkening path, are perhaps unexampled in the annals of unselfish loyalty. It was he who now induced her to persuade Louis XVI. (December 1791) to write those memorable letters to the Kings of Spain and Prussia, acquainting them with the true position and real sentiments of the Royal Family.  She herself wrote a most touching letter to Catherine II., defending her husband's acceptation, and concluding with these pathetic words: "We have not been led away by any feeling of cowardice.  Fear of personal danger can have no effect upon our minds.  The ceaseless degradations which we experience, the insults we are forced to sul  ι to . . . the atmosphere of villainy which surrounds us, the distrust we find everywhere, . . . is not all this a continuous moral death a thousand times worse than the physical death which delivers from every ill?  Your Majesty, who knows every kind of courage so well, must agree that the greatest courage of all is to endure torments such as these."  The remedy Marie Antoinette suggested was an armed Congress of all the Powers, to be held at a place sufficiently close to the frontier to terrify the Jacobins.  The ostensible aim of the Congress was to be the re-establishment of the balance of power in Europe ; but the French Royal Family was to be assumed to have nothing to do with it, and the *emigrés* in general, and the King's brothers in particular, were to be excluded from all participation in it, as their frivolity and indiscretion might do more harm than good.   A copy of this letter Marie Antoinette sent to Gustavus III., at the same time thanking him for his generous efforts, and exhorting him to keep the impetuosity of the King's brothers within due bounds.

The idea of a Congress, which originated with Fersen, was at first rejected unconditionally by Gustavus, who feared that it would give the Emperor too much influence in the proposed negotiations between France and the Powers. He also observed, very pertinently, that to admit the principle of a Congress of Powers assembled for the express purpose of discussing the question of the constitution of an independent state was laying down a very dangerous precedent for the future, and pointed out, besides, the almost insuperable formal difficulties of such a Congress.   Finally, however, the arguments of Fersen, the urgent letters of the King and Queen of France, the hesitation of Spain at the last moment to join the proposed Triple Alliance for fear of provoking another war with England, above all, Leopold's manifest shyness of any Congress whatever, converted Gustavus to a belief in it, especially as the political situation both in Germany and France had suddenly entered upon a new and altogether unexpected phase, which, with skilful handling, might be made, perhaps, to force the Emperor's hand.

The German Electors, who had from the first watched the progress of the French Revolution with instinctive suspicion and dread, now began to tremble for their own safety, and the Elector of Treves applied directly to Gustavus III., as one of the guarantors of the Peace of Westphalia, to espouse his cause, and thus earn "the lasting gratitude of the German Princes." Gustavus without delay instructed his Minister at Vienna to propose to the Emperor the holding of a Congress under the protection of a *Reichs-armée*, consisting of Austrian, Prussian, Russian, and Swedish troops, to protect the territories of the minor German princes bordering upon France. Prussia was to be compensated for her services (for without compensation she would not move a step) by some of the Indian possessions of France. Gustavus also considered it necessary to keep the *emigrés* at Coblentz well in hand. Hitherto he had looked through his fingers at their follies; but the mischief which their intrigues and indiscretions were manifestly doing to the good cause now induced him, at last, to try and bring the aristocratic rabble to their senses. The Princes, however, somewhat resented the dictatorial tone of their Swedish protector, and henceforth transferred their homage to the lavish and indulgent Tsarina. The Peace of Jassy had just freed her from the pressure of the Turk, and she was only biding her time to pounce upon Poland. " I have many unfinished jobs on hand,"[1] she said to her private secretary in one of her expansive moments; "it is necessary that they [the European Courts] should have something to do so as not to meddle with me." To embroil Sweden, Austria, and Prussia in a war with France was now the secret object of her intricate and apparently inconsequent policy. Besides, she did not believe in the practicability of an armed Congress, and events justified her scepticism, for the Emperor would have nothing whatever to do with it, and neither Prussia nor Spain would move a step without him.

Thus all the efforts of Gustavus III. had foundered against the supine apathy of the great Powers, and his restless imagination had already begun to devise fresh adventures

---

[1] Khrapovitsky, *Dnevnik.*

in fields much nearer home—in Norway and Poland, for instance—when he suddenly was joined by a new and welcome " ally," as he ironically called it, in the French Legislative Assembly itself, whose unexpected intervention in the political arena at this moment at once brought matters to a crisis

On October 1, 1791, the Legislative Assembly met for the first time, and any hopes that the Royal Family of France may have built upon it were instantly dissipated.  It has been well remarked[1] that, from 1789 onwards, the level of political ability in France dropped lower and lower from Assembly to Assembly, and between the Constituent and the Legislative the drop was deep indeed.  The Constituent Assembly had, at any rate, been freely elected, and had represented pretty fairly the wealth, the talent, and the grandeur of France; but 450 of the 750 members of the Legislative Assembly were obscure young lawyers or lawyers' clerks.  It was also the most juvenile Parliament that had ever come together, the eldest member of the House being not quite thirty.  Nor could it be called really representative.  The bulk of the nation, from apathy or cowardice, had kept away from the polling-booths altogether, so that, practically, the government of a country of 26.000,000 of inhabitants was disposed of by some 300,000 club politicians, men who, in the words of Andrew Chenier, himself a Republican of the Republicans, conspired against society in the name of society.  It is quite true that the Jacobins pure and simple numbered little more than a third of the whole Assembly, but their leaders, Pétion, Danton, and Manuel, had already appropriated most of the posts of authority and emolument in the capital, while in the House itself 136 "empty-headed, voluble visionaries" whom the district of the Gironde had sent up to Paris, dominated the feeble, vacillating majority "with the energy of fanatics and the

[1] Taine, *Origines*, *etc.*

expedients of scoundrels." The unhappy King was absolutely powerless. There was no such thing as an executive, as we understand it. In the whole of France at that moment there was not a man who had the right to give orders or the power to enforce obedience, and the most conspicuous figures in this "metaphysical polity," as Gustavus III. contemptuously called it, was a crowned puppet, who had to sign whatever was put before him, and paper Ministers, who, against the first principles of all parliamentary government, had neither votes nor seats in the Legislature.

The first sign of the coming catastrophe was the menacing attitude which the Assembly took up towards foreign Powers, not because there was any fear of an invasion (we have seen that there was absolutely none), but from sheer reckless wantonness. In fact, it was the ambition of the Girondists to provoke a general European war, and it was at this very point that the King's friends, headed by the new War Minister, M. de Narbonne, a radical nobleman of the Lafayette type, but not nearly so vain, and much more venturesome, fancied they saw a means of saving their master by skilfully turning the bellicose effervescence of the Assembly against the *emigrés* of Coblentz and the minor German princes, and, taking advantage of the temporary popularity which such a step could not fail to give to the King, bring about a counter-revolution with the assistance of the army. They accordingly persuaded the King to appear in the Assembly and announce that he had sent an ultimatum to the Elector of Treves, the special protector of the *emigrés*, giving him till January 15, 1792, to disperse their armies, under pain of being regarded as the enemy of France. The King's announcement was received with enthusiastic applause. A war credit of thirty millions on paper was granted unanimously, and Narbonne gave such an optimistic account of the state of the army and the fortresses, that not to take instant advantage of their overwhelming superiority seemed to the Girondists an unpardonable crime.

It was with no small satisfaction that Gustavus III. heard of this ultimatum, and he did his utmost to turn the war-like demonstrations of the Girondists to his own advantage, especially as, since the recall of his ambassador from Paris, December 1791, he had now little or nothing to fear from the wrath of the Assembly. Carisien, the Swedish Minister at Berlin, was directed to energetically represent to the King of Prussia how disgraceful it would be to submit to "the insolent dictation of the so-called National Assembly," and to assure Frederick William that the King of Sweden, as one of the guarantors of the Peace of Westphalia, would actively co-operate with him in any measure necessary for the maintenance of the dignity and integrity of the Empire. Nevertheless, all the efforts of Gustavus to provoke a war between France and Germany failed. At the very moment when the *emigrés* at Coblentz were rejoicing at the prospect of a sudden solution of all their difficulties by a general European war, the French Constitutional Minister, St. Croix, arrived at Treves with the ultimatum of the Assembly. The Elector of Treves, in great perplexity, at once applied to the Courts of Berlin and Vienna for instructions, and they sharply ordered him to at once dismiss the *emigrés* from his domains and give the French Assembly no just cause of complaint in the future. The unhappy Elector, despite the protests of the Russian and Swedish Ministers, was bound to obey, and the *emigré* host was dismissed accordingly.

Nevertheless, in the midst of these repeated disappointments, Gustavus had at last the satisfaction of a diplomatic triumph which dealt a severe blow at the French National Assembly.

In view of a possible war with Austria, the more prudent

of the Girondists began to look abroad for allies: Prussia and England seemed to them the most promising confederates, the former as the historical rival of Austria, the latter as being apparently more friendly disposed towards the Revolution than any other Power.[1] Count Segur was accordingly despatched to Berlin with the offer of an alliance, and Talleyrand, the ex-Bishop of Autun, who now comes before the world as a diplomatist for the first time, went to London on the same errand.[2] On hearing of these secret missions (the Queen keeping him well informed as to everything that was going on at Paris), the energetic Fersen took prompt measures to circumvent both envoys. He sent to Carisien, the Swedish Minister at Berlin, what purported to be a copy of Segur's secret instructions, full of the "most atrocious and damaging statements," as Segur himself expressed it, while Gustavus privately warned Frederick William of Segur's coming, and exhorted him to have no dealings whatever with "the Jacobin emissary." The consequence was that when Segur arrived at Berlin, he found, to his astonishment and mortification, that all the world was against him. The King turned his back upon him in the presence of the whole Court, the Queen went out of her way to snub him at a reception, so that, after an unsuccessful attempt at suicide, the unfortunate diplomatist returned to France empty-handed and broken-hearted.[3] Very little better fared it with M. de Talleyrand at London. He had frequent interviews with Pitt and Grenville, was even presented to the King, and, though ill-supported by his principals at Paris, and hampered at every step by the anomalous, unofficial character of his mission, conducted his negotiations with extraordinary ability. He soon con-

---

[1] Pallain, *Le Mission de Talleyrand.*
[2] Both missions were unofficial. *Ibid.*
[3] Akeson, *Gustaf III.*, p. 190 ; Pallain, *Mission de Talleyrand.*

vinced himself that England preferred peace to war, but would give no direct answer either way; but whenever he insinuated the expediency of an alliance between the two countries, he could make no impression upon the English Ministers. Fersen had taken his measures so promptly and thoroughly to "destroy the effect"[1] of Talleyrand's representations, that, after a six weeks' stay in London, the young French diplomatist, who seems to have dimly suspected[2] that some occult influence was at work against him, requested his recall and quitted London on March 9.[3]

It was now, too, that Gustavus III. made a final effort to rescue the Royal Family of France from the perils that were closing in upon them from every side. He argued, with great force, that so long as Louis XVI. remained in the hands of rebels,[4] he would be compelled to lend his name to acts of violence most contrary to his interests and his glory, while the fear of exposing him to danger would always be a fatal obstacle to the efforts of his friends abroad. Gustavus was deeply sensible of the dangers attending a fresh flight; but, "as it is the duty of a true friend to give the most useful counsels even if they be the most perilous," he held himself bound to exhort their Majesties to make the attempt, as being the only infallible means of rehabilitating their affairs. According to this plan, Louis XVI. was to escape to England, as being the nearest, most convenient, and least suspected place

[1] "Les ministères du roi de France ont imaginé d'envoyer en Angleterre l'évêque d'Autun pour s'assurer de cette cour et lui offrir même la cession de quelques possessions [*i.e.* Tobago, Talleyrand, however, did not deem it expedient to make the offer] si cela était necessaire. La reine me l'a mandé et me charge d'en prevenir V. M. J'ai déjà écrit à Londres à quelqu'un qui a de l'influence dans la ministère pour avertir de cette demarche et détruire les effets."—*Fersen to Gustavus III., Klinckowström,* ii. 131.

[2] Pallain, *Desp.,* xx. p. 47.

[3] This, Talleyrand's first diplomatic mission, lasted from January 24 to March 9, 1792.

[4] See the long and carefully composed despatch sent by Gustavus III. to Fersen, 22nd December 1791. Klinckowström, i. 281-293.

of refuge.   If he had any scruples about seeking an asylum with "the natural enemy, or, at least, the puissant rival of his race," he was to call to mind the example of his illustrious ancestor, Henry of Navarre, who was resolved to rather fly to Queen Elizabeth than fall into the hands of the Leaguers. The King of France, moreover, was to be careful to employ none but Englishmen,[1] and only two of them, one to conduct him from Paris to the coast, and the other to take him across the Channel.   To divert attention and gain time, the members of the Royal Family were to escape separately and by different routes.   When once Louis XVI. had regained his freedom, he was "to regard himself as re-invested with all his former authority, and in full possession of his inherited prerogatives," and his first act was to be the issuing of a manifesto repudiating everything that had happened since the opening of the States-General in 1789, and informing the sovereigns of Europe that, free at last, it was his intention to win back the throne of his fathers sword in hand.   Meanwhile, he was to do all in his power to distract and mislead public opinion in France by sanctioning all the absurdities of the Assembly, by changing his Ministers as often as possible, especially the Ministers of War and Marine, "so as to introduce the utmost confusion into those departments;" by choosing for his advisers the persons most agreeable to the multitude, and "therefore most ignorant of affairs," and by pretending to resume his negotiations with the Emperor.

Such was Gustavus's plan, and it must be admitted that it was equally remarkable for its craft and audacity.   But now a serious question arose; who was to carry it out?   By

---

[1] On this point Gustavus could speak feelingly.   He owed much to individual Englishmen.   Both he and Fersen were strongly convinced that *no Frenchman* was discreet or courageous enough for so difficult and delicate an enterprise.

this time the state of Paris had become so dangerous that it was scarcely safe for a foreigner to show his face there. If even accredited Ministers, like the Swedish *chargé d'affaires*, Bergstedt, daily trembled for their lives,[1] it seemed little short of homicide to send thither young Fersen, who was well known there, and, since his participation in the flight to Varennes, a marked man. Marie Antoinette herself implored the young Swede not to come, and Gustavus, regarding it as impossible that he could ever get there alive, proposed that he should go to England to prepare a friendly reception for Louis XVI., while Craufurd, who had in the meantime returned to Paris, should be at hand to help the Royal Family to escape. But, despite the mortal perils in the way, the devoted Fersen determined, for the Queen's sake, to venture upon another visit to Paris. Accordingly, on February 11, 1792, he left Brussels for the French capital attended by a single adjutant. They travelled as Swedish couriers *en route* for Portugal under false names, and, by way of additional precaution, Fersen had with him counterfeit credentials as Minister Plenipotentiary to Portugal. The journey was successful. On February 13 they reached Paris, and the same evening Fersen contrived to steal an interview with the Queen unobserved. The following day he was with the Royal Family from six o'clock in the evening till six o'clock next morning. Fersen very soon, however, convinced himself that a flight was " physically impossible." The King and Queen were kept under the strictest surveillance, and every vehicle that left the château was searched. The King, too, had his scruples. He had so often pledged his word not to quit Paris, that he held himself bound in honour to remain. Fersen, however, at last forced a promise from him that when the Allies invaded France he would attempt to escape on foot through the forests with the aid of

---

[1] Akeson, *Gustaf III.'s Förhallanden, etc.*

smugglers, who were to bring him to a safe place near the frontier, where a detachment of fifty light troops would be in readiness to receive him. This was the only crumb of comfort which Fersen could give his unhappy friends. Both the King and the Queen were in a pitiable state of anxiety and depression. "I know people tax me with weakness and irresolution," said Louis XVI., "but surely no one has ever been in such a position as mine." "He begged me," wrote the young Swede to Gustavus III., "to tell the Powers beforehand not to be astonished at anything he might do, for it would all be the effect of constraint. They must put me altogether on one side," he went on, "and let me go my own way." The King's pathetic account of his absolute isolation moved even the stoical Fersen to tears. Fersen's declaration that Gustavus and Catherine desired the restoration of the French monarchy in its absolute integrity, and were quite resolved never to sanction any "mixed government," won the warm approval of the Queen. The King, less daring but more far-sighted, doubted the possibility of restoring the old absolutism, but was at last brought to consent never to negotiate with rebels except to deceive them, and to look entirely to his friends abroad for deliverance.

All this time Fersen literally carried his life in his hands. So great was his insecurity that he dared not remain in Paris more than two days at a time, but made a journey southwards as far as Tours, as if on his way to Portugal, returning to Paris again on February 19. Despite the redoubled vigilance with which the Royal Family were now guarded (the rumour of another projected flight seems to have reached the ears of the authorities), he succeeded, on the afternoon of the 21st, in paying a *third* visit to the Tuileries, stayed there till midnight, and then, accompanied by his adjutant, and provided with a courier's pass from the

Swedish *chargé d'affaires*, they departed.   Thrice they were stopped and examined on the return journey, but finally reached Brussels again on February 27, "overjoyed at having succeeded so well." This perilous expedition had no substantial result after all, and has well-nigh been lost sight of altogether in the rush of epoch-making events which followed hard upon it.

After the dispersion of the *emigré* host by the Elector of Treves, at the Emperor's express command, it was clear that the European potentates were far too much occupied elsewhere to pay any attention to France.   Indeed, the Austrian declaration (November 29, 1791), in reply to the note of the French Government, had been sent with the express intention of strengthening the hands of the Constitutional party in the French Assembly, and thus maintaining peace in the west, to profit by the dissolution of Poland in the east.   Yet this pacific, not to say apologetic, declaration precipitated the very calamity it was intended to avert.   On January 17, 1792, Brissot rushed into the tribune and denounced the Kaiser as the real enemy of France.   The Electors, he said, were only his puppets, and the *emigrés* his tools.   He moved that the Franco-Austrian alliance of 1756 should be rescinded, and an ultimatum sent to Vienna threatening war within a month unless the Emperor gave explanations perfectly satisfactory to France.   In vain did the six sensible and courageous deputies in the House prove to demonstration that Leopold had neither taken, nor intended to take, a single hostile step towards France; on January 25 the Assembly adopted a resolution, which was at once a breach of the Constitution and a provocation to war,[1] giving the

---

[1] Cap. iv. sec. iii. art. 1 of the Constitution of 1791 expressly declared that it belonged to the King alone to communicate and negotiate with the foreign Powers.   Louis XVI. therefore was strictly within his rights when, in his message to the Assembly of January 28, he protested against this flagrant. breach of the Constitution.

Emperor till March 1 to declare definitively " whether he meant to live in peace and amity with the French nation, and renounce every compact directed against her sovereignty, independence, and security." Even this ultimatum could not open the eyes of the infatuated Kaiser, or turn him a hair's-breadth from his persistently pacific policy. It is true, he hastened, in sheer self-defence, to contract a fresh defensive treaty with Prussia (February 7), and increase his forces in the Netherlands ; but his reply (February 17) to the French ultimatum only reiterated his desire for peace, appealed to his dispersal of the *emigrés* in proof of the loyalty of his intentions, and protested that it was only the violence of the Republican minority in the Assembly itself which threatened a rupture between the two States. And so indeed it was. The vast majority of the Assembly was for peace ; but, cowed by the menaces and insults of the mob, it meekly bowed its neck beneath the Jacobin yoke. On March 10 the whole Ministry resigned to escape impeachment, and the King, thoroughly broken by the tidings of the sudden death of his imperial kinsman (Leopold II. died of a fit of apoplexy on March 1), was driven to the crowning humiliation of accepting a Girondist Ministry, with the adventurer Dumouriez as Minister of Finance, and the crotcheteer Roland as Minister of the Interior. On March 27 Dumouriez sent a fresh ultimatum to Vienna, and the reply of the new King of Hungary being considered unsatisfactory, war against the Empire was formally decreed (April 20) by the Assembly, only seven deputies having the heroism and the good sense to vote against it.

Thus the consummation so devoutly wished for and so strenuously striven after by Gustavus III. was at last an accomplished fact. He, however, never lived to see it. At midnight, on March 16, 1792, only a fortnight after the death of the Emperor, the assassin's bullet struck down the Swedish monarch in the very Opera House which his patriotic munificence had dedicated to the National Muses. The story of that most stupid and dastardly of crimes now remains to be told.

# CHAPTER XXIII.

## *THE REGICIDES—THE LAST RIKSDAG.*

Bitter hatred of the Swedish nobility against Gustavus—The regicides —Pechlin—Johan von Engeström—Bjelke—Ribbing—Horn and Liljehorn—Anckarström—Seclusion of Gustavus during the winter of 1791-92—Financial distress of Sweden—The King very reluctantly summons a Riksdag to Gefle—The elections favourable to the Court—Arrival of Gustavus at Gefle—Festivities and diversions—The first *levée*—Opening of the Riksdag—Speech from the throne—Suspicion and hostility of the nobles—The Secret Committee—Account of its sessions by an eye-witness— Regulation of the finances—Obstruction of the nobles—Anger of the King—Fears of a fresh *coup d'état*—Intervention of the Marshal of the Diet — The proffered olive branch — Gustavus dissolves the Riksdag—His last speech.

THE Swedish nobility never forgave Gustavus III. for annihilating their long political supremacy, but they had, at last, got to fear the gentlest of despots almost as much as they hated him. Recognising, however, the hopelessness of a further struggle with an antagonist who, equally invincible in the parliamentary arena and on the battlefield, had, besides, the mass of the nation at his back, the recognised leaders of the Opposition now retired from public life altogether, and affected to ignore what they could no longer prevent. But the rank and file of the Swedish gentry thirsted for vengeance. They could not forget the disgrace they had undergone, and determined to take advantage of the first opportunity to bring about a counter-revolution which should reduce the King to his old position of abject dependence on the Legislature as before 1772. But among these malcontents was a smaller group of malignants who professed to hate the King on principle. The first article of their political creed was that no reform could be carried out till Gustavus had been made away with, and in their eyes even a regicide was a justifiable means for so desirable an end. At the head of these fanatics, though no fanatic himself, was the redoutable and disreputable Pechlin, who, since the revolution of 1772, had been living in comparative obscurity ; but, for the last two years, he had been the soul of a conspiracy for subverting the Government, a conspiracy, so vast as to embrace nearly half the Swedish aristocracy and so secret as even to baffle the vigilance of Baron Liljensparre, Gustavus's ever-watchful Minister of Police.

All the rest of the conspirators were more or less actuated by personal spite, but, at the same time, sufficiently blinded by the Jacobin casuistry of the day to consider themselves patriots instead of felons. The least disreputable of the gang was perhaps Johan von Engeström, whom we have already learned to know.[1] He was the philosopher and doctrinaire of the party, and was to have drafted the new Constitution had the plot succeeded. Baron Ture-Bjelke belonged to one of the most illustrious families in Sweden, but his own career had been anything but distinguished, and he had all an unsuccessful man's hatred of those who were more fortunate than himself. His connection with the conspiracy is a mystery which he carried to the grave with him a few days after the King was shot, under circumstances which make it tolerably certain that he held in his hand the lost clue to the whole of this tangled skein of plots within plots. Count Adolf Ludwig Ribbing, an ex-officer of the guards, of resolute temper, handsome person, and fairly good parts, may be

---

[1] Chap. XVI.

said to have imbibed a hatred of the King with his mother's milk, for he had been taught from his earliest infancy to regard Gustavus as a monster of iniquity.    He had also been disappointed in his hopes of preferment, and when the beautiful and wealthy Miss de Geer rejected his suit in favour of Baron Essen, the most dashing of the royal equerries, Ribbing instantly jumped at the false conclusion that it was at the instigation of the King, and never rested till he had revenged himself.    Count Clas Frederick Horn and Captain Pontus Liljehorn were poor creatures.    The former was a good-looking, elegant, over-educated, weak-minded young officer, half coxcomb, half poetaster, personally beloved by the King, and a general favourite at court and in society.    The youth's father had been one of the most enthusiastic admirers of Gustavus III. at the revolution of 1772, but this enthusiasm had turned to the deadliest hatred at the Revolution of 1789, when the elder Horn was among the number of the arrested noblemen. The excitable son at once made his father's wrongs his own, and from that moment, as he afterwards confessed with tears, "was led away from the path of honour and duty by the powers of evil."    Pontus Liljehorn was the most contemptible of all the conspirators ; indeed, his crime should be branded rather as parricide than regicide. Beginning life as a court page, he had been transferred to the life-guards and rapidly promoted.    His lively spirits and engaging manners endeared him to the King, to whose generosity he owed all he had and all he was.    At that very moment he was drawing his pocket-money from Gustavus's privy purse.    A sordid suspicion that others were partaking of the royal bounty more freely than himself armed the ingrate against his benefactor.    So little was Liljehorn suspected, that he presumed, in company with some brother officers, to pay the wounded monarch a visit of condolence on the morning after the fatal masquerade, when his emotion excited general sympathy and respect.

But it was in the muddled brain and ferocious perverted heart of Jakob Johan Anckarström that the idea of a regicide, which had long been floating in the air, first assumed a practical shape. This miserable man was one of the many victims of the new revolutionary ideas then in vogue. His was the temperament of the true political fanatic—a feeble judgment, a confused moral sense absolutely at the mercy of a morbidly brooding fancy, and an inordinately violent temper. Anckarström's fixed idea was that Gustavus had forfeited the allegiance of his subjects by the *coup d'état* of 1789, and that it was a sacred duty to get rid of such a perjured tyrant by any means whatsoever. He was thus already a regicide at heart, when a prosecution for seditious language, unknown to the King, who actually remitted the well-deserved sentence, made the half-crazy zealot a regicide in deed. Private spite henceforth became the real motive of a crime which the deluded monomaniac still persuaded himself was solely undertaken for the common weal.[1]

It was towards the end of 1791 that Anckarström resolved to take the King's life. "I bethought me much," he tells us, "if perchance there was any fair means of getting the King to rule his land and people according to law and benevolence, but every argument was against me. . . . The King is more than gracious towards individuals,

---

[1] Anckarström was a brute by nature. From a very early age he delighted in public executions and in horribly torturing animals. Let us add that he was of a naturally quarrelsome, tetchy disposition. He owned some landed property, on which he had settled after leaving the army, and soon made himself odious to his neighbours by his litigiousness. The story that his animosity to the King was owing to the latter's breaking off the former's liaison with an actress is a mere fable. Anckarström, though a brutal husband, was rather a Puritan than a Lovelace, while Gustavus never interfered with the affairs of actresses at all.

but if anything is demanded or required for the commonweal, he gets nasty, and everything turns out as he wills
it. . . . 'Twere best to venture one's life for the commonweal, for to live ten years, more or less, of a wretched life,
is as nothing in comparison with making a whole nation
happy.  The misfortune[1] which happened to me personally
at the end of 1790 . . . knit together my resolves rather
to die than live a wretched life, so that my otherwise sensitive and affectionate heart [sic] became altogether callous
as regards this horrible deed."

Just before Christmas 1791, Anckarström made the
acquaintance of Horn at Hufvudstad, the latter's country
seat.  They began talking about the Government, and
Anckarström then said: "How unfortunate it is that we
cannot get rid of the King!"  "What's the good of talking about it?" replied Horn; "even if we all act *en corps*,
we can do nothing."  "You may think it odd," returned
Anckarström, "but I'd do it if I only got the chance."
Horn looked at him in amazement, but objected that murder
was perhaps "too inhuman an expedient."  Was there no
other way of removing the King?  He then suggested
that they should abduct Gustavus by night from his country
château of Haga, and keep him hidden till a political revolution had been accomplished.  To Haga the pair went
accordingly on a beautiful moonlit night at the beginning
of January 1792, and, after dodging the guards, walked
through the park right up to the château to reconnoitre,
and were startled to see the King standing close to one of
the windows of the ground-floor and gazing abstractedly
out upon the freshly-fallen snow.[2]  The conspirators at
once beat a retreat.  They had already convinced themselves of the impracticability of Horn's fantastic alternative.

---

[1] *i.e.*, his trial for sedition.
[2] Another account says that, as they watched him, they saw him suddenly turn
pale and faint away, whereupon a strange panic came over them and they fled.

A fortnight later Horn invited Anckarström to dine at Hufvudstad, where he met Ribbing for the first time. Horn and Ribbing fell a talking together of the badness of the times and the best way of mending them, when Anckarström suddenly intervened. "It will be no good till you get rid of Gustavus III.," said he. "God knows when that will be," cried Ribbing with a shrug. "I'd do it if I only had the chance," said Anckarström. Horn made game of him, and Ribbing laughed contemptuously, but Anckarström stuck to what he said, and two days afterwards they all met again at Anckarström's chambers in Stockholm. Ribbing and Horn seem at first to have had their doubts about Anckarström, but he now convinced them that he was perfectly in earnest, and it was agreed that an attempt should be made upon the King's life at the Opera House that very night. Horn supplied Anckarström with a good pair of pistols, Ribbing got him a private box next to the royal box, and they all three proceeded to the Opera House accordingly, but nothing could be done, because the King never left his box the whole evening. Anckarström had no better luck at the Swedish Theatre, or at a masquerade, whither he went all alone, with the same deadly purpose, a few days later, for on both occasions there were so few people present that detection would have been certain. "I went away," says Anckarström characteristically, "much discouraged, partly because none would lend me a helping hand, and partly because the unlucky deed had not been done, though I had pledged my word that it should be done without fail."

But now an event occurred which gave the King a six weeks' respite. The Riksdag met in mid January, at the little Bothnian seaport town of Gefle, known, from its out-and-out loyalty, as "The King's own borough."

During the winter of 1791–92 Gustavus III. had lived the life of a recluse. Much as he had gained politically from the revolution of 1789, socially he had lost still more thereby.   Ever since the day when Fersen's lovely daughters had come to the palace as suppliants for their aged father, and vainly waited for an audience in the Pillar Chamber,[1] the ladies of Sweden had turned their backs for ever upon the "royal charmer."   Henceforth the beauty, the grace, and the intellect of Sweden would have nothing more to say to the Court.   The royal *levées* and circles were so poorly attended that they had to be given up altogether.   Even the theatres were only half-filled ; the palace, once so brilliant, now became a " dreary desert," and the King had to be content with the society of his own servants.   But in truth, Gustavus was no longer the man he had been.   " I have never seen a greater change," says his friend and confidant Armfelt,[2] " than that which the King's conduct underwent from 1788 till his death.   Misfortune had done him much good.   Ever since the war, and amidst all the festivities which succeeded it, I cannot recollect having a single conversation with him which did not turn upon some serious subject, and if . . . a witty sally occasionally escaped his lips, it rather resembled a quotation from some one else than an expression of spontaneous mirth." [3]   And indeed the King had more than enough to disturb and sadden him.   Abroad his one ally was on the verge of ruin, and he could do nought to help her.   At home the political horizon was gloomier than it had ever been before.   Glorious as the Russian war had been to the arms of Sweden, it had been well-nigh ruinous to her finances.   The very festivities in celebration of the crowning victory of Svenksund had to be curtailed for want of money.   The army, for the same reason, had been paid off

[1] Adlerbeth.
[2] Elof Tegner, *G. M. Armfelt*, vol. i.
[3] Wallqvist, *Minnen och Bref.*

in depreciated notes; and it was only the firmness and courage of Toll that had prevented a mutiny among the disbanded sailors at Carlscrona, which would have been more dangerous than half a dozen Russian · victories. At the very lowest computation, 9,000,000 rixdollars (£700,000), an enormous sum in those days for so poor a country as Sweden, had been added within the last three years to the national debt, which now amounted to 43,000,000 rixdollars (£2,300,000), while the deficit for the current year was estimated at 900,000 rixdollars (£70,000). The Finance Minister had exhausted every saving expedient in vain, and nothing but the direct intervention and assistance of the Estates of the realm seemed possible to avert national bankruptcy. Yet still the King hesitated to convene the Estates. The dangers of a Riksdag were very real, its benefits quite problematical, and Gustavus shrank instinctively from a probable repetition of the scenes and the struggles of three years before. Still, even at the risk of offending him, his friends persisted in urging him to summon the Estates, and at last, during the temporary lull in Continental politics, in the winter of 1791–92, Gustavus gave way. A few days before Christmas a royal proclamation summoned a Riksdag to Gefle, the capital being no longer considered safe enough for the purpose. The precautions taken by the King on the eve of the elections eloquently testified to his anxiety as to the result. Divisions of the body-guard and of the light dragoons were encamped in the neighbourhood of Gefle, and the dashing Armfelt was sent down thither to take the supreme command. The burgesses and yeomanry of Gefle, whose loyalty was proverbial, were also ordered to be under arms. A royal circular was issued to all the departments of state and to the colonels of every regiment, forbidding every civilian or officer in the army to come up to the Riksdag without the King's express permission. This unprecedented order created a great sensation, and was rightly interpreted as an electioneering move to keep away from Gefle as many of the disaffected gentry as possible. At Court a gloomy silence prevailed. Every one there was nervous and suspicious, and Bishop Wallqvist, who waited upon the King at Haga on New Year's day, was much struck by his Majesty's unusual agitation.[1] The Court evidently feared much and expected little from the coming Riksdag.

Nevertheless, as the appointed day grew near, the outlook brightened considerably. The Nobility, as might have been anticipated, sent none but hostile deputies to the Riksdag, and the burgesses of Stockholm, disgusted at the preference given to Gefle, also voted against the Government; but, on the other hand, the vast majority of the representatives of the three lower Estates were ardent royalists, so that, despite the defection of the capital, the King was assured of victory beforehand.

On the evening of January 22, 1792, amidst the blare of clarions and the gleam of torches, Gustavus made his state entry into Gefle. His retinue, as usual, was numerous and splendid, and the pageant is described by those who saw it[2] as "most imposing." The night before leaving Stockholm he had attended a masquerade, mingling freely with the crowd, and almost rubbing shoulders with his would-be assassin without suspecting his danger. Still less did he suspect that his Nemesis was even now on his track, and would dog his footsteps all the time he was at Gefle. The King was received at the gates of the little town by the Primate of Sweden, the Lord-Lieutenant of the county, and a deputation from the three lower Estates, who escorted him to Gefle Castle, where he was to reside

[1] Wallqvist, *Minnen*.    [2] Ibid.

during the Riksdag.   Great enthusiasm was excited by the
appearance of the little Crown Prince, afterwards of such
melancholy notoriety as Gustavus IV., but now a gentle,
amiable lad of fourteen, who had accompanied his father
up from Stockholm and won all hearts by his simple and
unaffected courtesy.

The King had spared no pains to make the deputies,
whom he had thus summoned in the depth of an Arctic
winter to the remote little Bothnian borough, as comfortable
as possible.   He kept open table every day at court, and
his example was followed by the great officers of State,
who were lodged sumptuously, and provided with *chefs*
from the royal kitchen and liqueurs [1] from the royal cellar.
Nine ordinaries, at which 200 people sat down daily to eat
and drink, were maintained at the King's expense for the
parliamentary rank and file.   But the most magnificent of
these public banquets was that of the royal favourite Armfelt,
whose grand airs gave peculiar offence to the Opposition.   But there were other entertainments besides these
junkettings.   The King held frequent *levées* at the castle,
which were always crowded.   The Marshal of the Diet
gave afternoon receptions to the gentry, and balls every
Wednesday to the ladies of Gefle, while those who cared
for gaming frequented the hazard tables of young Armfelt.
A sort of fashionable gazette was also published every day
by Captain Holthausen, one of young Armfelt's " many
adjutants." [2]

The most embarrassing moment during Gustavus's residence at Gefle was his first meeting with the Nobility
at the *levée* held, the day after his arrival, in the State
bedchamber at Gefle Castle.   The crush was indescribable, all four Estates being largely represented, and some
curiosity, and not a little anxiety, was felt as to how his

[1] Adlerbeth, *Anteckningar*.          [2] Wallqvist, *Minnen.*

Majesty would welcome as his guests those very gentlemen whom he had sent to gaol only two years before.  Amidst the most disquieting silence the King went slowly round the large circle, addressing each one in turn with his usual graciousness till he came to the spot where stood young Count Brahe, the premier peer of Sweden, who during the last Riksdag had been the King's most persistent and uncompromising opponent.  Brahe had resolved on this occasion also to set his compeers an edifying example of republican stiffness and sternness ; but Gustavus, taking him familiarly aside, conversed with him so gaily that in three minutes the young man, to his own inward vexation, "quite lost countenance," and actually found himself smiling at the "tyrant's" pleasantries.  The King then serenely completed his rounds.  It was remarked that he overlooked none, addressing nobles, clergymen, burgesses, and peasants in turn with that discriminating tact and easy *bonhomie* which very few could entirely resist.  When he had gone quite round the circle, and remained standing in the centre of the room, there was another very awkward pause, whereupon the adroit Schröderheim at once advanced to the rescue by announcing, with a deep bow, that the heralds who were to "blow in" the Riksdag had arrived, and that the dragoons, whose duty it was to escort the Marshal of the Diet to the House of Nobles, were waiting in the courtyard below. At the same instant the imperturbable Taube threw open the doors of the tapestried screen that surrounded the bed of state, and the King immediately passed through and took his customary place at the bed-head.  The heralds were thereupon introduced and departed with the royal proclamation.  The next moment the roll of drums and the flourish of trumpets in the courtyard below announced that the grand herald had mounted his horse.  "We found ourselves," says Schröderheim, "on the eve of a grand

ceremony, and our courage revived." The King now took
from the bed the historical silver bâton with the gold grape-
shaped knob, with which so many great men had swayed
the House of Nobles, and beckoning forward from the
throng Baron Erik Ruuth, addressed a few gracious words
to him, and then placed the bâton in his hand, thus con-
stituting him Marshal of the Diet. Ruuth has been well
described as "one of the most energetic and industrious
souls whom the brilliant monarch ever attracted to his
side,"[1] and his loyalty and devotion had stood the severest
tests triumphantly. As Finance Minister during the war,
he had shown remarkable ability at a most critical time,
and the tact and courage with which he presided over a tur-
bulent House of more than 400 mutinous noblemen during
the present Diet well deserved the countship with which he
was subsequently rewarded by his grateful master. At the
same levée the Archbishop of Upsala took the customary
oaths as Talman or President of the Estate of Clergy, an
office which, as the King gracefully reminded him, he had
already held thrice before with distinction. A few days
afterwards Anders Wallin, Burgomaster of Stockholm, was
appointed President of the Burgesses, and Olof Thoreson of
Calmar President of the Estate of Peasants. Wallin's appoint-
.ient was a stroke of policy. He had been elected deputy
because of his Radical sentiments, and had come up to Gefle
ready to oppose everything. But, from the moment when
the King placed the Talman's mace in his hands, he began
to see matters in a different light, and hopes of further
preferment speedily converted him into a staunch royalist.

On February 27, the Court and the four Orders, each
headed by its president, proceeded in state to the cathedral, where Dr. Wiedemann, Bishop of Skara, preached a

---

[1] *Biog. Lex. öfver Sv. Namn. M.*, article "Ruuth." He had since been
superseded as Finance-Minister by Hakansson.

sermon which delighted the most critical ; while Wallqvist, Bishop of Wexiö, attired in new and costly vestments of the King's own devising,[1] officiated at the altar, assisted by the Gefle clergy in full canonicals.   After service the procession went in the same order to the Rikssaal, or Hall of Assembly, to listen to the speech from the throne.   The Rikssaal was a large wooden building built expressly for the occasion by relief gangs working day and night amidst the most tempestuous weather, there being no public hall at Gefle large enough to accommodate the Estates of the realm when they met in Congress.[2]   The ceiling, the floor, and the benches of the deputies were covered with purple cloth ; while the best of the *hautelisse* tapestries, which the kings of France had presented in former times to the kings of Sweden, were hung at intervals along the walls.[3]   As a spectacle, the opening of the Diet of Gefle was much inferior to the opening of any of its predecessors.   The absence of the royal Dukes with their suites was felt, and even the rich Burgundian costumes and flowing white silk mantles of the Lord High Steward and the Earl Marshal, who sat on tabourets one on each side of the throne; even the gorgeous red and black capes and scarves of the royal pages and drabants, the black and silver liveries of Armfelt's body-guards, and the picturesque costumes of the Russian, Polish, English, French, and Prussian Ministers, who were present on the occasion, could not supply the place of the ancient Senators,[4] whose rich

[1] Wallqvist, *Minnen.*

[2] Schröderheim, *Anteckningar ;* Adlerbeth, *Anteckningar.*   Of course each Estate had its separate hall for debating somewhere in the town.

[3] The hall was so vast, however, that Schröderheim says the *hautelisse* tapestries looked like tiny prints on a cottage wall.

[4] The Raad, or Senate, was abolished by Gustavus in 1789, as incompatible with a strong monarchy.   One of the clauses of the Peace of Westphalia fixed the rank of a Swedish Senator as equal to that of a Spanish grandee of the first class.

purple mantles, plumed velvet hats, and heavy golden chains had always been the most imposing features of such ceremonials. The day, too, was heavy with snow and bitterly cold, so that the light of day scarcely penetrated the few and narrow windows of the Rikssaal. The temper of the various portions of the audience was strikingly different. It was observed that while "involuntary applause beamed on the countenances"[1] of the deputies of the three lower Estates, who stood, as usual, on the left-hand side of the throne, the Nobility, who stood on the right, preserved throughout a sulky silence. The speech from the throne was worthy of the man who, besides his other great titles to fame, enjoys the rare distinction of being the one great orator whom Sweden has yet produced. It was delivered, too, with the declamatory force and dramatic skill of which Gustavus was so consummate a master. Simple and natural as usual, disdaining all rhetorical ornament or artifice, he appealed direct to the hearts of his hearers, and his tone throughout was patriotic and conciliatory.[2]

"One-and-twenty years have now elapsed," began the orator, "since first, as King of Sweden, I greeted you from the throne. The realm was then shaken to its very foundations; its independence was threatened; its ancient reputation, which your forefathers so nobly won for it with their blood, had gone; the army was in confusion, the fleet only existed on paper; . . . the realm, torn asunder by contending factions, was a prey to the ambition of a few magnates; the Bank was without ready money; there was no individual security—in a word, society was on the very verge of dissolution. Then the Most High, Whose mighty protection has so often saved this realm from destruction, once more upheld the body politic. Everything

---

[1] Schröderheim, *Anteckningar.*

[2] Any translation of such a masterpiece can, of course, only be tentative.

took, another shape.   Fourteen years of tranquillity succeeded these convulsions.   Unity, concord, mutual confidence lightened my labours, assisted my youthful inexperience, furthered my burning zeal for the restoration of the realm. The finances were adjusted ; agriculture revived ; the army was reformed and remodelled ; fleets were built ; commerce, beneath the protection of the Swedish flag, began to flourish anew, and they who then saw what the realm was, and recollected what it had been only a few years before, could scarce believe that so short a time had worked so great a change.

" I linger with a secret satisfaction over the memory of those first years of my reign, those happy times when no clash of opinions was to be heard, and a universal tranquillity seemed to guarantee a long felicity.

" But another time came.   It seemed as if we ourselves, weary of our very happiness, were unable any longer to endure it ; as if that secret longing which leads men to desire a change in their condition would not permit us to enjoy our tranquillity any longer.   That feeling weighed upon our minds and tore us violently away from our peace. Storms arose, the spirit of discord awoke once more ; the realm was shattered ; everything seemed utterly lost.

" I felt the effects of that terrible agitation ; I felt what I was venturing, but I trusted in the magnanimity of the nation, and I was not disappointed.

" I called you together.

" Grievous were your deliberations, but the realm needed a ready help, and you gave it.   The army showed itself Swedish, it showed itself not unworthy of its forefathers, it strove valiantly.   Finland was saved, and our external tranquillity was restored.

" Such, during the past twenty-one years, has been the course of events—events not altogether felicitous, perhaps

not altogether propitious, but at least honourable to. us,
and serving, at any rate, to remind foreign Powers of the
might of Swéden so long as Sweden is only true to herself. . . . Moreover, it was reserved for your courage,
your steadfastness, to set your contemporaries a great
example of unity and concord at the very time when our
most ancient ally, a nation once so powerful, presents so
horrible an instance of the hideous consequences of that un-
bridled license which brings about the destruction of States.

"An honourable peace has been the fruit of your steadfastness—a peace the more secure as being made between
two independent nations without any other intermediary than
the mutual respect which those who have manfully contended together cannot but feel for one another—a peace
confirmed, moreover, by an amicable union between two
closely-related allies, which promises the realm peace and
safety, and gives it redoubled dignity in the eyes of Europe.

"If I have been able to contribute something thereto,
my sole merit is to have never despaired of my country;
to have never doubted the imperturbable stout-heartedness
of the nation; to have known how to appreciate its steadfastness, its magnanimity, its zeal for the fatherland; to
have felt sure that the Swedish people would never forsake
its kings when they went before it into battle.

"It is after all these vicissitudes that I now welcome
you to-day, and with what emotion do I not behold you all
assembled before my throne, ye good lords and commons
of Sweden, my dear and dutiful subjects, when I recall
the zeal which each Estate respectively has displayed in
these troublesome times; when I recognise among you, ye
good lords of the nobility and chivalry, those whom I have
seen fighting by my side, those who by their talents, their
exploits . . . have approved themselves worthy Swedish
noblemen; or when I recall the loyal zeal which you, ye

good men of the reverend Estate of Clergy, have shown to
me and the realm, by encouraging the people to persevere
when fortune was least propitious, fulfilling to the uttermost the duties of your sacred calling by putting your
whole trust in God's providence, and strengthening the
bonds which unite together King, people, and fatherland.

"And in looking back upon these vicissitudes, how can
I ever forget the noble emulation which the Burgesses of
this realm displayed in rebuilding the flotilla when it needed
instant help, after an honourable battle against twofold
odds?   But if ever I should be so ungrateful as to forget
it, posterity will certainly never forget that remarkable
testimony to your resources and your patriotic zeal, ye
good men of the worshipful Estate of Burgesses, when it
comes to be recorded in our annals how almost every town
in the kingdom built and equipped a vessel, and how
Europe, in amazement, saw a new fleet, thrice as large as
the one it believed to be annihilated, spring up in six short
months from the sea, to wage battle on its waves and there
defend our coasts.

"And how can I express my gratitude to you, ye good
yeomen of the honourable Estate of Peasants, ye who have
shown yourselves what you have always been, what the
enemies, the oppressors, the deliverers of this kingdom . . .
have ever found you; ye who hastened, with one accord, to
the defence of the realm, leaving your ploughs, to man and
steer into battle the very vessels which your own hands had
equipped; ye whose stalwart arms dug up the very soil
they till to raise ramparts against the enemies of your
country !   To express my gratitude ∙I can find no other
words than these—you have shown yourselves *Swedes;*
you have shown yourselves worthy descendants of those
of whom Gustavus Vasa said that his trust was in God and
the peasantry of Sweden.

" But now that our external tranquillity has been restored, a work of equal importance remains to be accomplished—the regulation of our finances, which the conduct of the war has deranged. That is why I have called you together. From the reports which I shall lay before your colleagues in the Secret Committee, you will find that our resources are larger than was anticipated, and that if your resolutions are unanimous, it will not be necessary to lay upon you any greater burden than what you already bear.

"I have called you together at a time when a fanatical delusion is agitating nearly every land, at a time when few of my contemporary monarchs would have ventured without much misgiving to expose themselves to the disturbances which large assemblies spontaneously engender. But I fear them not. I rely upon your devotion and upon the straightforwardness with which I mean to lay before you the subjects which require discussion. And if your confidence only meets mine half-way, such a noble wedlock of wills can only produce such fruits as these—the good of the commonweal, the might of the realm, the respect of foreign Powers and universal tranquillity.

" May the grace and the blessing of the Almighty assist you in the accomplishment of this great work, and bring your weighty deliberations to a happy conclusion."

Now though the King's speech breathed nothing but conciliation (and his actions certainly did not belie his words), it failed to satisfy or soften the Opposition. The Nobility had come up to Gefle in a mood of mingled suspicion and alarm. The most absurd rumours had been circulating in the capital.[1] It was whispered that the detested Armfelt was to be made Marshal of the Diet; that the few remaining privileges of the first Estate were to be

---

[1] Armfelt ascribes most of these rumours to the ladies of Stockholm, the Fifth Estate, as he jocosely calls them, who, since the revolution of 1789, had been bitterly hostile to the King.

swept away by a fresh *coup-d'état;* that the guards had
secret orders to fire if necessary upon the leaders of the
Opposition, and much more to the same effect.  Most of
the noble deputies, therefore, feared, or affected to fear,
personal violence at Gefle, and many of them wore loaded
pistols beneath their mantles besides their swords.   But,
though still mutinous and defiant, they were sorely perplexed.   The lesson of the last Diet had not been lost
upon them.   If even then, on ground of their own choosing, and with absolutely everything in their favour, the
King had easily worsted them, how would it be now
when they were reduced to half their usual strength,[1] and
had none to marshal their forces ?   Their great leader,
Fersen, the veteran Fersen, whose immense influence,
unrivalled parliamentary experience, majestic bearing, and
manly eloquence had extorted even from Gustavus the
admission that " Count Fersen was the only subject
with whom a king might not disdain to cope," Fersen,
broken-hearted by his humiliation in 1789, had withdrawn altogether from public life, leaving none behind
to take his place.   Brahe was too young and unpractised ;
Pechlin, who kept discreetly in the background, much
too infamous ; while Clas de Frietzky, for more than half
a century the financial oracle of the Opposition and the
constant terror of speculative Finance Ministers, with all the
virtues which make a politician universally respected, had
few of the qualities which make a party leader implicitly
obeyed.   Moreover, the nobility were seriously hampered
by the persistent ill-will of the three lower Estates, which,
despite every precaution, frequently burst all bounds, and
caused no small disturbance.   Thus, at the very beginning of the Diet, a gentleman named Berghman, with a

---

[1] In 1789 nearly 900 gentlemen had sat in the Upper House ; in 1792 there
were scarcely 500.

few other noble deputies, paid a visit to the Burgess's Club, and were just sitting down to play cards when up came Abraham Westman, a rich Stockholm brewer and an ardent royalist, who publicly denounced Berghman as a spy, and, in spite of his remonstrances, had him summarily ejected. The affair caused a great sensation. The Estate of Nobles hotly espoused Berghman's cause and loudly demanded satisfaction, while the Estate of Burgesses as stubbornly stood by Westman. Fortunately the tact of the Marshal of the Diet prevented an actual collision, and the matter was finally allowed to drop.[1] The Estate of Peasants, too, was disposed to harry and vex the gentlemen whenever it could, so that its demonstrative loyalty rather required the curb than the spur. The King's policy, therefore, during this Diet was simple enough : he had only to keep the three lower Estates in a good humour and ignore the first Estate altogether, since it refused to be won. The Nobles, on the other hand, though "their worst growlers knew not to what divinity to turn,"[2] frequently showed their teeth and annoyed where they could not injure. Their one great opportunity was in the selection of delegates to represent them in the Secret Committee,[3] where all the real business of the Diet was always transacted, and this opportunity they made the most of. While the three lower Estates selected none but loyal committee-men, including some of the King's most trusted counsellors, the first Estate chose as their delegates men who were not only Gustavus's political opponents, but also notoriously disagreeable to him

---

[1] Adlerbeth, *Anteckningar.*

[2] Armfelt to his wife. E. Tegner, *G. M. Armfelt*, vol. i.

[3] The Nobility were represented in the committee by eighteen delegates, the three lower Estates by a like number, so that, including the four Talmen, it made a Council of forty, besides the King, who, as president, had a casting vote, and was always sure of a majority, as the Talmen were his nominees and the eighteen commoners his supporters.

personally, besides going out of their way to insult the
royal favourite, Armfelt.[1]  Fortunately the indispensable
Frietzsky and the moderate Lantinghausen were also among
the noble delegates, and both of them honestly did their
best to prevent unnecessary friction, and keep both their
sovereign and their own colleagues within due bounds.
The sagacity, the patience, the amiability, and the debating
skill of the King, who always presided on such occasions,
to say nothing of the constant presence of the little Crown
Prince by his father's side, also had a sobering effect upon
the Opposition, so that the deliberations of the committee
were, on the whole, peaceful and decorous.

The Secret Committee met together every day for five or
six hours in the Stone Saloon of Gefle Castle.  The King
always sat at the head of the table in an arm-chair, with
Charles IX.'s mace and a large silver inkstand in front of
him, the Crown Prince and the Lord High Steward occupying tabourets on his right and left respectively.  The
forty delegates sat on benches covered with purple cloth
on both sides of the table.  Schröderheim, who kept the
minutes of all the meetings, relates an incident of the first
session, ridiculous in itself, but significant enough of the
morbidly suspicious temper of the Opposition.[2]  " Behind
the King's chair was the chimneypiece, and, to prevent any
inconvenience from the fire, a screen was placed in front of
it which had been taken from one of the castle attics.  The
panels of this screen were painted with figures borrowed
from some old legend or other, but, unluckily, on one panel
was a representation of four monkeys bound with chains,
and led by a harlequin who was piping to their dancing.

[1] Armfelt not being able to attend in his place to vote on this occasion, had
sent his adjutant to the House of Nobles with his proxy, which was immediately pitched into the waste-paper basket.

[2] Schröderheim, *Anteckningar.*  Wallqvist (*Minnen och Bref*) has also
recorded his experiences in the Secret Committee.

The *frondeurs* [among the nobles] saw in this a scandalous
allegory [of the King leading the four Estates by the nose],
and would not allow anything to chance." To Schröderheim also we are indebted for an amusing description of
the behaviour of all the delegates during the sessions of
the Secret Committee. Most of the gentlemen, he tells us,
were either " cold and haughty " or " bitter but discreet."
Count Adolphus Hamilton, however, who, from being the
King's most intimate associate, had become his worst foe,
and had a great reputation for caustic pleasantry, occasionally ventured upon a passage of arms with Gustavus ;
" but," adds Schröderheim, " the King knew only too well
how to turn the laugh against him." The clerical delegates
were all men of great talent. Two of them, Wallqvist,
Bishop of Wexiö, and Prebendary Nordin, with whom
we are already acquainted,[1] were men of genius. The
bold and energetic Wallqvist talked incessantly, but always
to the point, while the timid but subtle Nordin " never
once raised his voice, but whispered all the more." The
Burgesses were delightfully comical. They bowed and
scraped whenever they were spoken to by the King, and
always referred most humbly to "my lord Finance Minister,"
the burly Hakonsson, who invariably replied " with a bored
but complaisant nod." Burgomaster Fagerström, " the
most spiteful reptile ever inhabited by human soul," tried
incessantly but fruitlessly to pick a quarrel with his colleagues of the first Estate, and coughed " most indecently
all the time." " I am quite sure," says Schröderheim,
" that the King would never have permitted the most lovely
Countess to appear at Court with such a cough." The
peasant delegates chattered in their homely way as only
peasants can, and the mischievous Schröderheim, who had
a keen sense of humour, jotted down their favourite exple-

[1] See Chapter XVII.

tives, with a view to subsequently parodying their proceedings for the King's amusement.

The deliberations in the Secret Committee continued from day to day their calm and even course. There was no hitch or obstruction of any kind, and the most dutiful submission on one side and the most gracious and friendly condescension on the other seemed to promise a swift and satisfactory session. Something like consternation indeed appeared on the faces of all the committee-men, especially the peasants, when Hakonsson first revealed to them the true state of the finances ; but Gustavus explained to their satisfaction that the new debt was a direct consequence of the inevitable war with Russia ; and after a careful and anxious investigation of a fortnight, the committee reported to the Estates that it was satisfied that the debt had been legitimately incurred, and recommended that the whole amount should be liquidated by the State, with the assistance of the Bank of Sweden, the extraordinarily prosperous condition of which institution was due entirely to the wise measures taken by Gustavus in the earlier part of his reign. The King also engaged to incur no fresh debts, in return for which assurance the committee advised the Estates to continue the present subsidies to the Crown till the next Diet. The matter was then debated by each of the four Estates separately in the usual way. The three lower Estates adopted the proposition of the Secret Committee in its entirety at the very first reading by acclamation ; but the Nobility demanded that the proposition should be laid upon the table for discussion, and discussed it was accordingly with fierce acrimony.

This obstruction, for it was really nothing else—the question having ,been already settled by the unanimous decision of three Estates out of four—very nearly led to a terrible explosion. Gustavus longed for the conclusion of

the Diet with indescribable impatience.[1]  He had a deadly
fear of the month of March, a fear which cannot fairly be
called superstitious, as, strangely enough, nearly all the
untoward accidents of his chequered career had happened in
that month.  He had been warned before leaving Stockholm
that if this Diet were prolonged much beyond February,
the consequences would be dangerous, perhaps fatal to himself; and, above all, he wished to have the early spring free
for his numerous foreign enterprises.  His wrath against
the Nobility, therefore, for resuming the dilatory tactics of
1789 was terrible.  He regarded their conduct as a criminal resistance to his plans, as an impudent attempt to
prolong the Diet against his own wishes and the wishes
of a majority of the Estates, and he determined upon
an instant and crushing chastisement.  The bitterest
blow he had ever struck against the Nobility was, as
we have already seen, the Act of National Security,
adopted during the last Diet, which practically abolished
the ancient exclusive privileges of the aristocracy by
throwing open all public appointments to competitors
of every class, regardless of rank or birth.  A most just
and liberal measure in itself, it nevertheless wounded
patrician pride in its most sensitive point, and the most
tremendous threats, nay, wholesale imprisonment itself,
had been powerless to bring the Nobles to recognise the
validity of the official signature of their Marshal surrepti-
tiously affixed thereto under compulsion during the last
Diet.  It was this same Act of Security which Gustavus
now resolved to force upon the first Estate.  It was
arranged that a deputation from the three lower Estates
should wait upon his Majesty with a humble petition that
the Act of Security should be incorporated among the Acts
passed by the Diet, in which case the Marshal of the

[1] Adlerbeth, *Anteckningar.*

Nobility would be bound to subscribe it in the name of his order. The Nobles were indirectly informed of the King's intent, but the tidings, so far from cowing, only stung them into desperation. They immediately let their Marshal know that they would never consent to the recognition of such a document; that they were prepared, if necessary, to oppose force to force ; that they would rather be buried beneath the fragments of their benches than be false to their convictions ;[1] that all who dared to support the King's violence should henceforth be marked men, and that Finance Minister Hakonsson, a notorious absolutist from conviction, and popularly suspected to be the originator of the idea, should be the first victim. The disquietude of the King's friends was great. They besought him, with tears in their eyes, not to rip up again old wounds that had begun to heal, or adventure his dignity and safety for so trifling a gratification. They might just as well have talked to the winds. Gustavus calmly continued his preparations for quelling the Opposition and dissolving the Diet on the same day, February 24. On the morning of the 23rd, there was a meeting of the Secret Committee. The noble delegates seemed more dead than alive. The Marshal of the Nobility looked as if he were about to be led to instant execution ;[2] the Finance Minister was horribly discomposed, and the Lord High Steward looked as black as thunder. Gustavus, on the other hand, was curt and peremptory, and after the transaction of some purely formal business, the Committee separated till the afternoon. It now seemed to the King's friends as if only twelve hours separated them from another revolution, the consequences of which were incalculable, and they trembled for his and their own security. Fortunately, at

---

[1] Adlerbeth, *Anteckningar*.
[2] Schröderheim, *Anteckningar*.

the last moment, the tact and judgment of Baron Ruuth, the Marshal of the Diet, saved the whole situation. He affected to take seriously the hasty threat of the Nobility against the Finance Minister, and drawing Hakonsson aside, confidentially informed him, as a friend, that the nobles had made up their minds to beat him to death the following. morning at a quarter to ten. Hakonsson declared defiantly that his conscience had nothing to reproach him with, and he therefore had no fear ; but the shaft had gone home, and the more he thought about the business, the less he liked it. The same afternoon he hastened to the King, and falling on his knees, implored Gustavus not to force the Act of Security upon a mutinous and determined nobility. He was warmly supported by Secretary Schröderheim, Baron Armfelt, the Lord High Steward, and the Marshal of the Diet, who all went into the royal cabinet one after the other, and declared that they would rather resign their posts than risk a third revolution. The King said nothing, " but his countenance was terrible." [1] Nevertheless he had already resolved to give way, especially as the Nobility, at the last moment, though very ungraciously, had consented to adopt the financial propositions of the Secret Committee without any alteration. The deputation from the three lower Estates was indeed received as arranged, but the King declared to them that the incorporation of the Act of Security among the resolutions of the Diet was now unnecessary. However, it should be annexed to the resolutions of the three lower Estates, and this compromise was accordingly accepted. Thus the one storm which had threatened the peace of the Diet passed quietly away.

After this, all went as merry as marriage-bells. The King and the Estates vied with each other in dispensing

[1] Schröderheim.

compliments.   It was unanimously resolved that a medal
should be struck, at the expense of the Bank of Sweden,
commemorating the glorious victory of Svenksund; an
address of thanks and congratulation had already been
presented to his Majesty for concluding peace with Russia,[1]
and a deputation to the little Crown Prince had presented
H.R.H. with a gift in money in anticipation of his wedding.[2]   In the joy of his heart, Gustavus was now more
than ever anxious to make his peace with the Nobility,
and this anxiety led to a most touching and dramatic scene,
which made the last meeting of the Secret Committee for
ever memorable.[3]   When the minutes had been duly read
and signed, and the four Talmen, after the usual complimentary speeches, had informed his Majesty that there was
nothing more to be done, Gustavus rose hastily, and, turning to the Nobility, thus addressed them : " But there is
one more thing for me to do.   I must, before closing these
sessions, express my satisfaction at the concord and the
mutual confidence with which, under the most trying circumstances, your deliberations have been uninterruptedly
conducted to so speedy a conclusion, and how can I better
do so than by giving the public and posterity a token of
my respect for real personal merit ?   I see amongst you,
my good lords and gentlemen, that grey-haired man who,

[1] The King replied to this deputation as follows :—" I receive with much
emotion the thanks of the Estates of the realm for the peace which the Lord
has vouchsafed us.   Your courage, ye good lords and commoners of Sweden,
your vigorous help, have prepared the way for it.   Your steadfastness, your zeal,
your valour in battle, your co-operation, have restored to the Swedish arms that
respect which they enjoyed in ages past, and peace has been the result.   As
the first citizen among you, I have only done my duty by striving to fulfil the
obligations laid upon me from the day when I first received the crown which
so many great heroes and immortal kings have worn before me," &c. &c.

[2] He was to have married one of the Russian Grand-Duchesses, but broke off
the match himself on coming of age.

[3] We have three separate accounts of this scene, by Schröderheim, Wallqvist,
and Adlerbeth.   Of these, Schröderheim's is incomparably the best.

at every Diet for well-nigh half a century, has won for himself universal respect and consideration. His insight, his unusual gift of giving eloquent expression to his opinions, to say nothing of the amiability of his society, have been useful and helpful to us all, and, need I say it? most delightful to me personally. Your eyes are already fixed upon Frietzsky. I know it. 'Tis he whom I mean. I name him Commander of my Vasa Order, and it is my intention to dub him before you all."

It was an impressive moment. Frietzsky, who was sitting on the last row of benches, turned as red as fire. The next moment he arose, advanced a couple of steps, raised his right hand as if about to speak, and bowed his head. His emotion was too strong for words. The faces of the Nobility showed that they were vexed at the King's magnanimity, and feared weakness on the part of their own champion. The Clergy, never indisposed to a compromise, beamed with satisfaction; but the Burgesses and Peasants suffered bitter twinges of jealousy at seeing such a distinction about to be conferred upon a member of the Opposition. At last Frietzsky found his voice. "Forgive my timid embarrassment, most gracious King," said he, "if I cannot sufficiently testify my gratitude. The favour offered me, so flattering to a subject in any case, is doubly so to me, because of the gracious manner in which it has pleased your Majesty to offer it, and the place, the time, and the circumstances attending it. Nevertheless, the least temptation on my part to accept the gift would make me unworthy of it. Near twenty years ago, when the Vasa Order was first instituted, it was I who spoke in favour of it from my place in Parliament. I was consequently suspected at the time of intriguing to obtain it, and in my anxiety to confute such suspicions, I bound myself by a solemn oath never to accept or wear it. No doubt, I went too far; but the oath was taken, and it prevents me now from accepting your Majesty's most gracious offer.   Your Majesty, I am sure, while appreciating rightly my self-abnegation, will never doubt my dutiful gratitude — a gratitude to which my few remaining days shall testify.   And besides, sir, what external sign of distinction can equal the honour done to me to-day, or the satisfaction which it affords me?"   The aged statesman stopped short, and tears ran down his cheeks.   He advanced, and seizing the King's hand, twice pressed it to his lips.   "Your Majesty is not displeased with me, I hope?" said he.   "No, my dear Frietzsky," replied Gustavus, much affected; "such a refusal as yours can certainly offend no one, for it is dictated by honour and virtue, and more than justifies my kindly intention towards you."   The King then closed the session of the Secret Committee with a spirited harangue, and quitted the room.   The moment he was gone, the nobles crowded round Frietzsky to compliment him, and one gentleman had the indecency to say, in allusion to the King, "Ah-ha! that fox went away with his tail between his legs." Frietzsky turned upon his colleague in noble indignation. "No insults!" he cried.   "Don't profane a noble action and a noble incident!   The whole of my order ought to share and sympathise with my personal gratitude to my King."

Two hours afterwards the Diet was "blown out" with the usual ceremonies.   "The bad weather, or rather stress of time," says Schröderheim, "saved us from the procession to church," divine service being held in the Rikssaal, where an altar and a sacristy, hung with Gobelin tapestries, had been hastily improvised for the occasion.   The King dismissed the Estates to their homes in a speech described by one of the Opposition as "full of the most flattering caresses and the most engaging promises."[1]   It has also

[1] Adlerbeth, *Anteckningar*.

the melancholy interest of a last speech.   Never again
were the men of Sweden to listen to the august and ample
periods of their greatest orator.

   " When I opened the Diet, which I dissolve to-day
amidst such happy circumstances," thus he began, " I told
you that I had not feared to call you together at a time
when a fanatical delusion was agitating nearly every land,
and that I relied upon your devotion to me, and upon the
magnanimous heart of the nation, to settle in tranquillity
and concord the weighty matters which were the occasion of your coming together.   My hopes have not been
disappointed, and after showing, amidst the flames of war,
that you were the same people whose valour of yore was
wont to shake or sustain thrones and empires, you have
now, amidst the blessings of peace, given your contemporaries a still nobler example of the sobriety, the perspi-
cacity, and the harmony with which the representative of
a wise and powerful nation know how to consider, discuss,
and determine the matters concerning which the head of
the State requires their counsels. . . .

   " And if, as the first of my fellow-citizens, . . . I am
bound, in the name of the Fatherland, to thus convey
to you an expression of thanks equally honourable to us
both, how much more must not my heart be moved by the
affection which you have shown to me and my son during
the course of this Diet, and with what love, respect, and
confidence ought not his youthful mind to be filled at the
sight of the noble nation which, from his very cradle, has
given him so many proofs of its devotion and regard !  You
have seen him follow the course of your deliberations ; you
have seen him initiated by me into the practice of that
great calling for which Providence has destined him.   I
want to accustom him betimes to the weighty charge which
will one day be his.   I want to make him, from his youth

up, learn to esteem the people he is to govern, love their
laws, and respect their liberties.   You have gratified the
wishes of my heart, a father's heart, and, anticipating the
future, so to speak, have hastened on the moment when
it will be your wish to see my race, perpetuated by him,[1]
secure the continuance of the dynasty and the stability of
the throne. . . .

   "You will now return home to your dwellings to resume
your callings in peace and quietness, and convey to your
fellow-citizens the satisfactory tidings that you have honestly
and zealously done all that in you lay to maintain the good
of the commonwealth and the might of the State.   I too,
I go to watch over your welfare and the welfare of your
country ; I go to provide for the improvement of agriculture, the increase of commerce, the utilisation of our resources, to guard the majesty of the laws, to see to the
equitable administration of justice ; I go to promote reverence for religion and maintain the dignity of the realm—
in a word, to devote myself to all those duties incumbent
upon my office, but still more binding upon my affections
and the gratitude which your devotion and your loyalty
awaken in my heart.

   "It is with such sentiments that I now dissolve this
Diet.   With the same sentiments will I welcome you again
before the throne when our common concerns again require
your presence.   In the meantime I commend you to the
protection of the Almighty, assuring you severally and
collectively of my royal grace, favour, and good-will."

---

[1] An allusion to the marriage gift presented to the Crown Prince by the
Estates.   It is melancholy to reflect that the progeny of this young Prince were
excluded in 1809 from the succession, and banished the country.

# CHAPTER XXIV.

## *THE MASQUERADE AT THE OPERA-HOUSE.*

Satisfactory result of the Diet of Gefle—Gustavus's foreign policy—France—Poland—Mysteriousness of his projects—Anckarström's state of mind—He determines to shoot the King on March 16 at the masquerade—Conference of the conspirators at Pechlin's house—Final preparations of Anckarström—Movements of Gustavus on the 16th—The anonymous warning letter—Gustavus ignores it—He is shot, but not killed—Consternation of the Court—Heroism of the King—He is removed to the Palace—Determines to appoint a Regency—Investigations at the Opera-House.

THUS the Gefle Diet, from which all manner of horrors was anticipated, was dissolved amidst mutual compliments and joyful pæans. The King's friends were quite bewildered at his good fortune. "Never since the creation of the world," wrote Armfelt to his wife with characteristic exaggeration, "has there been such harmony as has prevailed during this Diet."[1] Pessimists might regard the financial expedients adopted as mere palliatives, but they effectually relieved the King from his more pressing embarrassments, and thus left him a free and open course for the future. It was also obvious that he had lost nothing of his popularity, and such a fact could not but strengthen his authority both at home and abroad. Now that the finances had been regulated, he could employ every penny of the Russian subsidies, scanty though they were, in repairing his fleets and mobilising his armies, so as to be in readiness for any political conjuncture abroad. For it was upon the great

[1] O. Tegner, *G. M. Armfelt*, vol. i.

European theatre of events that his penetrating gaze was constantly fixed. What his real plans were at this period will never be exactly known. No man ever possessed the entire confidence of Gustavus III., and even his most influential favourites were always left in the dark till the very last moment as to their master's intentions. It has been well remarked that, expansive and sociable as he was in private life and on ordinary occasions, yet, in all the great crises of his life, he took counsel of none but himself. So much we may safely assume, however—his interest in French affairs, up to the very moment of his death, was as strong and as lively as ever. His last letters to Breteuil, Bouillé, and the French Princes breathe nothing but defiance to the French Revolution and its undisciplined hordes of National Guards.[1] "I hope," he wrote to Breteuil from Gefle, "that the year we are entering upon will be as fortunate as the year last past was unlucky. If my prayers are accomplished, you will see France saved and your sovereign re-established." Want of money alone retarded his operations. Young Bouillé had been sent by his father to Gefle with a definite plan of campaign. Gustavus approved of it, but very pertinently asked from whence the necessary funds were to come. He bitterly laments the millions squandered by Catherine II. upon the *emigrés.* "If the Powers," he wrote, "who sent the Princes such large sums, amounting to a total of more than 12,000,000 livres, of which not a single penny now remains, had only sent me a tithe of that money last autumn, perhaps we should now be the masters of one [French] province at least, and things would have been in a very different state to what they are now."

And complications were arising in the East as well as in the West. Early in March, Count Stackelberg, the Russian

---

[1] Akeson, *Gustaf III.*

ambassador at Stockholm, received orders from his Court to gauge the views of the King of Sweden as to Poland. Gustavus at once saw that a fresh partition of that unhappy country was at hand, and the question at once arose, How would such an event affect Sweden? Poland had always been an object of especial interest to Gustavus. At one time, indeed, he had actually aspired to the Sarmatian throne himself. He longed to quarter the White Eagle of Poland and the Horseman of Lithuania among the Gothic Crowns and Lions, and it would not have been the first time that a Vasa had worn the diadem of St. Stanislas. At the outbreak of the Russian war he had even offered the Republic a definite alliance; and his envoy at Warsaw, the virile and energetic Lars von Engeström,[1] had powerfully contributed to the passing of the famous Constitution of May 1791, Poland's last bold stroke for freedom against Russian tyranny. The Poles had accepted the assistance of Engeström with effusive gratitude, and had even sent one of their most illustrious magnates[2] to Sweden at the head of a splendid embassy, but nothing came of these political coquetries. There could, indeed, be no real bond of fellowship between a nobility which had degraded their own King into a mere puppet, and a King who would brook no interference whatever from his nobility. The Poles, with that fatal impatience of all control which was the chief cause of their swiftly impending ruin, preferred King Log to King Stork, so the projected Swedo-Polish alliance proved impracticable. At the same time Gustavus could not regard the disappearance of the Polish State with indifference, and Catherine's evident

---

[1] A brother of the regicide Johan, but too upright a man to do anything but loathe such a crime as assassination. His *Anteckningar* is one of the most important documents extant as to contemporary Poland. The literature relating to Gustavus's Polish policy is pretty considerable, but it is a subject I have been obliged to pass over. *Raphael's* is the best Swedish book thereon.

[2] Potocki.

anxiety to come to an understanding with him on the subject gave him reasonable hopes that Sweden, if only she played her cards well, might reap no small advantage from these fresh complications. At the same time, his past experience of Catherine's perfidious policy made him very chary in his dealings with her, and his despatch to Stedingk of March 13, 1792, written only three days' before his assassination, shows that in political astuteness he was quite a match for his "*bonne cousine.*" He regarded the Polish question, he said, "as a conjuncture which might offer some substantial advantages to Sweden." He must first, however, be more exactly informed of the real intentions of the Empress. It was possible that her affected interest in French affairs was merely a feint "to turn the attention of the neighbours of Russia and Poland towards another quarter . . . so that she might appropriate all the benefits accruing from a fresh partition of Poland." "In any case," he adds, "whether the Empress wishes sincerely, and without any ulterior views, to take [an active] part in French affairs, or whether she only wants to use France as a pretext for having her hands freer in Poland, it is of the utmost importance that I should know exactly what I am about, so as not to expose myself to vexatious disappointment, or lose the opportunity of deriving some advantage from so favourable a circumstance, should it take place."[1] In plain English, Gustavus meant that the Empress would have to purchase his neutrality. He knew very well that she had come to regard him as a Power to be reckoned with in any division of the spoil, and he was quite determined to do the best for himself and his country. What Gustavus hoped to gain from these unexpectedly favourable conjunctures, it is difficult to say. His real designs were, as usual, wrapped in impenetrable obscurity. Some have

[1] Akeson, *Gustaf III.*

conjectured that he meant to extort a Russian army corps and ample subsidies from the Empress for a vigorous on-slaught upon Paris in the early spring.   Others speak of a contemplated visit to London[1] to arrange a subsidy treaty with England.   Others again contend, with more show of reason, that Norway[2] was the object of his secret ambition, and that he expected Catherine to sacrifice Denmark to him in return for his abandoning Poland to her.   It is also by no means improbable that he looked for some territorial compensation on the other side of the Baltic, some extension of Swedish Finland perhaps, or possibly a slice of Livonia.   Unhappily for him, it was just at the very moment when the impending crisis was at hand, at the very moment when his keen political insight would have infallibly discerned where Sweden's real interests lay,[3] that Anckarström's bullet struck him down in the prime of his life and the heyday of his hopes.

For all this time Anckarström had never once lost sight of his victim.   He had taken his pistols with him to Gefle, and had waylaid the King every day; but the severe weather made Gustavus give up his usual walks, and the assassins dare not attack him in his carriage.   Despite his fanaticism, the miserable man, by his own showing, occa-sionally had qualms of conscience.   "All this time," he

[1] Fryxell, *Bidrag till Sveriges nyare historia efter* 1772.

[2] General Hugo Hamilton in 1854 related the following anecdote, told him by his father, who was one of Gustavus's gentlemen-in-waiting :—" Alongside or behind his plan of a coalition against France, Gustavus III., in 1792, con-cealed another.   Under the cloak of a French expedition, he meant to collect an army for a sudden invasion of Norway.   Hamilton used to observe about this time a number of charts and maps on the King's table which excited his suspicion.   One day the King said to him, 'Don't you think that our campaign against France will be a right down merry one?'   'I *think*,' replied Hamilton, ' that the campaign will rather be directed against Norway.'   Much startled, the King sprang up and seized Hamilton by the collar.   'Fellow,' said he, ' not a word to any one about what you *think!*   Recollect that in serious matters I'll stand no nonsense.' "—*Fryxell, Bidrag, etc.*, p. 184.

[3] Akeson, *Gustaf III.*

tells us,[1] "the thought kept on occurring to me : Is this right, or is it not rather sin? Nay, I would answer, 'tis thy bounden duty to love thy neighbour as thyself. If I were persecuted, I should wish others to help me, consequently I ought to help others. If I did the deed from selfish or malicious motives, it would be wrong, but now, it is the only comfort I possess in my most wretched state, which, with the help of the Great and Gracious God [sic], will soon be changed into a most happy condition of things."

On the first Friday after the King's return to the capital (March 2), a masquerade at the opera-house was announced. Ribbing, who seems to have at last convinced himself that Anckarström was no trifler, urged him to make a fresh attempt on the King's life, engaging to secure his escape. They both went to the masquerade, accordingly, and the King also ; but so few people were there, that nothing could be done. Another masquerade which had been fixed for the 6th was abandoned, and a week later the last masquerade of the season was announced for the 16th. The position of the regicides had now become critical. They had been so sanguine of success that they had imparted their secret to a number of political sympathisers, so that a single repentant or imprudent word might at any moment have brought the active plotters to the scaffold. It was plain that if the deed were to be done at all, it should be done at once. Accordingly, after a final conference at Hufvudstad, when Counts Horn and Ribbing promised to provide for Anckarström's children in case his estates were confiscated,[2] they all three

---

[1] Anckarström's confession, *Lex. ö. Sv. Namn. M.*, article "Anckarström." We must not forget that Anckarström had at this time a comfortable home, a good income, a flourishing estate, a loving wife and promising children—in fact, all that most men strive for all their lives !

[2] The Estates were granted to the heirs of the felon by the Prince Regent, but they had to change their names.

returned to Stockholm, quite resolved that the following day, Friday 16th, should be the King's last.

On the afternoon of the 16th there was a general conference of all the leading conspirators, except Horn and Anckarström, at Pechlin's house, where they ate and drank of the best, and soon became very merry and confidential. After coffee had been served, the host took Liljehorn and Engeström aside into his bedroom, where they discussed what form of government should be adopted after the King's fall. It was unanimously agreed that the moment Gustavus was dead, Armfelt, Taube, Ruuth, and all the other leading Gustavians should be arrested, the young Crown Prince proclaimed King with a council of regency, and the Estates summoned to do the rest. One of the conspirators is said to have jocosely exclaimed, " Fancy if the General [*i.e.*, Pechlin] should have a place in the Council ! " whereupon the old fox replied with a grin, that home was the best place for him. To every one of the conspirators was now assigned his proper *rôle*. Pechlin and Ribbing undertook to crowd the masquerade with accomplices ; Engeström was to draft a brand new radical constitution ; Liljehorn promised to answer for the Guards.

At four o'clock Pechlin's guests separated. Ribbing returned home to make his final preparations with Horn and Anckarström, who there awaited him. Anckarström employed the next few hours in getting ready his weapons.[1] He loaded each of his pistols with two bullets and fourteen pieces of lead and iron of various shapes and sizes, besides adding a few nails. Then he filed the blade of the huge butcher's knife, which he had purchased ten days before for the express purpose of completing his crime, to a razor-like sharpness, besides carefully barbing the point. This

---

[1] It is a fable that Ribbing and Anckarström tossed up as to which of them should have the privilege of killing the King.

improvised dagger has been described by those who saw and handled it as one of the most frightful weapons imaginable—a wound from it must have proved instantly fatal. A little before twelve Horn called for Anckarström, and at half-past they went together to the masquerade in black dominoes with white masks, and there met Ribbing and a number of Pechlin's acquaintances (Pechlin took care *not* to be there personally), all similarly attired.

We must now return to the King.

Gustavus III. had a peculiar horror of assassination. He once said to his faithful Schröderheim, " If I am to die a violent death, I pray that it may be publicly, on the scaffold, not by the hand of a Damien or a Ravaillac." His dread of the month of March we have already mentioned ; but he does not seem to have feared the March of 1792 more than its predecessors, and the fatal 16th found him apparently in the best of humours. In the morning he walked with one of his favourite equerries, young George Löwenhjelm, in the Haga Park, where the new palace which was to have rivalled the château of Versailles in grandeur and magnificence was just rising from the ground.[1] Löwenhjelm asked the King when the building would be completed. " Well," replied Gustavus, "if I reach the average age of humanity, I hope to dwell in it for a few years before I die." After that the King went in his sledge to Brunsvick, a picturesque little village near Haga, where a large sledging-party, including nearly all the Opposition, was running races. Gustavus, after watching the whole procession pass by the Haga Park, followed them, and was present during the sports as a spectator. He then returned to Haga with Löwenhjelm, who was in attendance for the day, and after dining there, drove the same afternoon to town and paid a visit to the

---

[1] The colossal foundations still remain to puzzle or astonish the tourist. The building was abandoned after the King's death, as too vast and costly.

French theatre, where *Les Folies Amoureuses* of Regnard was performed, thence proceeding to the opera-house, which they reached soon after eleven.[1]  The King had a little private apartment there, where he used to sup with a few well-chosen companions whenever he attended the masquerades.  There were with him on the present occasion, besides Löwenhjelm, Baron Essen, his chief equerry, and four attendants.  During the repast, the page Tigerstedt brought in a letter addressed to the King.[2]  Löwenhjelm, who was sitting at Gustavus's left hand, turned his head aside while his master was perusing it; but his curiosity being excited by Tigerstedt's gestures, he peeped over the King's shoulder and perceived that the mysterious missive was written in pencil, in a large round hand, without any signature.  Gustavus read the letter through twice, then smiled, and put it into his pocket without a word.[3]

After supper, Löwenhjelm asked the King whether they should mask.  "No," replied Gustavus; "run away to your

[1] I follow mainly Löwenhjelm's own account of the fatal event, first published by the historian Fryxell in 1882.  Sierakowski's circumstantial account of the murder (*Histoire de l'Assassinat de Gustave III. . . . par un officier polonais* [Count Sierakowski] *témoin oculaire*, Paris, 1797, which has hitherto been the accepted version, and of which the numerous French versions are only so many copies, may now be regarded as apocryphal.  I shall frequently have occasion to expose its errors.

[2] Sierakowski states that this anonymous letter was fastened with a wafer impressed by a seal, which led to the discovery of the writer.  This is incorrect.  We shall see presently how the writer of the letter was really discovered.

[3] The exact contents of this anonymous letter will never be known.  It was not printed as a whole in the official report of the trial of the assassins, and subsequently disappeared.  Fryxell, in his collection of original documents entitled "*Bidrag till Sveriges historia efter* 1772," has endeavoured to reconstruct this letter from the extant fragments, and there is little doubt that the result thus obtained is substantially correct.  Sierakowski, with impudent omniscience, pretends that the letter only contained these words, "Je suis encore de vos amis quoique j'aie des raisons pour ne le plus être.  N'allez pas au bal ce soir.  Il y va de votre vie."  Now, in the first place, the letter was a long one, and, in the second place, the writer expressly declares himself to be the King's foe, not his friend.

little sweetheart downstairs." Every one then withdrew except Essen, to whom the King now showed the anonymous letter. It professed to be written by a stranger "whose pen was directed by the voice of conscience," began by plainly informing the King that for some time past a conspiracy had been afoot to take away his life, and warned him that the murderers had fixed that night for carrying it out. The writer earnestly adjured Gustavus not to appear at the masquerade, and then proceeded, with a strange mixture of bombast and impudence, to extol his own virtue and patriotism, and to lecture his sovereign on his public and private misconduct, directly threatening him with future disaster if he did not amend the errors of his ways. The literary style of this singular effusion was as rough as its tone was rude. It evidently meant to convey the idea that it came from one of the lower classes. Essen, much disturbed, implored the King not to go to the masquerade ; or, if he did, at least to wear a coat of mail beneath his mantle. But Gustavus, laughing at his fears, selected a three-cornered hat, threw over his shoulders a so-called Venetian silk mantle, which left the decorations on his breast perfectly visible, and put on a half mask, which barely covered his eyes and the bridge of his nose. He was almost as recognisable as if he had been unmasked. He then took Essen's arm, and stepped into his private box, which commanded a view of the whole of the grand saloon.

Among the crowd of masqueraders whom the severity of the weather had not deterred from attending, the King's glance fell at once upon a group of black dominoes, who, whispering together, drew near to the royal box, but immediately dispersed again, as if fearful of attracting attention. The group in question actually consisted of the assassins, who had entered the opera-house at the very

moment when the King appeared in his box, and at once
perceived him standing there with Essen by his side.

After watching the scene for fully a quarter of an hour,
"as motionless as a picture in its frame," the King remarked to Essen, "They have lost a good opportunity
of shooting me. Come, let us go down; the masquerade
seems bright and gay. Let us see whether they will dare
to kill me!" The dancing was now in full swing, and as
Gustavus entered the saloon, leaning on Essen's arm, he
was quickly recognised by the decorations on his breast
and the vivacity of his movements. A murmur of "There's
the King!" ran through the room. He took a turn round
the saloon, and perceiving Löwenhjelm flirting in a corner
with "his little sweetheart," Gustavus stooped down and
whispered to her as he passed, "The pretty mask should
be very gracious to her cavalier there, for he was quite
in a hurry just now to run away from me to her." He
then disappeared with Essen into the green-room, Horn
and Anckarström, who had been at his heels all the time,
waiting for him close by the side-scenes among the dancers.
They had not long to wait. In a few moments the King
and Essen reappeared; but they had only moved a few
steps forward, when two large groups of black dominoes,
advancing from opposite directions, ran together so as to
catch the King in their midst and make further progress
impossible. Then a hand lightly tapped Gustavus on the
shoulder, and a voice exclaimed, "*Bon jour, beau masque!*"
This was Horn's signal to Anckarström, who instantly
pressing the muzzle of one of his pistols to the King's
body, discharged its contents into his back,[1] a little above
the left hip. Löwenhjelm, who heard the muffled report

[1] Aiguila (*Histoire du Règne de Gustave III.*) says that the King first felt the
pistol at his breast, and by a rapid movement turned it aside. But Anckarström,
in his confession, expressly states that he crept behind the King to make sure
of him.

from where he was sitting, and was under the impression that some practical joker had let off a squib, hastily quitting his partner, forced his way through the crowd to restore order. Surprised to find the King and Essen with their masks in their hands hemmed in on every side by a surging throng of black dominoes, he inquired what was the matter. "Some villain has shot the King!" exclaimed Essen, casting a searching glance around him. Too horrified to speak, Löwenhjelm drew his sword, and, standing in front of the wounded monarch, drove back the throng. A guardsman, following his example, drove them back from behind, till the two had a clear space around them as far as their swords could reach. But for their promptitude there can be little doubt that Gustavus would have been despatched upon the spot.[1] Anckarström, in his first amazement at the apparent failure of his pistol-shot, had dropped all his weapons on the floor. He now mingled with the crowd and raised a cry of fire, which was taken up by his accomplices to create confusion and facilitate escape. But above the din rose the voice of young Captain Pollett, one of the King's adjutants, ordering the sentinels to close all the doors, an order they instantly obeyed. The King had already commanded those about him to discover and seize but not to hurt the murderer. As the truth gradually became known, most of the spectators were filled with indignation, and those persons who wore black dominoes were roughly handled. The unfortunate monarch, still supported by Essen, and dripping with blood, was escorted back to his little room, where he reclined upon a red divan. He bade Löwenhjelm return to the saloon, see how things were going on, and say, in answer to all inquiries, that his

---

[1] Some accounts say the King staggered and fell immediately after he was wounded, but Anckarström, in his confession, attributes his failure to kill the King outright to his own surprise that the King did *not* fall.

wound was a mere scratch. Löwenhjelm found the music still playing,[1] for the orchestra and many of the dancers had apparently noticed nothing. On his own responsibility he sent for fifty dragoons of the regiment he commanded, besides issuing an order in the King's name that all the gates of Stockholm should be closed till further notice. On his way back to the King he was accosted by Ribbing, who asked how his Majesty fared. Löwenhjelm replied as he had been told. "Thank God!" exclaimed Ribbing; "may the murderer be brought to justice!"

A few moments after Anckarström's shot had been fired, the Prussian Minister, Brockhausen, and the Spanish Minister, the Chevalier de Corral, arrived at the opera-house. On being informed at the door by Löwenhjelm of the disaster, they at once solicited and obtained an audience. Gustavus received his visitors with a tranquil gaiety which they could not sufficiently admire, told them "with the utmost precision"[2] how the fatal accident had occurred, and added, "How unfortunate that, after having braved in warfare the fire of the enemy, I should have been wounded in the back in the midst of my own people!" Their conversation was interrupted by the precipitate entrance of young Armfelt, who should have been at the masquerade before, but had unfortunately been detained till nearly midnight at the house of the Danish Minister, Count Rewentlow. Hurrying home, he had donned a Venetian domino, and hastened to the opera-house.[3] On arriving there, he remarked nothing unusual.

---

[1] It would appear from this that the *violente agitation* of Aiguila, and the *terreur générale* of Sierakowski, are not to be taken too literally.

[2] Brockhausen's *Dépéche till sit hof rörande Konungamordet*, contained in Schröderheim's *Anteckningar*.

[3] Armfelt's Memoirs. See O. Tegner, *G. M. Armfelt*, vol. i. Armfelt's account of the King's last days is certainly the most graphic, and, on the whole, the most reliable we possess.

The Second Lifeguards, whose colonel he was, were on duty there for the night. He ascended the stairs to get to the King's private room through the grand saloon, but was stopped at the door by the porter, who said to him, "You may go in, General, but you will not be allowed to come out again!" Armfelt, fancying that the fellow was either mad or drunk, pushed by him without a word, and was opening the door for himself, when the man drew nearer and whispered, "The King has been wounded by a pistol-shot, and no one is to go out, because they want to catch the assassin." So overcome was Armfelt at this frightful news that all his strength seemed suddenly to desert him. His knees tottered. He staggered through a little antechamber to the grand saloon, which was dimly lit by a single candle, and close beside the stove sat a little page sobbing. "Where is the King?" asked Armfelt. "In there, on the red divan," said the boy between his sobs. "Wounded?" "Yes."— Armfelt rushed in without another word. Gustavus no sooner beheld him than he stretched out his arms and said, with a smile, "Who would ever have thought, my friend, that I should be wounded from behind?" In his utter agitation Armfelt did not know what to say, and the room reeled round with him when he perceived that the grey mantle which the King had wrapped round the lower part of his body was soaked with blood. "Don't be so alarmed, my dear Armfelt," cried the King cheerily; "you know from experience what a wound is, and I feel no pain." He then made the young man sit down; and after drinking a glass of water, Armfelt rallied all the physical and moral energy left in him, and asked if the surgeons had been sent for. Finding, to his astonishment, that they had not, he was hastening away for them, when the King beckoned him to his couch and whispered in his ear,

" Send and see whether La Perrière is at home ; I fancied I recognised him quite close to me in the crush just now." La Perrière was a French actor suspected of Jacobin proclivities. Gustavus thought at first that a foreigner had fired the fatal shot. He could not believe one of his own subjects capable of such an act. Armfelt instantly executed his commission, but found that the actor had been in bed for some hours. On returning to his master's side, he found the room thronged with sympathisers of all classes ; and making his way up to the divan, privately informed Gustavus that La Perrière was safe at home. " So much the worse," replied the King ; " then it is a Swede after all ! But don't let us talk about it any more now. There is something for you to read,"—and he thrust into the favourite's hand the neglected letter of warning.

Meanwhile, the news of the catastrophe had attracted the rest of the *corps diplomatique* to the opera-house, and the corridors leading to the King's private apartment were speedily thronged with diplomatists, court dignitaries, and the principal officers of state. The Russian ambassador, Stackelberg, was among the first to obtain admission. No sooner did he see the King than his emotion overcame him, and he exclaimed, " Sir, sir, in spite of such a warning, to have exposed a life so precious to your country and to Europe !" " Thank you, dear Count," replied Gustavus, " but when a madman has made up his mind to sacrifice his own life to obtain yours, he must succeed in the long-run." Most affecting of all was the scene between the King and his brother, the Duke of Sudermania. The Duke, who had been summoned from his bed at midnight by Lieutenant Reuterskjöld, was so overcome with grief and horror when he entered the room, that but for the assistance of the royal pages he would have fallen to the ground. " Brother Gus, brother Gus !" was all that he could say, and his voice was choked with tears. The King gave him a glass of water, or he would have swooned. It seemed to those who were present as if it were the Duke and not the King who had received his death-blow.[1]

By this time the doctors had come and did all that could be done under the circumstances. The first to arrive was Surgeon Hallman,[2] quite out of breath with rushing upstairs. The King laughed when he saw him, and said, "See how my portly Hallman puffs and blows!" Hallman examined the wound at once, but declined to give an opinion about it. "Nay," cried Gustavus sharply, "a King ought to know his danger, and you ought not to hide it from him." "I cannot tell, sir," replied Hallman, "till I have probed the wound with the proper instruments." It was determined that the patient should be removed at once to the palace, and his coach was quickly at the door. Gustavus now rose from the divan, but, after taking a dozen steps became so faint that he had to be carried downstairs in a sedan-chair, Armfelt, Essen, and Löwenhjelm attending him. As he was borne through the crowded hall, he gaily remarked that he resembled the Holy Father borne in procession from the Vatican to St. Peter's. Hundreds of persons of all classes followed the carriage, or walked beside it, while an immense throng of the common people, whom a report of the catastrophe had brought together, lined the way on both sides, wailing and wringing their hands. Short as was the way,[3] it seemed long

---

[1] The question whether the Duke was implicated in his brother's murder is one of the most obscure in Swedish history. The man who could order a lady to be flogged from sheer spite and connive at the murder of a nobleman he feared, was certainly capable even of fratricide ; but the evidence is so hopelessly conflicting that Charles XIII. must be allowed the benefit of the doubt.

[2] Löwenhjelm, *Minnen.*

[3] It is scarcely more than a five minutes' walk from the opera-house, which is close beside the Hôtel Rydberg, to the Palace, which is exactly opposite.— Since these lines were written the Gustavan Opera-House has been demolished to make way for another opera-house on an even grander scale.

enough to every one. The King suffered much from the
jolting of the carriage, but, on reaching the foot of the
grand staircase, where they shifted him once more into
the sedan-chair, he resumed his serene and cheerful air,
greeted and thanked every one in the most friendly manner,
and talked to all who were near him with that peculiar
blend of gaiety and tenderness which never failed to
excite sympathy or enthusiasm. All who had been with
him in his chamber at the opera-house, besides a great
many of the common people, now followed him into his
bedroom, so that he can almost be said to have been
undressed and put to bed in public. He continued to
converse with those about him, but it was observed that
he spoke most freely and most earnestly to the Russian
Ambassador, Stackelberg, and the English Minister, Robert
Liston, who never left his side. The throng in the bedroom, however, soon made the atmosphere hot and stifling,
and the doctors were at last obliged to order every one
out so as to give their patient a little needful repose.
The King accordingly took leave of the whole assembly
in the most gracious manner, and so serenely that he
seemed to feel neither pain nor uneasiness. It was then
that an affecting scene occurred which Löwenhjelm thus
records : "The English Minister, Liston, one of the coldest
men I ever knew, rushed suddenly up to the bedstead,
knelt down before it, and seizing the King's hand in his
own, kissed it repeatedly and covered it with his tears."

The room had no sooner been cleared than the King
beckoned Armfelt to his side, and said, "Don't let us hope
too much. This affair may be very serious. In any case,
I shall certainly grow much worse than I feel now, and
therefore a Regency must be appointed, so that affairs may
continue their course, and I may not be disturbed every
moment." Armfelt assented. Gustavus then said that he

would leave the investigation of the crime of which he was the victim entirely to the Regency. He wished, he said, to know nothing about it—not even the sentence was to be submitted to him. " I want to remain ignorant all my life," he added, " as to whether Swedish hands are really stained with my blood." Then, after a pause, " At all events, I feel sure the Jacobins must have suggested the idea. Swedes are neither cowardly nor corrupt enough to have conceived such a crime."

The King had no sooner left the opera-house than Liljensparre, his dreaded Minister of Police, a sort of Swedish Sartines, took possession of the grand saloon there, and lost no time in noting down the names and addresses of all the masqueraders, who had to pass out before him one by one between two files of soldiers with fixed bayonets. The assassins were not even suspected, and Horn[1] had managed to escape, not only from the room, but from the town, before Liljensparre had arrived. Anckar-ström lingered till the last, and said to the Minister, " You won't suspect me, I hope!" " Why you more than others?" asked Liljensparre, with a searching look, and from that moment Anckarström was a marked man. Immediately after leaving the opera-house, Liljensparre summoned all the locksmiths and armourers of Stockholm to the Ministry of Police to examine the pistols and the knife which had been picked up on the floor of the saloon, when Kaufman,

---

[1] Horn had fled immediately after the shot, and succeeded in escaping from the city before the gates were closed. Yet Sierakowski tells us : " Le Comte de Horn . . . parut [before Liljensparre] comme les autres. . . . Il attribua son air de contrainte . . . à la douleur d'avoir perdu son roi. . . . M. de Liljensparre ne crut pas devoir le faire arrêter [!]." This, however, is nothing to what follows : " Successivement," continues the veracious " témoin oculaire," " parurent les autres chefs du parti des mécontents, tels que MM. Ribbing, Enge-ström, Bjelke, Liljehorn, le général Pechlin. Ils répondirent tous a leur tour," &c. Now, with the single exception of Ribbing, not one of these men was present at the masquerade. The inference is, neither was Sierakowski.

the gunsmith of the bodyguards, recognised the pistols as having been lately repaired by him for Captain Anckarström. Anckarström was at once arrested at his house, and taken into custody three hours after the firing of the shot.

# CHAPTER XXV.

## THE SICK-CHAMBER.

Excitement and indignation in the capital—Energy and zeal of the
Minister of Police—Reconciliation of the King and the Nobility
—Terrible nature of Gustavus's injuries—Early hopes—Descrip-
tion of the sick-room—The patient's moods—Change for the
worse—Pleads for his murderers—The last moments—Dalberg—
The inkstand accident—The Bishop of Wexiö sent for—Farewell!
—Retrospect.

On the morning of the 17th March 1792 all Stockholm
awoke in terror and confusion.      sters had already been
placarded everywhere announcing the attempted assassination, but expressing a strong hope that his Majesty would
very speedily recover.    A   ward of 25,000 riksdollars
(£2000) had already been o..ered for the apprehension of
the assassin; but he was in custody before the public
advertisements to that effect had been printed.    The excitement in Stockholm was intense, and its first symptoms
were decidedly alarming.    Rumours of a widespread aristocratic conspiracy spread more and more every day, and when
it became generally known that all the regicides hitherto
arrested were gentlemen, the populace was only with the
utmost difficulty restrained from sacking the residences of
the principal leaders of the Opposition.    General Count
Horn, young Horn's father, was besieged by the mob in
his own house, and only saved from a terrible death by the
prompt arrival of a detachment of dragoons, who carried
him off to the palace ostensibly as a prisoner.    For the
next ten days there was not a nobleman in Stockholm

who did not tremble for his life. The people were furious against the murderers of their beloved King. Their old hatred against the aristocrats blazed up afresh, and if an able and audacious agitator had been on the spot at that moment to take advantage of the prevalent excitement, it is by no means improbable that every nobleman in the capital would have been massacred. The Regency, however, took the most energetic precautions against any such outbreak. Soothing proclamations bade the people keep within doors and abide the result of the judicial investigations. The burgesses of Stockholm were placed under arms, and patrolled the streets night and day to keep order. They were afterwards reinforced by 400 men of the Second Life-guards, whose loyalty was above suspicion. Fortunately for the public peace, the terrors and the suspicions of the people gradually subsided; but crowds thronged the churches, where the daily prayers for the King's recovery were frequently interrupted by the sobs and groans of the congregations, consisting, for the most part, of the lower and middle classes.

Meanwhile, with untiring energy and almost superhuman skill, Liljensparre was pursuing his investigations, and in a few days all the ringleaders of the conspiracy were in his hands. It was no easy matter to induce them to confess, it was still more difficult to reconcile their conflicting confessions, but Liljensparre's ingenuity triumphed over every obstacle. The anonymous letter was traced to Liljehorn through a baker's boy, whom he had bribed to deliver it to one of the royal pages. Bjelke, after destroying all his papers, took poison rather than face Liljensparre's cross-examination, telling the priest who attended him in his agony that the King would have nothing more to fear when he (Bjelke) was dead. Pechlin, arrested on suspicion, jocularly remarked that it was strange that no conspiracy in Sweden could be regarded as complete unless he was included in it. All Liljensparre's efforts failed to extract anything compromising from the wily old reprobate. Fresh arrests continued to be made daily, Ribbing and Horn having confessed to more than a hundred accomplices, and Liljensparre already possessed sufficient evidence to implicate half the Nobility,[1] when an order from the Council of Regency stayed the hand of the indefatigable Minister. The political atmosphere had suddenly undergone an important change. The Nobility now began to tremble for their own safety, and were anxious to make their peace with the royal martyr. Gustavus, with characteristic magnanimity and foresight, met them half way. On the morning after the masquerade he told Schröderheim that, if he recovered, the remainder of his days should be tranquil; and on the following day, in an interview with his brother, he not only declared his determination to forget the past, but solemnly adjured the Duke to conceal the names of the assassins from the infant Crown Prince. "As destined to rule this people," added he, "I do not wish the seeds of hatred and vengeance to be sown in his youthful mind." This tacit reconciliation may be said to have been formally ratified by Count Brahe's celebrated interview with the King on the following day, when, after begging for an audience as a personal favour, he knelt down at the bedside of his sovereign and implored forgiveness for an opposition which, though determined and uncompromising, had at least always been conscientious. Gustavus extended his hand, but immediately drawing it back, exclaimed, "Nay, embrace me, my dear Count! 'Tis indeed a happy accident which enables me to regain old friends so long estranged." He

---

[1] In the post-bag which left Stockholm on the morning of the 16th, scores of letters were found containing this simple phrase, "*A minuit il ne sera plus; arrangez vous sur cela*" (Aiguila).

then embraced Brahe, and assured him that everything
was forgotten.

The interview with Brahe had such an excellent effect
on the King's spirits, that at first, in spite of a naturally
delicate constitution and the terrible nature of his injuries,
strong hopes were entertained of his recovery.  On the
morning after the crime the wound was first examined.
The sufferings of the patient must have been excruciating.
We are told that the operating surgeon, Dr. Theel, thrust
his hand up to the wrist into the wound, from whence he
extracted a few iron spikes, without, however, being able
to reach either of the two bullets which still remained in the
patient's body.  During the whole operation the King held
Armfelt's hand, which he now and then pressed convulsively,
while his features were distorted with agony, though not a
cry, not a complaint escaped his lips.[1]  The doctors naturally
tried to make the best of what seemed to them from the
first a very bad job.  They comforted the patient with the
hope that the bullets might have taken such a direction as
to make it possible for them to remain in his body without
endangering his life ; " but," adds Schröderheim sorrowfully,
" fear and uneasiness left little room for such expectations."
The operation left the King faint and suffering.  His pulse
rose considerably, his respiration was thick and fast, and his
face was flushed ; but, to the very last, his large blue eyes
retained that piercing brightness for which they had always
been so remarkable.  At first, indeed, he was able to trans-
act much business and give frequent audiences ; but finding
that they wearied him too much, he gradually discontinued
them and limited his society to the circle of his friends and
family, but with them he continued to converse gaily up to
within twelve hours of his death.  It was while he was still
omparatively strong that Armfelt ventured to tell him that

[1] O. Tegner, *G. M. Armfelt.*

Anckarström had confessed his crime. " It is only a few
months since I saved him from a lawsuit," replied the King.
" And are there any more of them ?" " No, your Majesty,
but many are suspected." " So much the worse ! I don't
want to know their names, and let no one henceforth say
anything more to me about the matter. It is only their
political plan I should like to know about, some time or
other. I am curious to see whether there was anything
really sensible in it."

During the whole of his sickness the King lay in the
largest of the state bed-chambers.[1] The cold in the room
was indescribable, for a large *hautelisse* screen had been
drawn round the bed, quite excluding the warmth of the
fire, so that the watchers within the screen, especially at
night-time, were often compelled, while the patient slept, to
wrap themselves in fur cloaks and lie in the upper corner
of the room behind a table. A tiny oil lamp, with a paper
shade over it, flickered upon a little table within the screen.
It was the only light which the patient could endure, and
lent a peculiarly grim and gloomy aspect to the vast chamber.
On one of the columns, right in front of the bed, hung a
night-clock, well within the King's sight, yet he was constantly asking what the time might be. A gentleman of
the bedchamber, a page, and two or three domestics, were
in constant attendance. In the antechambers outside, most
of the high officers of state, and all those who had a special
right of entry, came and went at all hours of the day and
night. In the upper corner of the bedroom was another
screen, and behind it a table at which the doctors held
their consultations. At night a lamp burned there also.
Around the walls, partly resting on chairs, partly lying on
the floor wrapped in their mantles, were the relief watchers.
The doctors issued bulletins every morning and evening,

---

[1] Schröderheim, *Anteckningar*.

and Hofjunkare Wallencreutz was always in attendance to answer inquiries about the King's health.

During the first week Gustavus had long intervals of rest and quiet, sometimes sitting in his armchair and sometimes lying in bed; but after that he shifted his position incessantly, and got less and less sleep. Towards the middle of the second week the wound, at the least touch, and therefore almost constantly, emitted an offensive odour,[1] which made the patient so faint that he had to be drenched repeatedly with *eau-de-cologne.* Up to the last moment, however, he always managed to stand up and move without assistance from his armchair to his bed, and *vice versâ.* He seldom complained of his torments, but would keep on asking what o'clock it was, and who was outside. Sometimes, when his pains became unendurable, he would dismiss his attendants on the plea of getting a little sleep, and groan softly over and over again, when he fancied himself quite alone. This always seemed to give him more relief than anything else. At other times he would bid those about him maintain an unflagging conversation; but interesting subjects became more and more difficult to find every day. Politics were forbidden altogether as too exciting.[2] Domestic affairs worried him, and he soon lost all interest in literature and the drama, once his favourite subjects. Occasionally Armfelt and Schröderheim ventured upon religious topics. He would listen to them with attention and even interest, but say nothing. During the first few days he delighted in planning little excursions for his convalescence, but very soon saw their futility. There was no perceptible change during the first week. He was always preternaturally watchful, but gave as little trouble as possible, and was never either irritable or impatient.

[1] Schröderheim, *Anteckningar.*
[2] Thus he never knew of the death of the Emperor Leopold or of Dumouriez's ultimatum.

On March 25, the second Sunday after the catastrophe, Gustavus felt so much better that he called the ever-vigilant Schröderheim to him, and, after apologising for the trouble he was giving, bade his faithful friend depart at once and take a little rest. Schröderheim gratefully assented and went, but he had not been lying down more than a couple of hours when he was awakened by a messenger, who told him to return to the patient at once. He returned, and found the King in his armchair, unusually gay, "but," says Schröderheim, "his merriment was not my mirth. The cough had begun again, and there was a vehemence about his respiration and all his movements which alarmed me." And Schröderheim's alarm became downright terror when Gustavus, after hastily devouring a far better dinner than usual, ordered and ate an ice, a thing he had not touched for years. "I had frequently remarked," adds Schröderheim explanatorily, "that when under the influence of extraordinary agitation, he would recklessly eat what he usually never touched at all." Conversation continued briskly through the meal, but after it was over the King's gaiety began to flag, his cough increased, and at last he took to his bed again. His condition rapidly grew worse, and towards evening a violent fever and racking pains supervened. During the following days Gustavus sank rapidly, but on the evening of the 28th the cough suddenly vanished, and the patient seemed to rally once more.[1] So much stronger, indeed, did he feel, that he sent for the Duke and entreated for the lives of his murderers.[2] The Duke was deeply affected, but earnestly protested against such an abuse of clemency. "Charles," replied the King, "it is enough that I desire it. As your monarch I command, as your brother I beseech you to obey me, and you shall answer for it to me before God if you do

[1] O. Tegner, *G. M. Armfelt*, vol. i.        [2] Löwenhjelm, *Minnen.*
VOL. II.                                        O

not." This solemn appeal prevailed, the Duke consenting
to remit the capital penalty, save only in Anckarström's
case.[1] After this, the physicians, apprehending no immediate danger, went home, and Armfelt, tired out with
watching, withdrew earlier than usual for a little rest,
first sending a message to the Queen that her consort was
much better than usual. He was aroused at half-past four
next morning by Count Wachtmeister, who told him that
the King had only a few more hours to live. The favourite
was instantly at his master's side again. On entering
the bedchamber, he found the King seated in his armchair,
with his head leaning on the hand of one of the gentlemen-
in-waiting, who was supporting it. His face was much
changed, and the doctors whispered to Armfelt that gangrene had set in, and the end was nigh. On perceiving
the tearful face of his *protégé*, Gustavus rallied with a
great effort, and, stretching out his hand, said, " It. will
soon be all over with me. Don't forget your friend when
he is gone." A mournful silence prevailed in the room.
By the patient's side stood Dr. Dalberg, formerly the
King's body-physician, a vindictive and malicious man,
but indisputably the ablest doctor in Sweden of his day.
Gustavus, for very good reasons, could not bear the sight
of him,[2] and Dalberg, therefore, had not been called in
till the very last moment, when the other doctors had
exhausted all their art, and human skill could do no more.
Dalberg arrived at four o'clock in the morning, and, after
succeeding in giving the patient a little temporary relief,

---

[1] Anckarström was subsequently condemned to stand in the pillory and be
scourged three days in succession, to lose his right hand and his head, and to be
quartered. Bjelke's corpse was first hanged and then buried beneath the scaffold.
Ribbing, Horn, Engeström, and Liljehorn were banished, and most of them
changed their names. Pechlin died in confinement at Varberg four years later.

[2] Dalberg, after being dismissed from his post, had circulated the most
infamous libels as to the King's private life. His Memoirs, too, are an insult
to Gustavus's memory.

said to him, " I find your Majesty's condition anything but satisfactory." " Is it dangerous ? " asked Gustavus. " Yes, sir," replied Dalberg, " it is ; my honour and my conscience will not permit me to conceal the fact." " How many hours may 1 yet live ? " inquired the King. " Five or six," answered Dalberg, " and I implore your Majesty to employ them in seeking after your soul's welfare and providing for the security of the realm, in case you have any further directions to give." " That gives me, then, till half-past eleven," remarked Gustavus ; then turning to his attendant, he ordered Secretary Schröderheim to be sent for at once. Schröderheim came, and the King whispered him to draw up three documents for his signature—the first nominating tutors and guardians for his son, the second appointing Baron Evert Taube Minister of Foreign Affairs, and the third making Armfelt governor-general of Stockholm. Schröderheim immediately sat down at a table in a corner of the room where the King could see him, and while he was thus writing, Gustavus turned to his friends, who stood around his chair speechless with emotion, and said, " Let no one else come in without my orders. I want to die in peace. I shall never forget how King Frederick [of Sweden] died. His bedchamber was like a market-place." When Schröderheim had written out the three documents, he handed them to the King, who read them all through carefully, and signed them in the presence of Armfelt and Taube. No sooner had he done so than he was seized with such a violent fit of choking that all present fancied the end had come. Again, however, the patient rallied, and in a faint, almost inaudible voice, interrupted by frequent coughing fits, dictated to Schröderheim a codicil to his will, whereby the actual provisional regency was to continue to govern Sweden during the minority of his son.[1] It was

[1] This codicil was deliberately ignored by the Prince Regent. Armfelt, however, admits that it was drawn up so hastily as to be almost unintelligible.

while he was writing out this document that Schröderheim, whether from agitation or design it is impossible to say,[1] upset the inkstand over the document, and had to do it all over again. At last, however, it was rewritten, and Gustavus, after reading and signing, and getting Taube and Armfelt to witness it, ordered it to be deposited in the public archives. And now Dalberg again approached the King, and suggested that his Majesty should see to his soul's welfare and send for a priest. Gustavus at once inquired what clergymen were outside. Some one mentioned the Archbishop. "No," said the King, "I don't want *his* help. He has never done me cheerful service. Call hither the Bishop of Wexiö!" Wallqvist, who was already in attendance, came at once with the sacred elements. Gustavus then made his last confession with every sign of real compunction, and repeated the Creed and the Lord's Prayer after the Bishop with folded hands and a firm voice. Wallqvist then communicated him. After the Bishop had withdrawn, the King took leave of every one present in turn, thanking them all for their services, and addressing a few kindly words to each; none, not even the domestics, was forgotten. Armfelt he embraced with great tenderness, and solemnly bade him never forsake his son, but serve him with the same zeal and devotion that he had always shown to himself. He was then removed to his bed. His friends stood around him in mournful silence; but Armfelt was encouraged by a smile to ask his master whether he would not like to see the Queen and the Crown Prince once more. "Nay," replied Gustavus, "not now, I think. I feel sleepy, and a little rest may perhaps do me good." Armfelt drew back, and was

---

[1] Armfelt, who alone relates the incident, insinuates that Schröderheim did it purposely, so that the King might die before the document was ready. But Armfelt hated Schröderheim, and Schröderheim, though a trimmer, was not base enough to do such a deed.

just about to throw himself into an armchair before the
fire and doze a little till the King awoke again, when
Dalberg beckoned him back, and said, "'Tis all over!"
Every one instantly rushed to the bedside, but could see
no change in the King's face except that his eyes were
now closed.   "He is asleep surely?" whispered Armfelt
to Dalberg.   "Yes," returned the doctor, lifting one of the
dead man's eyelids, and exposing the sightless balls beneath,
"but it is the sleep of eternity."

    .     .     .     .     .     .

Gustavus III. died in the forty-sixth year of his age and
the twenty-first of his reign, and the political importance
of Sweden died with him.   His immediate successors [1]
were his bitter enemies, and they hastened, with indecent
alacrity, to reverse his policy, both at home and abroad,
and traverse all his plans, not because they were bad, but
because they were his.   During the subsequent rule of
his infatuated son, Sweden lost, swiftly and irretrievably,
the last remnants of her ultramarine possessions, and
thenceforth ceased for all practical purposes to be a Continental Power.   What might have happened if her last
great monarch had retained the sceptre for another decade
it is idle to conjecture; but we may reasonably assume
that his political sagacity and his diplomatic *savoir faire*
would not have fished in vain amidst the troubled waters
of European politics.   Sweden, in that case, would still
perhaps have remained a formidable, and Poland a respect-
able Power, and the map of Europe at the present moment
might not be quite the same as we know it.

[1] The Prince Regent, Duke Charles, and his Minister, the fanatical Reuterholm.   The Regency appointed by Gustavus was dissolved, and Armfelt, Toll,
and all the other leading Gustavians persecuted or expelled the country.

APPENDIX

# AN INTRODUCTION

# HISTORY OF SWEDISH BELLES-LETTRES,

## WITH ESPECIAL REFERENCE TO THE CLASSICAL OR GUSTAVAN PERIOD.

Causes of the late development of the Swedish literature—The Reformation—The Reformers' Bible—Sweden's political greatness an impediment to the development of her literature—Stjernhjelm, the father of Swedish poetry—His prodigious learning—Stjernhjelm at Christina's Court—His poems—"Hercules"—*Bröllöpsbesvär* —Stjernhjelm's school — Columbus — Lagerlöf—The Italianate poets—Dahlstjerna—Sophia Brenner—Jacob Frese—Spegel, Lucidor, and Halmström—Triewald the satirist—Effects of the Revolution of 1720 on the Swedish literature—English influence—Carl Gyllenborg — Modée — Stagnell — Dalin — *Argus*—Its character and enormous success—*Argus* an imitation of Addison's *Spectator* – Dalin's dramas and satires—Carlotta Nordenflycht—Early poems —Society for the Promotion of the Poetic Art—Creutz—G. F. Gyllenborg—The epics of Madame Nordenflycht and Gyllenborg— Creutz's *Atis och Camilla*—Tragic death of Madame Nordenflycht—Eclipse of the Swedish literature between 1762-1772— Tegner's opinion of Gustavus III.—State of the Swedish drama in 1772 — Gustavus introduces the opera — Dramas of Gustavus III. — *Gustaf Adolfs Ädelmod* — *Helmfelt* — *Odin och Frigga*—*Gustaf Adolf och Ebba Brahe*—Collaboration with Kellgren—*Gustaf Vasa* — *Siri Brahe*—*Den Svartsjuka Neapolitan* — *Natalia Narishkin*—Gustavus's characteristics as a dramatist — Foundation of the Swedish Academy — Gustavus's inaugural address — Gustavus's prize essay on Torstenson — Gustavus as a composer of epitaphs — The Gustavan poets— J. G. Oxenstjerna — Chief works — *Skördarna* — *Dagens Stunder* — *Hoppet* — *Oskuldens Religion* — *Disa* — Translations from Milton and Tasso—J. H. Kellgren—*Mina Löjen*—Foundation of the *Stockholm Post* — Its literary dictatorship — Kellgren's formalism and sensualism — Critical severity — His attack on Leopold—Appearance of Thorild—His Ode on the Passions—His literary tournament with Kellgren—Thorild in politics—His visit to England—General resemblance to Carlyle—Kellgren's later poems—Leopold—Intimacy with Gustavus III.—Unjust depreciation of Leopold by later critics—The National School of poetry—Michael Bellman—Lidner—Anecdotes of his lavishness and impudence—C. J. Hallman—Armfelt as a dramatist—Olof Kexel—Munificence of Gustavus III. towards his poets and play-wrights.

THE Swedish is, with the single exception of the Russian, the youngest of the European literatures.   Not till the middle of the seventeenth century do we meet with anything that can be seriously called a literature at all.   The causes of this long intellectual barrenness are not far to seek.   Sweden's remote geographical position almost as completely separated her from the centres of European civilisation as if she had belonged to another planet, and her first contact with the South might, perhaps, be better described as a collision. The unexampled tenacity with which her hardy barbarians clung to their savage rites, wore out the lives and, for a time, set at nought the labours of the heroic succession of missionary monks who first ventured across her pirate-haunted seas and kindled the light of the Gospel in her sombre and interminable forests.   That light, though faithfully guarded, for long flickered feebly enough.   There were Christians in Sweden as early as the eleventh century, but it was not till after the Council of Linköping, in the middle of the twelfth, that Sweden became an integral part of Christendom.   No wonder, then, if the soul-stirring ideas which agitated and inspired the mediæval world found little or no response in the distant North.   At the very time when all Europe, from Holland to Hungary, full of religious fervour, was arming to rescue the holy sepulchre from the infidel, it was a question whether the hardly reclaimed Swedes and Goths would not, after all, relapse into their original idolatry, while the great poetic revival, which was the ultimate expression of this great religious revival (for the Trouvères, the Troubadours, and their imitators, the Minnesänger, were, after all, but the spiritual progeny of the Crusaders), never even reached so far as the shores of the Baltic. How, indeed, was it possible for the poetry of chivalry to flourish in a land where valour was too rugged to be romantic, and where love was rather an instinct than a sentiment ? It is somewhat more surprising to find little or no trace of purely indigenous Swedish folk-songs, especially when we reflect that the Swedes were of the same kith and kin with the men who invented alliterative verse, and possessed the lost art of composing those unique and exquisite prose epics, the Sagas. Moreover, in this re-spect Sweden stands in striking contrast with her elder sister, Denmark, who can show in her ancient *Kœmpevisor* the most copious and beautiful collection of popular poetry in the world. But Denmark, chiefly through her intercourse with the West, had received Christianity (and civilisation along with it) ages before Sweden, and Denmark's pro-gress proved Sweden's detriment. From the middle of the thirteeenth to the middle of the fifteenth century the influence of Denmark was paramount in Scandinavia, and this influence even extended itself over the languages spoken throughout the Peninsula. The Swedish tongue was gradually merged into the dominant Danish dialect, till it was scarcely distin-guishable therefrom, and only the successful patriotic reaction in Sweden, after the failure of the Union of Calmar, saved the native language from disappearing altogether. Then came the Reformation, and its immediate effect upon Sweden was to paralyse the intellectual growth of the nation. Every-thing which did not immediately subserve the purposes of the Reformers was anathematised as dangerous and diabo-lical. Literature was for long entirely confined within the narrow circle of theological polemics. The ancient Church had been much more liberal. The first tender shoots of the national literature had budded beneath her fostering care. The Monastery of Vadstena, where learning and piety had ever gone hand in hand, had taken a deep, intelligent, and patriotic interest in popular education, and been mainly

instrumental in the preservation of the native language.
Nay, more, the Renaissance had found its earliest pioneers
in enlightened Catholic prelates, who had endeavoured to
cultivate the taste of their countrymen by familiarising them
with the works of the great Italian masters.  With the introduction of Lutheranism by Gustavus Vasa and the Petris,
everything was turned upside down.  As usual, the men of
the new doctrine destroyed the old system before they had
anything ready to replace it, and in the long interval between
demolition and restoration, the bulk of the population re-
lapsed into something very like semi-barbarism.  The numerous convent-schools entirely disappeared.  The University
of Upsala, pre-eminently a Catholic seminary, was suffered
to decay, and the young Swedish nobility flocked in hundreds
to Wittenberg and to Rostock for an education denied to
them at home.  It is true that the Reformers (themselves men
of good parts and relatively high culture) provided for a
better state of things in the future by their famous translation of the Scriptures, a translation which, despite its many
Germanisms, is a literary monument of which any nation
might well be proud, and, certainly, had the great merit of
fixing, once for all, the form and character of the language.
But the Swedish Reformers were in the unfortunate position
of men who, after having laboriously laid the foundations of
an ambitious edifice, are compelled to use the rest of their
building materials as offensive missiles against a host of foes
suddenly starting up on every side to oppose the further
progress of the work.  For, in spite of all the care and cir-
cumspection of the King, the change of faith was neither a
simple nor a peaceful process.  To say nothing of the frequent collisions between the clergy and the Crown, the
infant Church had for a long time to sustain a fierce struggle
with the Catholics from without and with the various Protestant sects from within who would not be comprehended
in her fold.  The best energies of the long life of Laurentius
Petri, the first Protestant Metropolitan of Sweden, were consumed in defending sacramental grace and the apostolical
succession against the violent assaults of the Calvinists, and

his immediate successors found, to their cost, that the Church could exercise but little influence upon the people at large till she had first established her own right to exist.   Thus, for some generations, polemical literature was the only literature possible in Sweden.

A century elapsed, and Sweden, emerging from what had seemed her natural obscurity, suddenly became a Power of the first magnitude.   The blue-yellow banner had carried into the remotest corners of Europe the knowledge and the dread of the Swedish name, while the triumphs of Sweden's great diplomatists were not inferior to the triumphs of her great captains.   But this unexpected and extraordinary political elevation was unaccompanied by any corresponding development in the national literature.   The hundred years which elapsed between the establishment of the Vasa dynasty (1544) and the Peace of Westphalia (1648) was, from the æsthetic point of view, absolutely barren.   Yet this was the very time when the good seed sown by the Renaissance was producing its glorious harvest all over Europe. This was the golden age of European literature, the age of Shakespere and Spenser, of Rabelais and Corneille, of Lope de Vega and Calderon de la Barca, of Ariosto and Tasso, and their numerous satellites.   But, in truth, material prosperity alone is no more a guarantee for the development of a national literature than the mere possession of wealth is a guarantee for the mental superiority of its possessor. No doubt a certain amount of prosperity is necessary to the intellectual life of a nation, just as a certain amount of soil is necessary to the life of a plant.   But the soil may be too rich as well as too poor, and it matters little whether the plant be starved or surfeited so long as the result is the same—barrenness.   So, too, with countries.   Political adversity and degradation may crush the spirit of a nation, and temporarily deprive it of the faculty of speech and song —Italy from the middle of the sixteenth to the end of the seventeenth century is a case in point.   But, on the other hand, the lethargy of a long and uneventful peace, a plethora of wealth and comfort, may even more effectually than the

most persistent calamity quench and stifle the spiritual
growth of a nation. What did Holland produce during the
eighty years of unexampled material prosperity which separated Vondel from Bilderdijk which is now worth reading?
Hungary, again, between 1848 and 1867, furnishes us with
an ever-memorable instance of a national literature flourishing vigorously amidst the most appalling national humiliation; while the singular example of Poland shows that a
literature may reach its highest perfection even after the
political extinction of the nation which gave it birth. After
all, individual genius is the informing principle of every
literature. Without the decisive, determining influence of a
master-mind, the most favourable circumstances, the most
indispensable predisposing conditions must remain inopera-
tive. The *lingua toscana* continued to be a struggling dialect
till Dante impressed it with the hall-mark of his genius, and
the compatriots of Gustavus Adolphus and Axel Oxenstjerna, not without reason, continued to look down upon
their native tongue as too rude, coarse, and barbarous for any
but the commonest uses of every-day life, till Stjernhjelm
came, and "taught the Muses how to play and sing in
the Swedish tongue."

George Stjernhjelm, the father of Swedish poetry, born
in the last year of the sixteenth century, came of a good old
stock from the Dales, but of Norse origin. His early history
is fragmentary and obscure. We know nothing certain about
him till the year 1625, when we hear of him as "ethices
lector" at the College of Vesteras; as making the grand
tour in Count Gyllenhjelm's suite, and as everywhere attracting attention by his dialectical skill and prodigious
learning. The newly-founded English Academy of Sciences
shortly afterwards elected him an honorary fellow, and the
great Dutch scholars of the day regarded him as a young man
of brilliant promise. In 1630 he was appointed assessor or
puisne-judge of the Court of Dorpat, finally becoming Vice-
President of the same tribunal. This was the period of the
rapid rise of the short-lived Swedish Empire, when ability
of every sort was eagerly demanded and exhaustively

employed to cement and consolidate the colossal and imposing, but essentially frail and brittle structure.  Misled, no
doubt, by the illustrious but altogether exceptional examples of the great Gustavus and his great lieutenants, the
Swedish nation had acquired an almost superstitious belief
in the boundless capabilities of individual talent.  From
the mode in which offices and charges were distributed, it
seems to have been pretty generally held as an axiom that a
man of superior parts was adapted for any and every sort of
work, and was bound to excel in whatever he chose to put his
hand to.   This popular delusion, which had its root in an
exalted patriotism, certainly stimulated ambition and ability
to do their utmost, and sometimes produced really wonderful
results; but it wasted quite as much energy as it utilised
by distributing it over too wide an area, and it created
an adventurous, superficial type of character, which frequently did little by attempting too much.  Stjernhjelm was
one of the best specimens of this type.  The versatility of his
talents was astonishing; his contributions to every department of human knowledge seem almost fabulous, although
the innumerable gigantic fragments which he left behind him
show rather what he might have been than what he was.
As Atterbom has well remarked, he was not so much a man
of letters as a whole literature.  He was equally at home
in philology, metaphysics, jurisprudence, history, statistics,
mathematics, and natural science.  He compiled an Anglo-
Saxon dictionary, which was the first of its kind in Sweden.
He attempted the quadrature of the circle.  He edited the
Icelandic sagas, and commentated the ancient laws of
Sweden.   He investigated the origin of music, and laid
down rules for discriminating the true from the false in cases
of sorcery.  He published the Gothic text of Ulfilas, with
commentaries in Latin, Swedish, German, and Icelandic.
He wrote a series of Latin dissertations to prove Swedish to
be the parent tongue of all modern languages.  He laid the
groundwork of a new philosophy which was to reconcile
science with revelation.  He popularised algebra and trigo-
nometry; invented a universal standard of measurement,

the *Linea Carolina*—and all this in the leisure moments he
was able to snatch from his numerous and arduous public
duties.

But after all, it is as a poet, as the first great Swedish
poet, that Stjernhjelm is now chiefly remembered. His
scientific speculations, however ingenious and profound, possess for us but an antiquarian interest; his poetical and
critical works, on the other hand, form the bases of modern
Swedish literature.

Stjernhjelm's muse was very slow of speech; not till he
was fifty years old did she make her voice heard. In 1648,
Stjernhjelm was forced to fly from Livonia before one of the
periodical Russian invasions from which that province then
suffered, and losing by shipwreck the little he had snatched
from ruin on land, reached Stockholm in utter destitution.
This apparent calamity proved to be the stepping-stone to
fame and fortune. His great reputation readily procured
him an introduction to the Queen, and in the following year
we find him occupying the dignity of Hof-Kansler, part of
whose duty it was to receive, present, and reply to the
Foreign Ministers. It was now that his career as a poet
began. Christina, the youthful daughter of the great Gustavus, then adorned the Swedish throne. That brilliant
but eccentric princess, herself a genius of the first order, was
quick to detect and stimulate genius in others. Stjernhjelm's
ready wit, inexhaustible humour, and intimate knowledge
of men and books attracted her from the first, and he soon
rose high in the royal favour. The Queen used playfully
to call him and his poetical fellow-countrymen, Stjernhök
"my Dalestars,"[1] and by her command he composed, in
various languages, a series of ballets or operatic sketches
for the amusement of the Court. They are all mere trifles,
full of grace and melody, remarkable for the variety and
facility of their versification, and show with what ease the
strong and supple master-hand could bend the stiff and
stubborn Gothic tongue to its will. Even in the best of

---

[1] The word *Stjern*, appearing in their names, means " star," and both poets
were Dalesmen.

them, however, *Then fangne Cupido* (The Captive Cupid)
there is absolutely nothing to warrant Hammerskjöld's
extravagant comparison of his illustrious countryman with
our own great Shakespeare. These were the happiest
years of Stjernhjelm's life, but in the nature of things
they could not last long. For all his boisterous gaiety,
easy nonchalance, and a Mark Tapley sort of disposition
to make the best of everything, Stjernhjelm was a man
of high principles, delicate honour, and the most fervent
patriotism. Nay, even through his buffoonery there ran
a peculiar but very genuine vein of religious earnestness.
Once saved, as by a miracle, from shipwreck, and cast half-
naked upon the inhospitable Bothnian shores, he roused his
fellow-sufferers from their despair by dancing, singing, and
performing all manner of strange antics, till he had succeeded
in restoring them all to good-humour, when he suddenly
changed his tone, solemnly exhorted them, as men and
Christians, not to lose heart in disaster, and succeeded in
saving them all. Such a man was not made to thrive at
such a court as Christina's. The heartless frivolity and the
reckless prodigality of the Queen, the cynicism with which
she wasted the revenues of the crown, the unpatriotic
subservience to foreign Powers which marked her policy,
her contemptuous treatment of the most sacred things, her
preference for worthless favourites—all these things filled
Stjernhjelm with shame and indignation. He was never the
man to hold his tongue, and his wrath now found expression
in a series of pungent epigrams, in one of which Christina
chose to see an obscure but offensive allusion to herself.
She peremptorily ordered him back to Dorpat. The poet
obeyed without a murmur, but subsequently revenged himself by satirising his sovereign under the personification of
*Flättja* (Frivolity) in his great didactic poem, " Hercules."

The " Hercules " is an adaptation of the venerable fable of
the choice of Alcides. The youthful hero arises early one
morning full of doubt as to the true problem of life, and while
debating the matter with himself, is accosted by a fair woman—

" Light of look and easy of manner,"

decked out in gorgeous gold-embroidered garments. Her name is the Lady Lust, and after introducing Hercules to her three daughters, *Lättja* (Sloth), *Kättja* (Lewdness), and *Flättja* (Frivolity), and her son *Rus* (Fuddle), she congratulates him on his youth, strength, and beauty; implores him, with many winning words, to make full use of them while he may, reminds him that human life when once it has set—

" Never ariseth again, but abideth in darkness eternal,"

and assures him that she and her family will cater for all his wants. A panegyric of her daughters follows, which is a masterpiece of irony, and she concludes by inviting him to follow her—

" Where the way is even and broad, 'mongst roses and sweet-smelling lilies."

Hercules, with the ready credulity of youth, is about to obey, when another female form, dressed in simple white, stately and imposing, but lean, sunburnt, and weather-worn, appears upon the scene, and bids Hercules stay and give heed: we need hardly say that this is the Lady Virtue. Swedish critics have blamed Stjernhjelm for not making Virtue more winning and attractive; but we would ask, when was Virtue ever other than austere on first acquaintance ? At all events, the second Genius loses no time in preambles, but comes to the point at once. She ridicules the promises and unveils the designs of Dame Lust, but is forced to admit that the alternative she has to offer is, at first sight, uninviting :—

" Narrow at first is my way, 'midst tree-stumps and rough stony places,
    Uneven, through mud and through mire, overgrown, too, with thorns and with thistles."

But Honour and Glory will crown him on the distant heights, and Strength and Comfort will sustain him along the steep and slippery path. Finally, she reminds him that however serene and promising the morning of life may seem, its even-

ing must always be sad, for it ends in death, and death
means failure.   Her concluding description of the misery of
a " virtueless old age," in part a paraphrase of Ecclesiastes,
rises into tragic intensity, and leaves behind a painful impression, and, perhaps, a suspicion that the picture may be over-
drawn.   The choice of the new Alcides is left undetermined ;
but we feel that, after listening to the exhortations of Dame
Virtue, he could not have accompanied Dame Lust and her
daughters in anything like a comfortable frame of mind.

The "Hercules," like all didactic poems, has too obvious
and too practical a tendency to be ranked as pure art ; but
even those who quarrel most with the species are bound to
concede that it is a masterpiece of its kind.   The style and
colouring have been often and justly admjred, and as the
earliest attempt to write Swedish hexameters it was a daring
and brilliant achievement.   Judged indeed by the more perfect standard of modern times, the Stjernhjelmic hexameter
often seems rough and somewhat irregular, but at least it
is always sonorous and majestic.   The poem abounds with
passages of great vigour and beauty.   The reflections upon
Death's omnipotence (lines 67–79) contain the finest piece
of alliterative verse in the language, and there is a refreshing
irony of the robuster sort in the description of Miss Frivolity's library, which Lady Lust recommends young Hercules
to read when his mind is more matured and time hangs
upon his hands.

If *Bröllops-besvärs-ihugkommelse* (Recollection of the
Plagues of Wedlock) be, as is generally supposed, the work
of Stjernhjelm's old age, it not only speaks well for the
vitality of his Muse, but also displays many of the qualities
of a great humorist.   It is an amusing lament over the petty
ills which wait upon and follow after wedlock, and though
the fun is often a little broad, it is always honest and innocent.   The hexameter (Stjernhjelm's favourite metre) is
again employed, and shows an advance in smoothness and
suppleness upon the hexameter of the "Hercules," but no
loss of vigour.   But indeed there is scarcely a known
metre which this protean poet did not attempt.   He it was

who acclimatised the Alexandrine in Sweden, and first cultivated the sonnet there. Like Milton, however, he had a
decided preference for blank verse.

Stjernhjelm left the Swedish Muse, like his own Hercules,
between opposite alternatives. Before her lay the only safe
and sure, but withal hard and rugged road to a truly national
literature, which he himself had opened up for her. But
another voice was at her ear, insinuating difficulties, and
suggesting a less high and heroic path to the stars than that
indicated by the master, and to this siren's voice the young
Swedish Muse in an evil hour unfortunately listened. The
temptress who thus beguiled her was no other than her
Southern sister, the grotesque and mincing Italian Muse of
the *Secentismo*, who had succeeded, for a time, in turning
some of the best heads in Europe (our own "fantastics," for
instance, to say nothing of Gongora and Quevedo in Spain),
and for whom the ground in Sweden had only been too well
prepared by the peculiar favour which the Vasas had always
shown towards the Italian tongue. At first, indeed, it seemed
as if the Swedish Muse would remain faithful to her Stjernhjelm. Samuel Columbus (1642–79), his intimate friend
and biographer, cultivated the lately-naturalised hexameter
with success, and wrote some very sweet hymns and some
very bitter epigrams, while Peter Lagerlöf, the national his-
toriographer and professor of logic at Upsala, was reckoned
the best religious poet of his age. Both these learned men,
however, wrote Latin and German much better than their
native tongue (Columbus's *Odæ Sveticæ* even earned for
him the title of the Swedish Flaccus), and in any case they
could not stand before the wave of Italianism which now
swept over the country. The first symptom of the malady
was an inordinate fondness for the pretty platitudes, artificial graces, and sweetly mawkish sentimentality of Guarini
and his followers. For a time the *Pastor Fido* of that poet
enjoyed an extraordinary popularity in Sweden, no less than
four independent translations appearing within forty years.
A long regimen of this unsubstantial fare produced at last
an intellectual anæmia which hankered after stronger stimu-

lants, and found them in the perverse ingenuities and the bombastic extravagances of the Neapolitan Marini and his German imitators, Löhenstein and Hoffmanswaldau. It is true that the Swedish Marinists never attained to the sublime absurdity of their German rivals, and never even attempted their grotesque obscenities; but they thoroughly perverted the national taste, and, for a time, made a national independent literature an utter impossibility. The vagaries of this school flourish most luxuriantly in the triumphal odes of Gunno Dahlstjerna (1650–1709), the panegyrist of Charles XII., who treated the Swedish language as dictatorially as his great master treated the Swedish nation. Yet Dahlstjerna was not without a gleam of genius, and the frequent grains of pure poetic gold which shine amidst so much chaotic slag show that he was really capable of better things.

Dahlstjerna, as we have said, was the chief representative of the high-flying, fantastic style; the crawling commonplace, on the other hand, into which the much-abused didactic poem finally sank, found its chief expositor in Madame Brenner, the first lady-poet of Sweden.

Sophia Elizabeth Brenner (1659–1730) was the thrifty wife of a well-to-do citizen and the mother of fifteen children. She employed the fag-ends of her time in learning nearly all the languages of Europe, living and dead, and as it was the ruling principle of this busy matron to turn everything she knew to practical account, she took up her pen as she took up her rolling-pin, and turned out volume after volume of poems in much the same matter-of-fact, methodical way in which she turned out puddings and pasties. We call them poems because her contemporaries complaisantly accepted them as such; but in reality they are dry rhyming dissertations on courtship, wedlock, housekeeping, and cognate subjects, which go to prove that their estimable author was perhaps the most prosaic of her sex who ever existed. For how else can we regard a woman who had so little romance in her composition that she could only regard matrimony from the purely culinary and domestic point of view? Nevertheless, her own generation regarded the poetic effusions of

this fruitful and energetic matron with a wonder and a satisfaction somewhat akin to the admiration with which Mr.
Boffin regarded the erudition of the wooden-legged Wegg.
She was styled the tenth Muse, the Northern Sappho; nay,
more, her fame spread far abroad, so that we even hear of
an enthusiastic Mexican gentleman hailing her across the
seas as the great Minerva of the Goths.  Madame Brenner,
moreover, wrote many German poems, which, curiously
enough, are not only vastly superior to her Swedish verses,
but display a freedom, not to say friskiness, of treatment
which we should not have expected from so sedate a person.
But perhaps the best thing she ever wrote is a single
Italian sonnet, which Guarini himself might not have been
ashamed to own.

In those days, however, Madame Brenner's prodigious
learning was nothing unusual.  All the Caroline poetasters
went about with such loads of learned lumber in their heads,
that their brains had very little room for anything original.
If they had something to say, they usually said it in Latin,
German, or Italian ; it was the bare refuse of their thoughts
that they gave to their despised mother-tongue.  Amidst
the jarring Babel only one faint but sweetly pathetic note
strikes melodiously upon the ear.  The Finn, Jacob Frese,
a true lover of nature, who learned to think and feel deeply
on a life-long bed of suffering, has left some exquisite lyrics
— *Var-betraktélser under Sjukdom* (Spring Meditations
during Sickness)—breathing a gentle resignation under the
most painful affliction, and an earnest longing after a better
world, where the weary are at rest.  Stjernhjelm himself,
though his range was far wider and his touch firmer and
bolder, is neither so tender nor so sweet as Frese.

But Frese, after all, was but a solitary voice crying in the
wilderness.  If we except Spegel's spiritual songs, a single
madrigal by Liljensted (1655–1732) entitled *Klagan öfver
Iris afresa* (Lament over the Departed Iris), a few songs
by that strange waif, "the unlucky Lucidor," as he called
himself, and the amusing doggrel of Isaac Holmström
(1660–1708), Charles XII.'s field secretary, and the only

man capable of drawing a smile from that saturnine young
hero, the whole Caroline period (1660–1718) has nothing
to offer us.   Turgid, sesquipedalian triumphal odes, syco-
phantic eulogies, epithalamia and epitaphs, acrostics, and
chronograms—such was the literature of that dreary period.

Such a state of things could not last for ever.   The Swede,
in common with the other members of the Teutonic family,
has no lack of humour, and is always ready to laugh at his
own absurdities when they are brought home to him.   The
man who opened the eyes of his countrymen to their folly
was Samuel von Triewald (1688–1743), the earliest Swedish
satirist.   Triewald was a warm admirer of Boileau, and in
his epigrams and satires, of which the *Satir mot vara
dumma poeter* (Satire against our Stupid Poets) is the
most famous, happily caught the tone and style of his
master.   Nervous, pregnant, and downright, fiercely indignant
and coarsely energetic, his sarcasm is not the polished,
jewelled rapier of a Pope, or the penetrating, envenomed
stiletto of a Heine, but a bludgeon of good stout Swedish
oak, well studded with knobs of the best Swedish iron,
wherewith he drove from Mount Helicon, amidst the hila-
rious applause of the Swedish public, the profane herd of
hireling rhymsters who had so long befouled the waters
of Hippocrene, laid presumptuous hands upon the Muses,
and well-nigh ridden Pegasus to death.

Triewald's lot was cast upon evil days.   He not only had
the bitter mortification to survive the collapse of Sweden's
political greatness, but himself died an exile.   He lived long
enough, however, to see one wish of his heart gratified—he
lived to see the French influence, which he had done so
much to introduce, taking root in the national literature and
bringing forth much good fruit.

The momentous year 1720 was the commencement of a
new era in Swedish history.   The time had been when
nothing short of a powerful coalition could hope to contend
with Sweden on equal terms.   Henceforth, however, Sweden
could not even hold her own in the North without foreign
assistance, and she sought and found such assistance in her

ancient historic ally, France.   For more than seventy years
French influence was paramount in the Scandinavian peninsula.   Fatally mischievous as that influence was in politics,
in literature it was altogether beneficial.   Even in its decline,
the French literature was incomparably the finest in Europe,
and the best heads in the North very soon perceived that
they could not do better than closely follow French models.
Thus a French school began to arise in Sweden.   The
change, however, was gradual.   The provident, patriarchal
government of Count Arvid Horn (1720–38), which nursed
exhausted Sweden into convalescence, looked askance upon
France, drew near to England, and, for a brief period, English
ways and modes of thought began to be studied and imitated.
Horn himself, who had once been the right arm of the most
despotic of kings, idolised Oliver Cromwell in his later days,
and professed an almost superstitious reverence for the
English constitution.   His disciples, the Caps, were always
ardent Anglophils, and the ablest of them, Bishop Serenius,
compiled the first Swedish-English Dictionary, and introduced the rite of confirmation, on the English model, into
the Swedish Church.   In literature, however, strangely
enough, the English influence was first represented by a
man who, politically, was England's most bitter foe.   This
was no other than Count Carl Gyllenborg, Horn's successful
rival, and the originator and leader of the young Hat party.
Gyllenborg had for fourteen years, 1703–17, been attached
to the Swedish embassy in London ; had married Miss Sarah
Wright ; thrown in his fortunes with the Tory party ; been
implicated in Charles XII.'s plot to restore the Stuarts ; been
arrested and imprisoned in consequence, and ever afterwards
bore an inextinguishable hatred towards the Whigs.   With
current English literature Gyllenborg was well acquainted,
and he translated Steel's "Lying Lover" and other English
plays into Swedish.   But his great achievement is his original
five-act comedy, *Svenska Sprätthöken* (The Swedish Coxcomb), in which, with great vigour and much humour, he
ridicules the Gallomania of his noble compatriots.   Compared
indeed with Holberg's inimitable *Hans Frandsen* on the

same subject, Gyllenborg's satiric drama is but poor stuff, yet it has many and great merits. The intrigue, though somewhat too complicated, is ingenious; the characters are real flesh and blood; the vivacity and sparkle of the dialogue make it readable even now; but of course it is chiefly remarkable as being the first original Swedish drama.

But Gyllenborg, though the best, was by no means the only dramatist of the Frihetstid. Reinhold Gustaf Modée (1698–1750), the eminent jurist, performed the difficult and highly creditable feat of writing three charming comedies (*Fru Rangsjuk, Hakan Smulgrat,* and *Darhuset*), which, though written after French models for audiences accustomed to French pleasantry, contained not a single *double-entendre*, not a single equivocal jest—nay, not so much as a single coarse or crude expression. Modée's style is stiffer and heavier than Gyllenborg's, but in the delineation of character he far excels the witty Count, and no Swedish dramatist, except Gustavus III., ever had a keener eye for stage effect. To him, moreover, belongs the peculiar honour of inventing a new variety of the Harlequin or Jack-Pudding, the parasite Trulls, who figures in all three comedies, whose characteristic feature is a fabulously inordinate appetite, and whose ideal of felicity is a good dinner. Modée's original dramatic talent was thrown away upon the Frihetstid. It was his misfortune to have been born thirty years too soon. Gustavus III. would certainly have made a great dramatist of him.

In strong contrast to Modée stands John Stagnell, who also wrote three original plays—coarse-grained, highly-seasoned comedies, brimful of drastic humour, but with all the cynical indecency, and nothing of the grace and polish, of our own Wycherley and Etherege. Some idea may be formed of the coarseness of Stagnell when we mention that one of the principal characters in the comedy *Den lyckelige Banquerotieren*, Madame. Colique, has the graceful and easy habit of frequently interrupting her conversation with sonorous belches.

It was in Olof Dalin that the English influence reached its highest point and produced its best fruits. Dalin is

now perhaps chiefly remembered as a skilful entertaining courtier, as the ingenious and insinuating instructor of the youthful Gustavus; but it is as a man of letters, as the creator of
modern Swedish prose, that he here claims our attention.

In December 1732 there issued from the press of Printer
Schneider of Stockholm the first number of a small badly-
printed eight-paged quarto journal, entitled *Then Swänska
Argus* (The Swedish Argus), with the Horatian motto:
"Omne tulit punctum qui miscuit utile dulci." *Argus*,
which was offered to the Swedish public at the modest
price of something less than a halfpenny of our money per
number, professed to be the joint-composition of a society
which meant "to talk about everything tending to the
pleasure and profit of our countrymen;" in other words,
it was a satirico-moral journal, intended to hold up a mirror
to the follies and vices of the day. In the following number we are introduced to "the members of this society."
The first is a man about town, "endowed with every mental
and bodily advantage, who has passed his whole life at
court, and well knows all its ways. From the fashion of
his legs, methinks he should be called Sir Menuet. The
second is a soldier, Mr. Bluffhearty, whose good old Swedish
motto is 'Pluck and piety.' The third is a learned man,
whose physiognomy tells me that his name is Rackbrain—
a droll sight to look at, for his peruke mostly sits awry,
and his dress is not always in the best of order; you would
never imagine how much of wit and wisdom has taken up
its abode in that skinny head. . . . The fourth, a veteran
of the bar, takes the name of Goldenbalance. There was
a time when he was able to give what colour he would
to a process at law. . . . But now he hates his ancient
handiwork, regrets and repents of his former chicaneries,
and desires to give to God what he has taken from man
The fifth is a merchant, who calls himself Patriot, who has
travelled far and wide in his youth, has served his time in
two of the most famous mercantile houses in Europe, and
is well qualified to advise those who seek their country's
good and their own prosperity."

For the next five years *Argus* and his five imaginary associates continued to entertain the town. With the single exception of politics, there was no subject of human interest, no department of human knowledge, which they did not explore and illustrate. The barest summary of this ency-clopædia of wisdom, wit, and humour would fill a bulky volume; nor is its protean versatility less remarkable than its width of range. Dialogues, dramatic interludes, poems, moral lectures, satires, aphorisms, social studies after La Bruyère, apologues in Swift's manner, essays in imitation of Addison, legends, romances, fables, and anecdotes alter-nate in swift succession in its charming pages. Even to us, familiar with a *Spectator*, a *Tatler*, a *Rambler*, *Argus* is not without interest. Amongst the Swedish public at the begin-ning of the eighteenth century it produced a great sensation. It was practically the first periodical of its kind, and its suc-cess was instantaneous and extraordinary. In a very short time it became not merely one of the necessaries of life to the reading public, but also a real power in society. "Most of us still remember," wrote Bishop Celsius more than thirty years after the publication of the last number, " with what eagerness we looked forward to the day when this sheet came out, and how we fell upon and devoured it with the greediness of men who go to table with a hungry stomach." Speculation was busy as to the author, or rather authors, for it was universally held that no single head was capacious enough for such an undertaking. The favourite opinion seems to have been that the word "Argus" was itself an anagram composed of the initials of the real authors, and it was therefore with something like a shock that the incre-dulous public learnt, at last, that *Argus* was not the joint-production of a junto of distinguished philosophers and experienced men of the world, but the work of a junior clerk in the Foreign Office, young Olof Dalin.

It will be seen that in form, substance, and design *Argus* was a close (and we need hardly add an inferior) copy of the English *Spectator*. It is especially noteworthy, moreover, that *Argus* is weakest where the *Spectator* is strongest.

The most original and most taking feature of the English
Review is the happy invention of the Spectator Club, whose
chief members, Sir Roger de Coverley, Will Honeycomb, &c.,
are real living personages, who give a strong dramatic interest
to the narrative. The pretended authors of *Argus*, on the
other hand, the elegant Lord Honour-Menuet, the learned
Mr. Rackbrain, and honest Mr. Patriot, are mere abstractions,
of no interest to the reader. Dalin himself had the sense to
see this, and as early as his twenty-seventh number rid
himself of his characters by the simple expedient of sending
them to the country for the benefit of their health. In this
he acted wisely, for the last seventy-eight numbers of *Argus*
are incomparably superior to their forerunners.

In point of style, too, *Argus* is far below its English prototype. Perhaps, however, a comparison between them in
this respect is scarcely fair. In the English tongue Addison
found an exquisitely finished tool ready to hand, whereas
Dalin, less fortunate, had to make his own tools before he
could set to work, for he was actually the creator of modern
Swedish prose. No doubt it is perfectly true that had there
been no *Spectator*, *Argus* would never have seen the light of
day; still it is no mean feat to have gleaned laurels where
the *Spectator* had reaped beforehand, to have said something new on every subject which Addison had already made
his own.

*Argus* was Dalin's passport to fame and fortune. He
was pensioned by the Estates, petted by the Court, promoted successively to the posts of State Librarian, Tutor to
the Crown Prince, and Lord High Steward. His court life,
however, has been told elsewhere,[1] and the story of his subsequent literary career may be related in a very few words.

*Argus*, though very unequal, and full of a young author's
inevitable blunders, still remains Dalin's masterpiece. The
moral satirico-didactic essay exactly suited his peculiar genius.
He had a keen eye for the superficial foibles and absurdities
of human nature, and his pungent wit and saturnine humour
hit them off to admiration. But he did not penetrate very

---

[1] Vol. i. chap. ii.

far beneath the surface; his characters are types rather than personalities. This superficiality is most apparent in the couple of dramas which Dalin wrote for the newly opened Swedish theatre, the comedy *Den Afundsuke* (The Jealous Man), and the tragedy *Brynilda*. Of these two, the comedy, remarkable for its ready wit and facile dialogue, is decidedly the more successful, although as much inferior in plot to Gyllenborg's *Svenska Sprätthöken* as to all Modée's plays in the characterisation. *Brynilda* possesses a purely historical interest as being the first Swedish tragedy. It is a feeble imitation of the French classical drama, written in monotonous Alexandrines, with a superstitious observance of the unities, and shadowy abstractions for characters. Three years later Dalin returned to his older and happier vein, and wrote what in point of style are his most finished works, the poetic satire, *Aprilverk om var härliga tid* (An April Essay concerning our Glorious Times), remarkable for its melodious versification and exquisite irony, and the masterly *Saga om hästen* (The Tale of the Horse), obviously suggested by Swift's "Tale of a Tub," in which the fortunes of the Swedish people, from the Union of Calmar to the death of Charles XII., is told under the transparent disguise of the good steed Grolle, who, after faithfully serving many hard masters, is harnessed to a four-wheeled car (the Riksdag with its four Orders), and learns to go at an easier and less perilous pace.

Of Dalin's remaining works we need only mention his *Svenska Friheten* (Swedish Liberty), a politico-patriotic ode written to rouse the drooping spirits of his countrymen after the disastrous Finnish war of 1743-44, and eagerly seized upon as a saving plank by the foundering Hat Government, and the much more considerable *Svea Rikes Historia* (History of Sweden), the first serious attempt at a critical history of Sweden in a popular form. This great work, undertaken at the express desire and at the cost of the Estates of the Realm, not only cost its author years of the most laborious research, but also involved him in a disreeable, and, as the event proved, dangerous dispute with

the Order of Clergy, who professed themselves unable to
reconcile Dalin's theory of the origin of the Scandinavian
peninsula with the Biblical account of the Deluge.

Dalin stands alone in the Swedish literature. He owed
much to French and English sources; he was the connecting
link between the Caroline and the Gustavan schools; but he
neither belonged to any school nor did he found one. His
art, like Stjernhjelm's, was peculiar to himself and it died
with him. The same cannot be said of his illustrious contemporary and countrywoman, Madame Nordenflycht, who
is to be regarded not only as the pioneer of the French
school in Sweden, but also as the immediate precursor of
the classical Gustavan period.

Hedvig Charlotte Nordenflycht was one of those tender,
romantic natures who are ill-adapted for the rough wear
and tear of a busy matter-of-fact world, one of those beings
whom Misfortune seems to lead by the hand from their
cradle to their grave. Her parents, austere, practical people,
who held that a girl knows quite enough if she knows how
to cook, spin, and keep accounts, were horrified to catch
their little daughter reading plays and poems on the sly.
But though repeatedly and severely punished for it, she
could not be cured of this vicious habit, so that at last (but
not till her fifteenth year) she was allowed to follow her
natural bent, with the stipulation, however, that she was not
to learn French. About the same time a young mechanician
named Tideman, a sort of overseer on her father's estate,
became a member of the little family. Tideman possessed
great natural ability improved by extensive reading. He
was also a man of a singularly pure and noble character.
Charlotte was thrown much in his way, and she soon began
to regard him as a superior being, a sort of second Socrates.
He enlarged her views, directed her studies, taught her
to reflect on what she read, dissipated a growing tendency
to religious scepticism—in a word, became her spiritual
Mentor. But this was all. For if Tideman was as wise,
he was also as ill-favoured as Socrates. Sickly, deformed,
and prematurely old, he was certainly, the last person in

the world whom a lively and lovely girl of seventeen would
think of as her lover. When then Charlotte's father, on
his deathbed, joined Tideman's hands in hers, and expressed
the wish that they should be man and wife, and she at the
same time discovered that her master had all along been her
ardent admirer, a feeling of unutterable disgust overcame
her. "As a philosopher," she tells us, "I loved to listen
to him; but as a lover, the sight of him was unendurable."
Tideman was deeply hurt at the change; but, with characteristic nobleness, at once resigned himself to his fate. His
generous conduct touched her impulsive heart, and, over-
coming her aversion, she rewarded him with her hand. For
the next three years she was little more than his nurse, and
then death dissolved the unnatural union. Twelve months
of loneliness followed, during which she took up the study of
French under the direction of a handsome young clergyman,
of engaging manners and brilliant talents, named Fabricius,
the chaplain of the Huguenot Church in Stockholm, whom
she married after four years of dreary waiting, her family
for long refusing to let her throw herself away on a poor
parson. Seven months of what she has called "the mos
blissful life that any mortal can have in this imperfect
world" was rudely interrupted by the death of her beloved
after a nine days' illness. Her grief was so violent that
for a time both her life and her reason were in danger, and
when at last she arose from a three months' illness, it was
to conceal her griefs from the world in a secluded little
island cottage, where "my eyes seldom rested and my harp
played nothing but lamentations." It was now that she published her first collection of poems, entitled "The Sorrowing Turtle-dove, dedicated to the sweet and tender Philomel"
—harmoniously tender elegies, which excited a deep interest
in the fair eremite. Her friends, anxious for her health,
now compelled her to quit her retreat for the capital. Here
she drowned her sorrow in fresh and arduous studies,
and in 1744 was induced by her literary acquaintances to
publish a poetical annual entitled *Qvinligt Tankespel af en
Herdinna i Norden* (Aphorisms for Women by a Shepherdess

of the North). There is much mere verbiage and no end
of false sentiment in this poetic miscellany ; but it contains
many songs which have lived to the present, day, and deserve to live, for they are models of noble simplicity and
pathetic sweetness. The Aphorisms continued to appear
regularly during the next six years, and the Shepherdess
of the North gradually became one of the celebrities of the
Swedish capital. Her name was mentioned with interest and
respect at court, where she found a bountiful protectress in
Queen Louisa Ulrica. Her little house at Stockholm became
the favourite resort of the *élite* of Swedish society, a sort of
anticipation in miniature of Madame Geoffrin's *salon* at Paris,
with a more romantic colouring. Her fame even spread
abroad, and the great Holberg as well as the leading men of
letters at London and Paris were among her correspondents.

But Madame Nordenflycht was to be something more than
the enchanting mistress of a refined and literary *salon*. In 1753
she was persuaded by the enthusiastic circle which she had
gathered round her to become the Directress of a " Society
for the Promotion of the Poetic Art in Sweden," a society
which henceforward met several times a week at the house of
the "Swedish Aspasia." Almost simultaneously, the Swedish
Academy of Arts was founded by Queen Louisa Ulrica and
Dalin, but it soon appeared that the influence of this new
royal and national institution was far less than that of the
" private union of like-minded friends " which rallied round
Madame Nordenflycht. Dalin remained the solitary original genius the Academy could boast of ; whereas the more
modest Society attracted and appropriated the very men who
were to reform the Swedish literature and raise Swedish
poetry to hitherto unattainable heights. The secret of this
success is to be sought in the rare and peculiar art whereby
the talented lady knew how to convert inquisitive visitors
into enthusiastic friends. Madame Nordenflycht must indeed have been one of the most amiable of her sex. Love
and friendship were necessities of her nature. Her heart
literally overflowed with tenderness, benevolence, and compassion. She possessed that exquisite instinctive tact which

does everything at the right time, and seems always in the
right place.  If she was peculiar, she was never odd; and
her taste, though often fastidious, was always distinguished
by a noble simplicity.   Beautiful she could scarcely be
called; many denied that she was even pretty; but the
longer one looked into her large blue eyes, the more one
listened to her soft persuasive voice, the more one became
intimately convinced that she was both pretty and beautiful.  "It is possible," says one who knew her intimately,
"it is possible to have a prettier figure and more attractive
features; but not gentler ways or a more touching expression.  Her eyes," he adds, "beamed and sparkled with the
fire of intellect and the repose of innocence."

Conspicuous among the frequenters of Madame Nordenflycht's *salon* were two young noblemen, who, after brilliant
academic careers, had come from opposite ends of the country
to seek their fortunes in the capital.   The elder of the two,
Count Philip Creutz, from Finland, was at first sight anything but prepossessing.  His yellow, haggard features habi-
tually wore an expression of lassitude and distraction.  He
seemed to lack not only the light of intellect, but also the
vivacity of youth.  Yet whenever he chose to please (and he
chose pretty often), his eyes would sparkle with an enchanting radiance, a ruddy glow would suffuse his thin cheeks, and
all his gestures became irresistibly eloquent and winning.
His companion, Count Gustaf Frederick Gyllenborg, a tall
and handsome stripling, whose lustrous large blue eyes won
many a gentle heart, belonged to a family that had already
made a name for itself both in politics and literature.  Creutz
and Gyllenborg were truly idyllic natures, romantic, sensitive, deeply poetic souls, burning with a noble enthusiasm
for virtue and humanity.  Community of tastes and sentiments bound them together from the first in a friendship
which death alone could sever, yet no two dispositions could
have been more different than theirs.  The sociable, versa-
tile nature of Creutz was a peculiarly charming combination
of sprightly vivacity and the most romantic tenderness.   No
heart could long resist him, and at a later day he was to

be equally dear to the cynical Voltaire and the sentimental Marmontel. Gyllenborg, though by no means inferior to his friend in wit and fancy, was of a more serious turn of mind. His idea of perfection was a Stoicism tempered by Christian charity, and all his life long he attempted to act up to this high standard. Few careers have been so stainless. The vices which ordinary men find irresistible had not even any temptation for him. But his philosophy, though it beautified his life, trammelled and stunted his art. He seemed to consider it his duty to tie leaden weights to the wings of his fancy, and even to clip her pinions, lest she should venture upon too daring flights. There were even some departments of poetry, innocent in themselves, which his conscientious scruples forbade him to cultivate at all.

It was beneath the loving care of Madame Nordenflycht that these youths developed powers of which they themselves were at first barely conscious, and which found their expression in some of the most melodious verses in the Swedish language. " I can never forget," cries Gyllenborg, recalling those happy days, " I can never forget the pleasant moments we spent together. We regarded each other's productions as if they were our own; laughed at our mistakes, and were the first to acknowledge them. Correction was offered without pride and accepted without humiliation. We gave to men of letters an example which will never be imitated so long as self-love cannot endure to submit to the judgment of others, or pride is wounded by correction, or bitterness accompanies criticism and secret envy awards the prize."

The fruits of this literary intercourse were a series of volumes of polite literature which contain the masterpieces of the accomplished trio. Madame Nordenflycht contributed an historical ode on Charles XII.'s passage of the Duna; a religious ode on the existence of God; a learned satire in defence of women ; a philosophico-poetical dissertation as to whether knowledge or ignorance contributes most to the happiness of mankind ; and, finally, an epic poem in rhyming hexameters on Charles X.'s famous passage across the frozen

Belt, a subject afterwards attempted by Gyllenborg on a more ambitious scale and with a closer attention to historic accuracy, but with far less originality and poetic force. Both these *soi-disant* epics, so much admired in their day, must now be regarded as failures. The period chosen was much too recent for epic treatment, and the constant intervention of the personified powers of nature, and the allegorical representations of moral qualities very soon becomes insufferable. Gyllenborg, whose Muse was always a little too much given to prose and preach, contributed one or two satires, which are now very dull reading; a number of didactic poems, which have rather rhetorical than poetical merits, besides being more or less overcharged with moral admonitions; and two very beautiful descriptive idylls— *Vinter-qvädet* (Winter Song) and *Varqvädet* (Spring Song). The former, in particular, is perhaps the poet's most successful work, and has been well described as "fresh, bright, and clear as a fine winter's day."

But of all the essays of the three poetic friends, Creutz's exquisite pastoral, "Atis and Camilla," is incomparably the best. In the "Arcadian meads far from cities proud," dwells the fair Camilla, dedicated from her birth to the service of Diana, whose precepts she bears in her heart. On the eve of a great festival to "the sacred, shadowy, cold and constant queen," the fair vestal is tormented by evil-foreboding dreams, but, comforted by her faithful friend Doris, is able to present herself next day at the great portal of the temple to receive the throng of sacrificers. Among them is the young huntsman Atis, who drags thither in chains a wounded lion as a votive offering to the goddess. Hitherto "his cold, heroic breast has borne a heart untamed," but on perceiving Camilla, his peace of mind, his icy scorn, depart, and taking the majestic priestess for the very goddess, he falls down before her, and is only prevented from worshipping her on hearing from Camilla's own lips that she is a fellow-mortal. Atis leaves the temple amazed, dumb, and pensive. Consumed by a quenchless fire, and haunted by Camilla's form, he wanders aimlessly through wood and field, and despairing of ever possessing the fair vestal, calls upon Death to end his woes. Nor is Camilla in much better case. The sight of Atis has destroyed her repose also, and in her tender bosom, where "virtue and tenderness have made their nest," where never a thought has arisen to which "angels might not have listened," there burns a secret flame which is something very different from the sacred fire of Diana. She wanders disconsolate and alone where the waters flow and murmur, beneath the linden trees, a prey to conflicting doubts and fears. "Diana," she cries, "let me die before I prove so weak," and yet she adds, "Is not Nature's law as holy as thy own decree?" An accident brings the disconsolate lovers together again. A wounded hart, flying from the hunters, seeks refuge beneath the tree where Camilla is pining, and dies in her compassionate arms in the very act of gratefully licking her hand. The pitiful and indignant Camilla jumps rather hastily to the conclusion that Atis is the assassin, and perceiving him slowly approaching her on the river's bank, immediately reproaches him for a barbarian, and commands him to depart for ever from her sight. Atis naturally casts himself the same night from a high cliff; but Cupid breaks the desperate lover's fall, and leads him to the Temple of Hope, where, in a mirror, he sees the smiling image of his Camilla with outstretched arms, is comforted, and resolves to seek her out once more. Camilla, who has ever since been reproaching herself for her severity, is easily persuaded to grant him an interview in a "dark neglected grove to silence dedicate," hated of bird and beast ever since young Daphne died there "deceived and desperate," where the awful stillness is only broken by the wailing voice of a sunless little brook. Here, hidden as they hope even from Diana's eye, the lovers meet, pour out their souls to each other, and swear eternal fidelity. But in the very instant of their supremest joy a loathsome serpent steals unperceived through the rank grass, winds itself round Camilla's neck, and buries its mortal fangs in her fair bosom. Atis's avenging arm is raised too late. The serpent dies in vain, for Camilla breathes her last sigh in her lover's arms. Atis, in despair, sucks the venom from his lady's wound, madly upbraids the unrighteous powers which so "deceive innocence and have no punishment left for vice and wrong," and piteously appeals for help to the unknown god the ruins of whose temple remain in these sombre shades.  His prayer is heard.  The soul of Camilla returns from the shades, and Diana, suddenly revealing herself in all her majesty, releases her vestal from her vows and bestows her benediction upon the grateful lovers.

"Atis and Camilla" has well been called the most beautiful idyll which the Swedish literature possesses, and one can well understand the extraordinary enthusiasm excited on its first appearance.  It was reserved for a later age to discover that the plot was as insignificant as it was impossible, and the *denouement* forced and feeble.  Then, however, the public was not so critical, and had only eyes and ears for the manifold beauties of the poem, its indescribably caressing, metrical harmony; its simple, tender pathos; the wonderful purity and beauty of its language, and, above all, the exquisite descriptions of Nature with which it abounds.  In "Daphne" and his later poems, Creutz paints his scenes with richer colours, and attains to a still higher excellence of form, but we miss the noble simplicity and the guileless grace which fascinate us in every line of "Atis and Camilla;" his Muse, to use his friend Gyllenborg's fine phrase, "has lost her first innocence."

The ten years which elapsed between 1753 and 1763 were perhaps, on the whole, the happiest years of Madame Nordenflycht's life.  The centre of a brilliant circle of admiring and adoring friends; enabled by the bounty of the Court to devote herself to her favourite pursuits without any fear of the future; equally famous at home and abroad for her talents and her virtues—everything seemed to bode a serene and tranquil evening for a career which had hitherto resembled a variable April day, more shower than sunshine.  But it was not to be so.  These ten years of idyllic sweetness and repose were to end with tragic abruptness.

In 1761 a new aspirant for literary honours joined Madame Nordenflycht's little circle, young Johan Fischerström, whose agreeable conversation, ready wit, and deep learning deserved and speedily won the friendship of his amiable hostess. Fischerström, like so many others, had come up to make his fortune, and it would appear that Madame Nordenflycht used what little interest she had in high places in his behalf. At first, therefore, the relations between them were strictly those of protectress and *protégé*, mild benevolence on one side, devoted gratitude on the other. And here, it might reasonably have been supposed, matters would have rested. Between a young man on the very threshold of life and an elderly matron, plagued by many infirmities, with scarcely a vestige of her former comeliness, and old enough to be his mother (she was seventeen years his senior), there seemed no room for such a thing as a romantic attachment. Unfortunately, hearts like the Northern Sappho's never grow old, and even at fifty she had by no means lost the art of pleasing. Fischerström, like all who approached her, was fascinated. She mistook mere admiration for a warmer feeling, and before she herself was well aware of it, had fallen violently in love with her *protégé*. A mere accident brought to light the secret of which she herself was half-ashamed. Fischerström himself had been wooing a long-obdurate belle, who at length consented to listen to his suit—and to whom could he more naturally confide the secret of his felicity than to his benefactress? The agitation with which she received the news first opened the eyes of the young man to the real state of the case. With rare chivalry, he at once offered to sacrifice his attachment for her sake. She, of course, would hear of no such thing, and affected to be resigned to her fate; but the shock was too much for her feeble health. In a fit of frenzy she leaped into a stream which separated her little property from that of her rival, was rescued more dead than alive, and expired three days afterwards from the effects of exposure. Such seems to be the true version of a variously told and still much-debated story.

Madame Nordenflycht's influence upon Swedish literature was very considerable and decidedly beneficial. She was, as we have already said, the connecting link between the Caroline and the Gustavan schools, but she belonged far more to the latter than to the former. Her talents and her best writings are tinged through and through by French currents of thought, and her pupils Creutz and Gyllenborg may be regarded as the first genuine poets of the new era.

From 1763 to 1772 the Swedish literature lay under a total eclipse. Carlotta Nordenflycht and Olof Dalin died within a few weeks of each other; Creutz, exchanging letters for diplomacy, had, as Swedish Minister at Madrid, entered upon that brilliant political career which ultimately was to bring him to the Swedish Chancellorship; the Academy of Belles Lettres, founded by Queen Louisa Ulrica, was dying of inanition, and Madam Nordenflycht's literary circle had not survived her. Gyllenborg still remained indeed; but he had no longer any heart to sing, for there was none to listen. The attenuated voice of the Swedish Muse was drowned in the discordant hubbub of that ferocious party strife which shook and shattered the Swedish state during the last decade of that period of parliamentary absolutism which the Swedes with unconscious irony call their " Frihetstid" or "Age of Freedom." Politics, or what passed for politics, engrossed all the energies and all the attention of the nation; the last convulsive struggles of the expiring Hat and Cap factions, prolonged through three successive barren, brawling Riksdags, found an echo in every castle, manse and cottage in the land, and

> "On the grave of Letters and the Arts
> Waxed, rude and rank, 'the Daily Advertiser.'"

Then came the famous revolution of 1772, and in an instant the whole face of things was changed. The world is still undecided as to whether the influence exercised by Gustavus III. upon the Swedish literature was bad or good; but every one who thinks at all cannot but agree with Tegner that, "the man who swayed a whole nation as he did, must have been one of the rarest, most highly-gifted beings with whom history is acquainted. For," continues the greatest of the Swedish poets, "it was not gradually, but instantaneously that his spirit flew like an electric spark through the benumbed and torpid nation. . . . He exercised over the popular imagination a dominion which, depending though it did simply and solely on the recognition of his personal superiority, yet had not a shadow of fear in it—a dominion which I will call the theocracy of genius, and which is the mildest, the least humiliating of all dominions.  It was not merely the greatness of his genius which made him what he was to his people, for very few were capable of appreciating how great that genius really was.  No, it was not so much to the greatness of his genius as to its peculiarity that he owed his influence.  For indeed there was in his nature something chivalrous as well as something great.  In him the high heroic strength of genius revealed itself not with sword and shield, but in the Graces' lightest robe.  He was, it is true, a great romantic epic, with its adventures and its enchantments ; but the tender outpourings of an affectionate heart and the gaiety of an exuberant frolicsomeness ran through the whole story. . . . His influence was like the influence of the atmosphere.  His age was, if I may so express it, the age when the Swedish intellect held its high festival. . . . His great soul had room not only for the plans of the hero and the statesman, but also for the graces of art and the joys of life.  He was a Hercules' club entwined with laurels and roses.  He was like the diamond, the hardest of precious stones, yet the same gem whose surface shows the richest and most beautiful play of colours."

Gustavus was no sooner firmly established on his throne than he vigorously addressed himself to the task of reviving the national literature.  It was to the theatre that he turned his attention first of all, not only because he loved it best, but also because it needed his assistance most.

The Swedish drama indeed had sank so low that it seemed beyond even the power of genius to raise it from its abject degradation.  At the best of times it had been but a delicate nursling, barely kept alive by the unremitting care of a vigilant patriotism, so that when Queen Louisa Ulrica,

with her French plays and her French players, banished it
from the Court, it speedily fell into disrepute. Soon it became
the mark of *bon ton* to ridicule the very idea of a Swedish
drama. If a native tragedy ever appeared upon the boards
at all, it was to supply the place of a French farce. The
whole play was turned topsy-turvey, commencing with the
last act, and ending with the first. The audience compelled
the actors to laugh where they ought to have wept, and to
weep where they ought to have laughed. In fact, very often
the spectators took as great a part in the acting of the piece
as the players themselves. To the patriotic soul of Gustavus III. this was an abomination. His first act as King
was to dismiss the French *troupe;* his second was to found
a Swedish theatre and appoint Baron Ehrensvärd its first
manager. The difficulties of the enterprise were almost
overwhelming, but they were encountered with equal courage and ingenuity. As there were neither native actors nor
a native *repertoire,* the King determined to commence with
a grand opera, not because he had any peculiar fondness for
music (which indeed he only cared for on the stage), nor,
as some have supposed, because he had no sense for pure
tragedy (his own tragedies are living instances to the contrary), but because an opera, while uniting in itself all other
theatrical *media,* could best conceal the deficiencies of the
chief medium of all—the language, which, as yet, was considered too weak and rude to stand by itself on the stage.
For a time, therefore, nothing but operas were performed.
The first, *Thetis och Pelée,* collaborated by Gustavus and
Johan Willander, was acted for the first time on January 18,
1773, and ran for twenty-eight nights, till nearly every one
in Stockholm knew it by heart. "Thetis and Peleus" has
but little poetic merit, and certainly cannot be compared with
Gustavus's second opera, *Berger Jarl,* composed in honour
of his brother's marriage, and written in collaboration with
Gyllenborg and young Count Gudmund Göran Adlerbeth,
afterwards so famous for his reform of Swedish prosody,
and for his masterly translations of the Latin classical
poets.

But " Thetis and Peleus " and *Berger Jarl* were, after
all, but the first rough trials of a promising prentice-hand.
The King himself saw the need of further study and preparation, and an interval of no less than eight years
separates *Berger Jarl* from his more mature dramatic
essays. In 1782, however, he again took up his pen, and
produced, in rapid succession, that famous series of original classical plays which, despite their many shortcomings,
are still regarded as the unsurpassed masterpieces of the
Swedish theatre.

The first of the series was *Gustaf Adolfs Ädelmod*
(Gustavus Adolphus's Magnanimity). The plot is briefly as
follows:—The Lady Märta Baner, whose parents were
among the many victims of Charles IX.'s cruelty, has been
brought up from her tenderest infancy by her aunt, the
Countess Stenbock, who intends marrying the girl to her
cousin, Erik Sparre—in fact, the young people have been
betrothed from their cradles. Sparre grows up a low and
brutal tyrant, with no thought for anything but his horses
and his dogs. Märta, who is secretly in love with young
Erik Johansson, Sparre's plebeian foster-brother, a chivalrous, noble-minded youth, loathes her intended bridegroom ;
but gratitude to an aunt who has been more than a mother
to her, and a sense of honour which forbids her to break
her plighted troth, make her sacrifice affection to duty. The
scene of the play is laid at the castle of Hörningholm, the
Countess Stenbock's country residence. It is the morning
of Märta's wedding-day, and the guests are only awaiting
the arrival of the young King, Gustavus Adolphus, who is
coming expressly to give away the bride. The Countess has
little cause to welcome the son of the man who murdered her
nearest kinsman, but is, nevertheless, instantly and entirely
won over by the gracious *bonhomie* of the young monarch,
who seems resolved to make " the friends of his forefathers "
forget the painful memories of the past. It is the young
lady's happiness, however, that most concerns the King.
He knows from experience the bitterness of a loveless marriage, and, in a private interview, invites Märta to forget

that he is her sovereign, and open her heart to him as her
friend. Is the match really to her liking? Märta, after
some hesitation, confesses that she owes her hand to Sparre,
but that her heart belongs to another. Pride or modesty,
or both together, prevent her, however, from confessing her
love for Erik Johansson; but Gustavus suspects the truth,
and the emotion displayed by the bride the same afternoon
when, at the King's request, she decorates young Erik with
the scarf of nobility for valour in the field, convinces him of
the correctness of his suspicions. He forthwith examines
the Countess as to the real sentiments of her niece, and discovers that although Lady Stenbock considers herself bound
in honour to carry out the match between Märta and Sparre,
there is very little love on the young lady's part, and that
even the aunt's interest in Sparre would be far less if he
were not the surviving child of her eldest and dearest kinsman. Hereupon the King produces a letter, confided years
ago by Sparre's dying mother to her friend, Chancellor
Oxenstjerna, certifying that, to save little Erik from his
father's fate, she induced his nurse to substitute her own
babe for the rightful heir, and that consequently Erik Johansson is the true Sparre, and Sparre is really Erik Johansson.
The conversation is interrupted by the report of a musket.
The false Sparre, in a moment of jealousy, has waylaid and
shot his foster-brother, who, however, is happily only
stunned, and recovers sufficiently to be married the same
day to Märta, the King restoring to the young bridegroom
the confiscated estates of his father. The curtain falls as
Gustavus Adolphus rises from his chair to lead off a minuet
with the happy bride.

  *Gustaf Adolfs Ädelmod* was acted for the first time on
June 11, 1782, at the palace of Gripsholm. The decorations and costumes are described as splendid, and the select
audience could not sufficiently applaud. Even the King's
chief political opponent, Count Frederick Axel Fersen, always
ready with a sneer and a jibe, admits that " the piece was not
without genius," and that " few kings, now-a-days, would be
able to write a better." The King's brother, Charles, played

Gustavus Adolphus; G. M. Armfelt, the royal favourite, with his handsome face, noble bearing, and superb figure, made a good Sparre, but Baron Barnekow, as the amusing pedant, Magister Figelius, one of the best comic characters Gustavus ever drew, took the palm. The motive of the piece, the substitution of one infant for another, is borrowed from Voltaire's *Comtesse de Givry ;* but the treatment is quite original. The dialogue, always graceful and facile, is coloured throughout by that romantic sentimentality and fervent patriotism which characterise all Gustavus's plays. The tame *denouement*—the *deus ex machinâ*—the intervention of Gustavus Adolphus, is the weak point of the piece, but all the other strictures upon it are, we think, either frivolous or mutually contradictory. Thus Friedlander objects to the dialogue between Gustavus Adolphus and Märta Baner as too stiff and ceremonious; but surely in this respect the royal author has been truer to nature than his critic, for how could we expect a proud-spirited, sensitive girl to be expansive and gushing in her first interview with one who, however amiable, was still the son of her father's murderer ? Friedlander further remarks that the play leaves a painful impression behind it because we see a woman lying helpless beneath the obligations of birth without the least power to gratify the wishes of her heart or vindicate her rights as a human being. But this is to be over-nice, for, in the first place, Märta can but will not break her bonds; and in the second, it is just the struggle between her sense of honour and her love which makes the piece so interesting, whilst the *denouement* at once releases the heroine from her sufferings and the audience from their anxiety on her behalf. Malmström, on the other hand, dislikes the piece for seemingly countenancing the caste prejudice that gentle birth is bound to assert itself even under the most adverse circumstances, whereas a plebeian, however favoured by fortune, will and must always remain a blockhead. But the whole drift, the very title of the piece shows that the King's sole intention was to magnify the generosity of his favourite hero, Gustavus Adolphus, though even if he had intended to illustrate dramatically the inherent superiority of blood, he would only have been following the eminent (we had almost said the infallible) example of our own great Shakespere.

The most puerile criticism of all, however, comes from Fersen, who was present at the first performance. "What made the whole thing ridiculous," says that caustic patrician, "was the scene in the last act which represented Märta Baner's wedding, when Gustavus Adolphus rose from his chair with much gravity to dance *en chaconne*, and danced it very badly." We really fail to see anything ridiculous in the good King condescending to so gracious an act, which, indeed, was no more than what we should have expected of a monarch who loved above all things to be regarded as the friend and father of his people.

On the 8th April of the same year a new piece from the royal pen, entitled *Helmfelt*, as superior to *Gustaf Adolfs Ädelmod* as *Gustaf Adolfs Ädelmod* is superior to *Berger Jarl*, was performed at the palace of Ulriksdal. Throughout this play there runs a vein of moral (nay, almost melancholy) earnestness, which we do not often meet with in the works of Gustavus III. "Bear in mind," says the hero in the concluding monologue, "bear in mind that without a good conscience, the glories of ambition and the gifts of fortune are but so many heavy burdens!" These words strike the keynote of the whole drama, the plot of which we will now briefly examine.

Jakob Grundel, a Stockholm merchant, ruined and dishonoured by the profligacy of a vagabond son, has hidden his head in a remote Scanian village, where, under an assumed name, and in the midst of his little family circle, consisting of his brother, his daughter-in-law, and their children, he vainly attempts to forget the past. Meanwhile the son, adopting the name of Helmfelt, has gone to the wars, gradually risen to the rank of Fieldmarshal, and returned home full of grief and remorse, but eager to atone for his former sins, feeling that "he who is capable of a real repentance is farther from sin than he who has never been tempted." The play opens with his arrival as

Governor-General in the very province where his kinsmen, whom he has vainly sought in Stockholm, live as poor cottagers, and the whole plot turns upon how the long-suffering family find in the great hero, whose exploits ring through the whole land, a repentant husband, son, and father.

Fersen, who had some words of praise for *Gustaf Adolfs Ädelmod*, can see nothing at all in *Helmfelt*, which he calls "a trivial, dull performance, without any elevated sentiments, poor in ideas, with nothing new or piquant, many long dialogues and repetitions masked by varying phrases." In delivering such a judgment, the noble Aristarchus only condemns himself; for all the great Swedish critics except Geijer (who prefers, rightly, we think, *Siri Brahe*) are agreed that *Helmfelt* is Gustavus's dramatic masterpiece. Its patriotic tone, its *naïve* and natural descriptions of simple country life, its sympathy with and knowledge of the ways and thoughts of the Swedish peasantry, above all, its fine contrast between the stirring odyssey of a warrior's career and the joys of a calm, idyllic country life—all these things have often and justly been admired, and produce, as Friedlander says, "a truly sublime and striking effect."

In the summer of 1783 the Court flitted to Drottingholm, where its theatrical *repertoire* was enriched by two fresh pieces from the same hand, a one-act comedy, *Odin och Frigga*, and a heroic drama in three acts, *Gustaf Adolf och Ebba Brahe*. The comedy is curtly dismissed by Fersen as bald, tedious, and meagre, and for once we agree with him. "Odin and Frigga" is indeed a miserable piece of work, altogether unworthy of the royal dramatist. Of *Gustaf Adolf och Ebba Brahe* it is possible to speak with more respect, but we certainly had the right to expect that the author of *Helmfelt* would have made very much more of a subject which lends itself so admirably to dramatic treatment as the pathetic loves of Gustavus Adolphus and Ebba Brahe. In his over-anxiety, however, to show off his great ancestor to the best advantage, Gustavus has not only neglected all the other personages, but even sacrificed the main plot to what should only have been an episode. In particular, the character of Ebba Brahe is true neither to history nor to nature, and she whom we have been always taught to regard as the most pathetic example of an undeserved dereliction, as the tender, fervent, deeply wounded, but piously resigned victim of the cruelest political expediency, is here transformed into a finished court lady, whose sole rule of conduct is "Honour's law." Nevertheless, this play also has been very much admired. Even Hammerskjiöld, the Zoilus of Swedish critics, who is always especially hard upon the classical school, considers that the contrast in *Gustaf Adolf och Ebba Brahe* between the sufferings of patient love in the royal palace and its calm and playful progress to an innocent consummation in the peasant's hut is very well conceived and poetically executed.

Hitherto the audience of the royal author had been confined within the narrow limits of his own Court, but with the opening of the superb Opera-House, 1782, built at Gustavus's own expense and dedicated by him to the National Muses, the great public was also enabled to participate in the new and noble joys which their King had prepared for them. About the same time, moreover, Gustavus was fortunate enough to find at last a *collaborateur* after his own heart in the person of the famous Johan Henrik Kellgren, whom we shall presently learn to know as the oracle of Swedish *belles-lettres*. No literary partnership was ever so successful. Each of the poets was unsurpassable in his own line, and each possessed precisely what the other most lacked. Kellgren had no deep dramatic instinct, but his astonishing facility as a versifier made him the most successful of librettists. Gustavus, on the other hand, had little ear for either rhyme or rhythm, but no one ever possessed such an intimate knowledge of the manifold resources of the stage. Of the first productions of this joint authorship, *Eneas i Kartago* and *Kristina*, we need only say that they prepared the way for better things; but Killgren's metrical version of *Gustaf Adolf och Ebba Brahe* was a great literary and dramatic triumph, far surpassing the original, and containing some of the most beautiful passages in Swedish poetry, while in *Gustaf Vasa*, a lyric tragedy in three acts, the united efforts of Gustavus III. and Kellgren achieved their masterpiece. This opera, whose subject (the deliverance of Sweden from the bloody Danish yoke by Gustavus Vasa) was sufficient of itself to move every Swedish heart, was performed for the first time on the 19th June 1786. No pains had been spared to make the representation as magnificent and imposing as possible. The music was composed by Naumann, the Kapelmeister of the Elector of Saxony ; the famous scene-painter Desprez came all the way from Paris to superintend the decorations, and, with the King constantly at his elbow, worked away at them night and day for months together. The piece was received with tumultuous enthusiasm, and had a run of twenty-three nights before a crowded audience.

Still, after all, as we have already said, Gustavus only regarded the opera as a means to an end, as a crutch to support the faltering steps of the Swedish Thalia till she was strong enough to walk alone, and his patriotic efforts had proved far more successful than he had dared to anticipate. The taste for dramatic representations became universal, and the best poets of the day vied with one another in contributing dramas to the *repertoire* of the new-born national theatre. In 1787, therefore, the King went a step farther, and founded and endowed the Royal Swedish National Theatre, which continued to interest him warmly for the remainder of his life, and for which he wrote another historical play, *Siri Brahe ;* a melodrama, "The Jealous Neapolitan ;" and three comedies, "The Hoodwinked Pasha" (*Bedragna Bachan*) ; "The One for the Other" (*Den Ena för den Andra*), and "The Birthday" (*Födelsedagen*). *Siri Brahe* was first performed on March 8, 1788, and immediately won a success accorded to none of the other pieces of Gustavus III. ; a success it certainly deserved, for it is not only the royal playwright's masterpiece, but also by far the best original drama which the Swedish theatre possesses. It is also the only Swedish play which has found favour abroad, and has already appeared in a French, an Italian, and a German version.

The Lady Siri Brahe, secretly married to the outlawed Johan Gyllenstjerna, who has followed King Sigismund Vasa to Poland, finds a refuge in the house of her aunt, the Baroness Bielke, Johan's mother, who, with the rest of her family, supports King Charles IX., Sigismund's younger brother and successful rival. The Countess, little suspecting that Siri is already the wife of her eldest son, has plighted away her hand to Count Erik Bielke, who, on the opening of the play, has arrived at Calmar Castle, the Countess's residence, to press his suit to an issue. On the same day, Johan Gyllenstjerna, braving a thousand dangers to see his young wife once more, has crossed the seas, made his way disguised into his mother's castle, and is concealed by Peder Stolpe, a faithful old steward, in a vault known only to Stolpe, where he is to await a favourable opportunity of carrying off his wife. Unhappily the secret of the vault and the mysterious stranger is discovered by the prying eyes of Siri's youthful sister Anna, and her playmate little Stina, Stolpe's daughter, and they, in an unguarded moment, re-veal it to Erik Tegel, Charles IX.'s crafty and hypocritical minister, who has an old grudge against the Gyllenstjernas, and whom a secret suspicion that Polish conspirators are lurking in the neighbourhood has also brought down to the castle. Siri, warned by Stolpe of her husband's peril, re-veals her secret to her suitor Count Bielke, appeals to his magnanimity, and pathetically implores him to save his favoured rival. Bielke, though stunned by the shock of such tidings, chivalrously promises to protect Gyllenstjerna from Tegel; but it is already too late, for Tegel's soldiers have discovered the vault and captured the fugitive, whom they are about to lead to the block, when the youthful Gustavus Adolphus, returning in triumph from the Polish wars, arrives just in time to discomfit Tegel and save Gyllenstjerna.

Even this brief analysis of the plot will suffice to show that *Siri Brahe* abounds with startling dramatic incidents, and it is due to its author to say that he has made the most of them. The brief dialogue between Stolpe and Stina plunges us *in medias res*, and the well-sustained intrigue proceeds rapidly and naturally to an intensely exciting and unforeseen *denouement*. The characterisation, usually Gustavus's weak point, is here very successful. Honest old Stolpe, with his blunt, soldierly fidelity; the sly, insinuating Tartuffe, Tegel; the pert and prying Anna, with her *confidante*, saucy little Stina, are real, living characters. Both in the tragic and comic scenes, too, the author has achieved his highest success. Siri's agonised appeal to her rejected lover to save her husband, and the savage triumph of Tegel when he fancies his victim is well within his clutches, are the best examples of the former; the sprightly dialogues between the two mischievous young girls, the best examples of the latter.

The two-act sensational drama, "The Jealous Neapolitan," displays, perhaps, greater technical skill than any of the author's other plays, and the copious and minute stage directions accompanying it show him to have been the most consummate of stage managers. But the subject is both unpleasant and impossible, and all the characters are so grotesquely unnatural that the general effect is a disagreeable one. We therefore pass on, without further comment, to *Alexis Michaelowitsch och Natalia Narishkin*.

There is no more eloquent proof of the elasticity of Gustavus's genius and his complete independence of circumstances than the fact that this delightful little comedy, so full of unaffected gaiety and good-humour, should have been designed amidst the hurly-burly of camps, and written in the brief interval between two pitched battles. The plot is of the lightest. Tsar Alexis, disguised as a young squire, has won the heart of the beautiful Natalia Narishkin; but, anxious to test the stability of her affection, orders her to be sent to the palace with a bevy of beauties, from among whom, according to ancient custom, the Tsar is to select his bride. A courtier, who personates the monarch, vainly

tempts Natalia to sacrifice her lover for an imperial crown,
till Alexis, who has all the time been trembling in the background, can endure it no longer, throws himself at the feet
of his devoted Natalia, and proclaims her Tsarina, to the
mortification of all the other beauties. The most piquant
parts of this charming play are the conversations between
the three chief competing belles, the haughty Sophia, the
languishing Theodora, and the mischievous Eudoxia, the
prototypes of whom, unless we are much mistaken, are to
be found in Gustavus's own court.

Of the three comediettas, the amusing *Den bedragne
Bachan*, *Den Ena för den Andra*, and *Födelsedagen*, we
need only say that they are sparkling trifles in the King's
best style, and sufficient of themselves to stamp him as a
humourist of no mean order.

As a dramatist, Gustavus III. is a disciple of the French
classical school, though by no means a servile disciple;
for he very frequently sacrifices the unities to theatrical
effect, and his stage is always much more crowded than
is usual with Racine or Corneille. But, if French in form,
in substance and idea he is intensely national, and the most
superficial acquaintance with his works will convince every
one that the royal author drew his inspiration, to use Oxenstjerna's words, "from his love for everything Swedish, his
desire for the honour of the Swedish name, and his zeal
for its universal triumph." Gustavus Adolphus is the real
hero of all his historical dramas, and his greatest opera
is little short of an apotheosis of Gustavus Vasa. This
patriotic enthusiasm, indeed, is apt to weary the patience
of those who do not themselves enjoy the privilege of
being Swedes. One tires even of Gustavus Adolphus at last.
Moreover, the exuberant, often high-flying, romantic sentiments which abound in these historical plays are apt to pall.
One wishes sometimes that these high-born magnanimous
heroes and long-suffering heroines were a little more natural
and human, real persons rather than virtuous personifica-
tions. To English playgoers in particular, accustomed as
they are to the strong meat of Shakespere, the cakes and

comfits of the Gustavan drama appear insipid, and often mawkish. But *Siri Brahe* and all the comedies, except *Odin och Frigga*, are always charming; and with regard to the other dramas, it should never be forgotten that they were intended not for the cabinet but for the stage. They should be seen on the boards to be properly appreciated. No one so thoroughly understood the resources and expedients of the stage as Gustavus III., and it may safely be said that as regards ingenuity of intrigue, skilful combinations, and well-calculated stage effects, they have never been surpassed in Scandinavia.

From Gustavus's dramatic works we now turn to his academic labours.

The year 1784 was a very memorable one for Sweden, for it was then that Gustavus III. resuscitated the Academy of Polite Literature, and founded the Academy of Arts and Sciences.

Volumes have already been written on this interesting subject, but the best account of it, after all, is to be found in the King's own letter to Count Carl Fredrik Scheffer. "To-day (March 22)," wrote Gustavus to his former Governor and ever faithful friend,—"to-day I have summoned up from the grave the Academy of Belles-Lettres, which, if not altogether dead, had, anyhow, fallen into a trance, which threatened to become a mortal lethargy, beyond the reach of medicine. I have employed such a potent exorcism, however, that the rapacious Acheron has finally relinquished his prey. It is true that she has changed so much that you would hardly know her, but it is something to have raised her up at all. As, however, she is still barely convalescent, and too much fresh air, at first, might therefore do her a mischief, she has only shown herself in private to-day to celebrate the anniversary of her foundation, for it is now thirty-three years since the late King gave her her first statutes. To prevent her from relapsing, moreover, I have administered to her such a strengthening tonic that she ought to be able to defy all changes of temperature for centuries to come. In plain Swedish, I have given her new

statutes, and so richly endowed her as to completely set her
on her legs again. . . . I have withdrawn the departments
of linguistics and Swedish poetry from the Academy's control; but, on the other hand, I have added antiquities and
numismatics, and have charged her with the task of com-
piling a history of coins and medals from the commencement of the monarchy to my father's death.  Nothing else
has been altered, however, and the Academy will continue
to cultivate polite literature in the learned and principal
foreign languages, namely, Latin and Greek, French and
Italian.  The Academy will also distribute every year, on
the 20th March, four prizes, to wit, a medal worth twenty
ducats for an historical essay, a medal of the same value for
a piece of poetry or a philosophical dissertation in one of
the above-named languages, a smaller medal worth fifteen
ducats for an antiquarian treatise, . . . and finally, a medal
worth twelve ducats . . . for mottoes and inscriptions. . . .
So there you have a concise description of this institution.
After having thus released the Swedish language from the
late Academy's encyclopædic embrace, I have founded a new
Academy for the cultivation of our own language on the
model of *L'Académie Française*.  It is to be called the
Swedish Academy, and will consist of eighteen members.
. . . The great Gustavus's birthday has been fixed for the
first distribution of prizes.  Both these Academies are amply
endowed, and I have made the funds provided for the purpose inalienable. . . . I have also provided out of the same
funds four pensions, each of 150 rdv. sp. (£32, 10s.), for
foreign scholars who are corresponding members of the
Academy of Belles-Lettres; . . . two similar pensions for
Swedish men of letters; and six pensions of 100 rdv.
(£22, 10s.) each, for Swedish scholars."

The speech with which Gustavus inaugurated the Swedish
Academy is not only, or even chiefly, a display of eloquence:
it is a pregnant and suggestive dissertation on the value of
the arts in general, and shows that the august orator regarded
literature especially not merely as the amusement of a refined
and select few, but as a matter of grave political importance,

as the surest means of enlightening and ennobling society, of stimulating and sustaining public spirit.

"To promote everything which may redound to the welfare of the realm is always my highest object; to contribute to the honour òf the Swedish name my dearest desire. The fame which has followed the Swedish arms throughout the length and breadth of Europe has too often been won at the cost of our individual happiness. It remains for us to achieve another and a greater triumph—the triumph which waits only upon polite literature and bookish arts, the triumph which defies time, and is indifferent to the precarious glory which vanishes with hardly won and lightly lost material conquests. Such triumphs are only attainable in quiet times, when concord at home and security abroad permit genius to freely feed her self-illumined flame, which, if often kindled, is still oftener quenched, in troubled times. And yet if a long peace, an undisturbed tranquillity, is necessary to the welfare of a state, is necessary to the felicity of subjects, too often, on the other hand, it develops a spiritual sluggishness which produces barbarism and paralyses those great minds which in other and better times might have become the honour and the glory of their native land. For men are so constituted that only enthusiasm can inflame them to great deeds. Some sharp stimulus is requisite to awaken the gifts with which nature has endowed them. The emulation, the energy, excited by the cultivation of the arts and sciences, are the only means in quiet times to nurse that fervour of mind which may be of such service to the commonwealth, and to fashion in the womb of peace those citizens capable of saving the realm when storms arise." After a brief but masterly characteristic of the eighteen members (they included Senators Höpken, Carl Scheffer, A. F. von Fersen, and Hermansson; the poets Gyllenborg, Adlerbeth and Kellgren; the historian Botin; Bishops Celsius and Wingard; and Secretary Schröderheim) of this high court of ultimate appeal in literature, in which the peculiar gifts of each are summed up in a few felicitous sentences, the orator thus continued: "With judges such as these, the Swedish language may

look forward to a new and glorious era; nor is the duty of
protecting her unworthy of those who have already dedicated
all their time to the service of the State.   I know there are
some who think that bookish arts and polite literature are
unnecessary; that they belong to those luxuries which ener-
vate the mind, which are only fit for the pastime of an effemi-
nate people, which ought to be banished with anathemas
from the midst of a serious, a valiant nation.   But for what
reward shall merit strive if not for a deathless name?   For
what shall a useful minister sacrifice his repose; suffer the
unjust calumnies of his contemporaries, the opposition of
envy, if not for the hope that an enlightened posterity may
one day do justice to his memory?   And how can this be
hoped for unless those whose genius can preserve his name
for a future world be found among us?   And what more
delightful duty for a cultivated intellect, what nobler pastime
for a statesman, than to endeavour to recall constantly to
mind the memory of those who have been their country's
benefactors? . . . To honour the memory of great men is
to invite their descendants to imitate them.   It is as much
as to say: Warriors, judges, statesmen, fellow-citizens!  Ye
who have inherited the names, ye who now stand in the
places of these bygone heroes, come and behold the offer-
ings which a thankful posterity dedicates to their memory, and
merit if ye can—merit, I say, similar memorials!   Remember
that your names will one day be arraigned before the tribunal
of posterity!  Do not debase them!  It rests with you
alone to make them as renowned as the names of your
ancestors.   Such, then, are the achievements to which I
now invite you.   I have done my part; 'tis for you to do
yours!"

It is well known that the King himself won the Swedish
Academy's first prize by his panegyric on Field-Marshal
Leonard Torstenson, the most brilliant of the great Gustavus's great lieutenants.   Like everything which Gustavus
wrote, the Torstenson eulogy was thrown off at one spurt.
It is especially remarkable for its warm, impetuous style,
lucid exposition, and deep and tender pathos.   The MS.,

fair copied by the King's *valet de chambre*, Fredrikson, was sent to the Academy anonymously. None of the Academicians had the faintest notion as to its real author. Botin, the historian, criticised it severely; but it favourably impressed the majority, and the first prize was unanimously awarded to it. An advertisement in the Gazette then invited the author to declare himself. The King, still preserving his incognito, got a friend to write to the Secretary of the Academy for a copy of the criticisms on the anonymous essay, which were to be sent to Hendrick Hendriksson at Svederus's bookshop. The Secretary pointed out in his reply that the Academy had altered a few ungrammatical passages, which were doubtless attributable to the carelessness of the copyist. Another Academician observed that many of the constructions were French rather than Swedish. Finally, the unknown author was ordered to appear at the extraordinary session of the Academy on the 20th December. The King then made himself known, and consented to receive the prize, but only at a special meeting of the Academy from which the public was to be excluded. The gold medal was handed to him by the President, the poet Kellgren, with a complimentary speech. We are told by an eye-witness, that, at first, Gustavus seemed embarrassed, and toyed nervously with the hilt of his sword while Kellgren was addressing him, but finally he looked up with a smile, and said with charming simplicity: " I thank you! Such a reward is an honour even for a King, especially as I have so many friends among you." Gustavus was also a very facile composer of epitaphs, a species of composition very much affected in Sweden at that time. Perhaps the best he ever did was the following for an inscription on the tomb of the unfortunate Erik XIV., who was poisoned, most probably at the instigation, and certainly with the connivance, of his brother John, who succeeded him :—

Here lies
ERIK XIV., formerly
King of Sweden.
His life showed the frailty of men,
His death
Their cruelty.
Vehement rather than tyrannical,
From being his brother's lord
He became his thrall.
Greater in adversity
Than in prosperity,
For one great crime's sake
He fell the victim of a greater.
He died, betrayed
By his brother
And abandoned by his subjects,
The 26 Feb. 1577, at Orbyhus.

It was Gustavus III. who ordered that the sceptre in the hand of King John's effigy in Upsala Cathedral should be removed and placed on the tomb of his foully injured brother, King Erik XIV., in the Cathedral of Vesteraas.

It was round this Northern Augustus, who thus laid down his sceptre at the feet of the Muses, and concealed the monarch's diadem beneath the laureate's chaplet, that the illustrious poetic group gathered which was to make the Gustavan era for ever memorable.

Gyllenborg, the last surviving minstrel of the Frihetstid, was the first whom Gustavus drew to his side. The Prince surprised the poet one afternoon reading a recently composed work to the Queen-Dowager; insisted upon his recommencing; was so delighted with it that he desired the privilege of his friendship, and for the next four years Gyllenborg, irresistibly fascinated, followed Gustavus about like his shadow. But Gyllenborg's ambling, refractory Pegasus could not or would not keep pace with the ambitious, soaring flights of his royal friend, and the staid, sober, contemplative, absent-minded poet, half-stoic, half-student, was an oddity rather than an ornament to a laughter-loving Court. No one saw this more clearly than Gyllenborg himself. He gradually dropped out of the glittering circle and returned with joy to his books and his ancestral groves, but not before he had had the satisfaction of seeing a brilliant nephew, whose fame was to utterly eclipse his own, take the first place in the favour of his King; that nephew was Johan Gabriel Oxenstjerna.

Gustavus III. used always to account it a great piece of good fortune that he too, like his great namesake and ideal, should possess his Oxenstjerna, a lineal descendant of Sweden's most illustrious statesman, who was also to stand highest in his royal master's affections and nearest to his master's throne.   Fortune, moreover, with singular propriety, gave to each of the Gustavuses the Oxenstjerna most after his own heart.   To the ambitious warrior-king she gave, by way of counterpoise, a guide of equal genius but calmer temperament; but to his volatile and fastidious descendant she gave a delightful and brilliant companion, who was to amuse his leisure and charm away his chagrins.

It was on the occasion of one of Gustavus's frequent visits to the University of Upsala that Oxenstjerna first attracted his attention, by the ability with which he defended an academical thesis set by the Queen-Dowager, namely, "Why great men are more abundant in one country than in another." The young student (he was then only seventeen) performed his part so admirably that Gustavus (then Crown Prince) publicly expressed his satisfaction to the Chancellor, and asked who the young disputant was.   On being told that it was Johan Gabriel Oxenstjerna, he exclaimed, "What a pity his name is not Axel!"[1]

Oxenstjerna came of a poetic stock (his mother was a Gyllenborg), and his early intercourse with his uncle Carl and with his uncle's friend, Count Creutz, led to a precocious development of his own great gifts, for he was certainly "a poet by the grace of God."   His poem "Night" (*Natten*), written while still a boy, was crowned by the literary society *Utile Dulci*, and procured him admission into that mystical Academy, which published all his earlier works.   From 1770–1772 he was attached to the Swedish Embassy at Vienna;

[1] An allusion to Gustavus Adolphus's great chancellor, Axel Oxenstjerna, "the axel on which the world turns," as the French diplomatists said.

but "the tyranny of cyphers," as he called his secretarial
duties, oppressed the mercurial young poet, and it was with
joy that he hailed the Revolution of 1772, which restored
him to his native land. In 1774 he was appointed Kam-
merherr to the King, a post which opened to him the golden
gates of the most delightful of courts, where no rank but
that of genius was acknowledged, and where the love of
letters and the arts was the ruling passion of the monarch.
Oxenstjerna's eminently sociable nature thrived and expanded
in this genial atmosphere; his talents were directed and con-
trolled by a master whom he loved indeed with enthusiasm,
but whom he also looked upon as a superior being; and if
his childlike gentleness and gaiety won him every heart, his
ever-ready wit and astonishing facility as a versifier made
him absolutely indispensable to the enjoyment of that brilliant
circle. It was not in Oxenstjerna's heart to refuse anything
to any one, so he strewed around him with lavish hand
thousands of occasional pieces, *vers de société*, odes, epigrams,
sonnets—all of them models of playful badinage and good-
humoured vivacity, always gay and graceful, very seldom
bitter or even sharp, and never equivocal or indecent. But
these fugitive trifles, for all their elegance and grace, were but
the surface froth and sparkle of Oxenstjerna's gorgeously
exuberant genius. We can form no idea of the richness
and sweetness of the nectar which lay beneath till we betake
us to his great descriptive idylls, *Dagen's Stunder* and *Skördarna*; his allegoric poem, *Hoppet*; his philosophico-religious
*Oskuldens Religion*; and that little masterpiece of playful,
ironical humour, *Disa*.

The poem *Skördarna* (Harvest), in nine cantos, which
occupied the poet for twenty-five years, is certainly Oxenstjerna's most ambitious masterpiece. It is a series of loosely
connected tableaux of country-life in Sweden, interwoven
with numerous narrative episodes, which pass gracefully
and naturally into moral and philosophic reflections. In
none of the author's other works is that love of the gran-
diose and the gorgeous seen to such advantage. As Tegner has so finely said: "The radiance of a southern sun is

reflected from these splendid pictures. Oxenstjerna's muse yearned after a warmer clime, a more luxuriant nature, a greater wealth of colour, than met his eyes in Sweden. It would almost seem as if it were by a mere lucky accident that she has strayed into the distant north, where only the wealth of her imagination can add freshness and lustre to Nature's duller hues."

*Dagen's Stunder* (The Hours of the Day), a sort of miniature *Skördarna* (for the longer poem stands to the shorter "as summer to a summer's day"), is a beautiful natural allegory. "For indeed the changeful day is a most appropriate type of the phases of human life. From the first faint morning twilight to the moment when the silent night, with the eternal stars, looks down upon the graves of men, there is, in truth, not one of the hours of the day which does not present, in a figure, the changes and chances of this mortal life." The poem is divided into four cantos, which sing respectively of Morning, Noon, Evening, and Night. "Count Oxenstjerna," for we must again follow Tegner, "had his own way of regarding our northern Nature. None of her peculiarities escaped him ; but they are projected on to his canvas . . . as through a silver lens. We recognise the lakes and groves ; but the purple dawn rests continually upon the transfigured meads ; a rosy sheen lies over the whole scene, reminding us of more southern skies. It is as though the grass were fresher, the air warmer, and the sky of a deeper blue. We cannot realise that we are in the cold north. We see before us a nationalised Eldorado full of radiance and glory."

Passing over that "fantastic mid-summer night's dream," the allegoric hymn to Hope, whose gossamer temple is finely represented as poised on the faint, transparent horn of the new moon, as well as the beautiful and touching *Oskuldens Religion* (Religion of Innocence)—"the sermon-on-the-mount of poetry," as it has been called—which reflects, as in a mirror, the pure, pious, and tender soul of the amiable poet, we come to the comic romance of *Disa*, the most original, and, at least in our opinion, the most delightful of Oxenstjerna's poems. Wieland himself has produced nothing more

gay and more graceful than this charming little romance,
which reveals the poet in the new and unexpected light of a
great humourist.

*Disa* is a comical version of an ancient Swedish legend.
The realm of King Sigtrud of Sigtuna is visited by a grievous
famine. The King, in despair, takes counsel of the high
priest, who consults the oracles, and so discovers that there
is but one remedy—the slaughter of one-half of the population for the sake of the other half. This cruel expedient
can only be avoided if a lovely virgin presents herself at the
palace to plead for the people; but, as if to make the alternative absolutely impossible, the fair intercessor must be
neither clad nor unclad; she must neither be walking, riding, nor driving, and she must come when the moon is
neither on the wax nor on the wane. This oracular response is at once advertised by proclamation. There are
many sceptics, however, who have their doubts about its
celestial origin, and are inclined to ascribe it to a secret
agreement between the finance minister, who cannot find
food for the people, and the high priest, who would fain
rid himself at one blow of all incorrigible heretics. The
oracular sentence reaches young Disa's ears through the
*Morning Post.* Her tender heart overflows with pity, and
she at once devotes herself to save her country. Scandal
whispers, indeed, that female vanity is at the bottom of this
generous resolve. But scandal will say anything, and Disa
justly considers that if the welfare of the state occasionally
demands that the warrior should draw his sword, it may
also be sometimes necessary for " beauty to bare *her*
weapons." So while King Sigtrud is bitterly cursing the
mawkish prudery of the court ladies, who will not move
a finger to save half the population from destruction, he
hears a distant murmur, which speedily swells into a roar,
and hastening out, perceives a huge crowd approaching the
palace, in the midst of which is the strangest spectacle ever
beheld by the folks of Sigtuna. In a light car, drawn by
two white harts, the naked loveliness of the ingenious Disa
shines through a transparent, light-blue netting. One leg

of the fair Hebe, booted and spurred, Amazon fashion, rests on the neck of a ram running in harness by the side of the car; and thus, with a girdle of roses round her waist, and a wreath of intertwining myrtles and lilacs in her dark brown locks, Disa, secure in her virtue, and not a little proud at having successfully interpreted the oracular enigma, ascends the palace steps amidst the gleam of a thousand torches, and regardless of the spiteful giggles of the ladies and the languishing looks of the gentlemen, throws herself at the foot of the throne to plead the cause of the people. Who could resist such an appeal? Sigtrud, full of emotion, arises, spreads his royal mantle over the shoulders of the prostrate suppliant, declares her his consort, dismisses the finance minister and the high priest, and the land is happy and contented ever afterwards.

Scarcely less famous than Oxenstjerna's original poems is his translation of Milton's "Paradise Lost," in the original metre, which is certainly the happiest foreign version of that great religious epic. With Tasso's "Jerusalem De-livered," on the other hand, he was, strange to say, far less successful, though there was a strong affinity between "Christ's Laureate" and the author of the "Religion of Innocence." Oxenstjerna, by his own confession, stumbled at the *ottava rima*, grew weary of the interminable exploits of Godfrey and Tancred, and found it difficult to enter into the glowing religious fervour of the Catholic poet. He got no further than the twelfth canto, and his fragment is but a pale reflection of the original.

Perhaps no poet of equal rank has so exposed himself to the charge of carelessness as Oxenstjerna. His most grievous stylistic sins, indeed, such, for instance, as the not unfrequent participial constructions, so foreign to the genius of the Swedish language, betray the influence of his educa-tion; for, like his royal friend, Oxenstjerna loved the French tongue so well and knew it so intimately that he half un-learned his own in the process. A less serious but more obvious fault is his frequent nonchalance on the score of rhyme and rhythm, which are frequently faulty; but this is due to the very fluency and spontaneity of his genius, and to his invincible aversion to alter anything that he had once written. Finally, Oxenstjerna's genius was more clear than deep, fine rather than bold. He was richer in images than ideas; he was more original in representation than in invention. Tegner has drawn a masterly comparison between him and the two other great descriptive poets of the Gustavan period, Creutz and Gyllenborg. "With Creutz," says the most poetical of critics, "poetry is a vine which twines itself around real life and clothes its stem with leaves and glowing grapes. But Gyllenborg stands alone, like an oak, hoary but stalwart, sometimes, perhaps, stretching out naked branches, but branches that always point high and heavenwards. Oxenstjerna's song, again, I would compare to a slim, pyramidal poplar whose stem from root to summit is scarcely visible for the foliage, but the bright gold of the sunshine and the gems of the early dew gleam and sparkle on each single leaf."

And yet the foremost place among the classical poets of Sweden belongs to none of this noble trio, but to another of lowly birth and unhistoric name. It is Johan Henrik Kellgren, whom his contemporaries, with one consent, pronounced "the glory and delight of the Gustavan age."

The little we know of the early life of this extraordinary man is soon told. The future arch-enemy of creeds and clergy sprang himself from a clerical stock, and after an exceptionally brilliant academical career, the young professor of poetry and belles-lettres (he was only six-and-twenty) settled in Stockholm as tutor to the children of the lovely Countess Meijerfelt, one of the three graces who led the revels at the Court of Gustavus III., and whose *salon* was the favourite rendezvous of the great and gay world. Kellgren, like his English counterpart Pope, with whom he has often been compared, may be said to have lisped in numbers; but his austerely critical taste (and he was as severe towards himself as towards others) long made him distrust his own poetical capacity. For in Kellgren the creative and the critical faculties went hand in hand,

and he whose fastidiousness constrained him at the close of his career to exclude from his collected works much which his protesting friends regarded as absolutely perfect, made him, at its commencement, shrink from producing anything which fell short of the very best. But the bright eyes of the lovely Countess kindled the ambition of the young poet, and it was beneath her roof that all his earlier masterpieces were written.

It was with the famous satire, *Mina Löjen* (My Laughter), that Kellgren took the town by storm. In an instant the obscure young *magister* became the favourite of Swedish society, the delight and admiration of the wittiest of courts, the terror of dulness and imposture. Soon all Stockholm knew the poem by heart, and during the next generation every couplet became a household word. The Swedish literature since Kellgren's time has advanced with giant strides, and achieved wonderful things; but it has produced nothing half so graceful, gay, insinuating, and melodious as *Mina Löjen*. Kellgren's contemporaries, moreover, were even more delighted with the philosophy of his exquisite *jeu d'esprit* than with its form, for it contained the quintessence of that refined, indulgent Hedonism which had spread like a flood from the banks of the Seine all over the rest of Europe, and was openly accepted in the highest circles as the most sensible substitute for Christianity. Long indeed before Kellgren's time, the new gospel of pleasure and indifference had made many distinguished but secret converts in Sweden (Höpken, for instance); but it was young Kellgren who first came boldly forward as the apostle of the new creed. The only divinity whom he recognises is the kind and gracious god, who laughs in the flowers of spring, breathes in the zephyr, blends with the nectar of the grape, and gives fire and sweetness to Glycera's kisses. The religion of suffering and sorrow, of fear and repentance, he utterly repudiates as fit only for a race of fools who plague themselves with imagined woes; and he invites the sportive hosts of laughter—
" laughter, the one divine, distinguishing mark of humanity "

—to follow him through all the phases of life, and teach him to weave the blithesome dance on the very edge of the dark grave.  Then, with smiling scorn, and delicate, epigrammatic irony, he ridicules in turn all sorts and conditions of men ; first, the great and noble, "for it would be infringing the privileges of rank not to laugh at the highborn first ; " next, the "children of Levi," and here the satirist forsakes his bantering tone, and plies the scourge with savage glee.   Then comes the turn of the learned strawsplitters and the meagre tribe of poetasters.   The satire concludes with an apostrophe to the race of "pretty fools called by a gracious heaven to enable us to wage war with sadness, and guide our footsteps more swiftly and surely along the flowery path which leads to the abyss "—a delightful piece of badinage whose graceful impertinences and contemptuous half compliments leave one in doubt whether the wicked wag adores or despises his fair friends the most. *Mina Löjen* was followed by a few erotic lyrics of exquisite form and melody, whose cynical voluptuousness, glowing colour, and mythological nudity of expression have greatly scandalised the moralists of a later and purer generation. The notes of such a lyre as Kellgren's could not fail to strike at once the ear of such a connoisseur as Gustavus III. The poet was persuaded to write a prologue for a court fête, and was afterwards presented to the delighted monarch, who warmly congratulated him, and promised to provide for him. It was not till two years later, however, that Gustavus actually took the poet by the hand, and made him his librarian and private secretary.   Kellgren's pension was charged on the funds of the richest hospital in Stockholm ; and on the envelope containing his certificate of appointment the King wrote, with his own hand, the following lines from *Mina Löjen* :—

"Who smote thee, then, with blindness?—say !
As following fame and fortune's call
You took the Heliconic way
Which brings you to—the hospital?"

But in the meantime Kellgren had risen by his own exertions to a position which made him independent of court patronage.

On the 29th October 1778, in conjunction with his friend Lenngren and a few others, Kellgren published the first number of a literary-critical review, the *Stockholm Post*. The programme of the new periodical was to provide occupation, enlightenment, and relaxation for a "moody and ignorant population, so much engrossed in the past by political squabbles as to have neglected and despised the refined and innocent joys of the understanding." Political discussions the journal renounced from the first as altogether unnecessary, now that the realm, "formerly plunged in the deepest degradation, confusion, and corruption, had been raised to the summit of honour, order, and prosperity." The people, it was declared, under a monarchical government were released from all anxiety as to their future welfare, for things had reached that happy stage when there was *one* who laboured and millions who enjoyed. This naive belief in the superiority of a one-man system of government may sound strange and even revolting to the ears of nineteenth century politicians; but in the year 1778 it was the firm belief of the whole Swedish nation, still in the first glow of its boundless enthusiasm for an amiable young monarch. To accuse Kellgren, therefore, as some have done, of sycophancy, is almost as absurd as to accuse him of being a Swede, or to condemn him for being a patriot. Besides, it was not in Kellgren's nature to truckle to any one. Even as a schoolboy, as a student, he had been remarkable for a haughty reserve, a sturdy independence, a critical superciliousness. He was always far more prone to sit in judgment upon his official superiors than to offer them incense. And when in later days he became the literary partner of his royal benefactor, the panegyric was always to him the most distasteful and difficult of compositions. "The public knows very well," he said on one occasion, "that one degree of praise in ordinary prose is equivalent to two in oratory, four in poetry, and at least eight in the ode."

As we have said, polite literature was the special department of the *Stockholm Post.* In all questions relating to literature and criticism it claimed to be a court of ultimate appeal, and for the next fourteen years it really exercised the most absolute dictatorship over the national literature. French classicism was the standard of excellence; Voltaire the idol and the oracle of this new æsthetic autocracy. A thing was judged good or bad according as it came up to or fell short of this *beau idéal,* whilst everything which seemed to run contrary thereto was branded at once as absurd or barbarous. Hence Kellgren's admiration for the English literature of Queen Anne's time, and his unmitigated contempt (at least in the first instance) for the rising literature of Germany. But artificial and narrow as its principles undoubtedly were, the immediate influence of the *Stockholm Post* was distinctly beneficial. The Frihetstid had left Sweden spiritually as well as materially bankrupt. At the close of that dreary and destructive period, the national literature was like a weed-grown wilderness, with only a straggling rose-bush here and there to remind the passers-by that it had once been a garden. Kellgren was the master-gardener who reclaimed this desolate waste, making it an artificial paradise abounding with everything pleasant to the eye and delightful to the taste, and rigidly excluding from its sacred precincts the rude and ragged herd of vulgar scribblers, whose native element was riot and confusion. It is ungrateful as well as fastidious for those who inherited the fruits of his labours to exclaim against his French formalism because his gorgeous flower-beds are perfectly symmetrical, his magnificent lawns faultlessly smooth and even, his grottos and terraces of uniform classical severity. But the accusers certainly have both right and reason on their side when they charge him with planting a upas-tree here and there among his myrtles and laurels; with suffering flowers of ravishing beauty indeed, but also of poisonous perfume, to have a place in his elegant *parterres;* and with rearing statues to the garden-god as well as to the muses and the graces. For it is idle to deny that the Voltairean

Kellgren was deeply tainted by the refined, self-indulgent, conscienceless sensualism of the day which contemptuously rejected the ethics as well as the dogmas of Christianity. We need not dive very deeply into the poet's life to discover that his intercourse with the nymphs of the opera-house was at least as frequent and familiar as his intercourse with the daughters of Apollo, and a glance at the pages of the *Stockholm Post* (to say nothing of his early erotics) will discover verses worthy of Gresset's most wicked moods and facetiæ which Poggio could scarcely have distinguished from his own. It is only too plain that the absolute freedom from prejudice on which Kellgren prided himself so much, made him regard the morally ugly with favour if only it were perfect in form and graceful in expression. Nevertheless it is going too far to say that he deliberately set himself to preach frivolity and licentiousness. On the contrary, the serious and noble ambition of reforming the national literature was, after all, the task nearest to his heart, and, on the whole, he performed it worthily. A consummate master of style himself, and so keenly sensitive of the beautiful and the elevated in art as to regard every low expression, every false sentiment, as "a buffet on the cheek of good taste," he was not likely to spare the Grub Street poets of his day, nor did he. One by one, the surviving poetasters of the Frihetstid were flogged, flayed, and vivisected by the merciless humourist, to the exquisite delight of the public, and driven with scorn and derision headlong from the republic of letters. Nor did mediocrity, however amiable, escape the blows of his iron sceptre. Thus the prosy and interminable Liliestraale was long one of Kellgren's favourite butts; and the flaccid Bager and the turgid Bjugg owe to the Gustavan satirist the same sort of immortality which Bavius and Mævius owe to the Augustan.

And Kellgren flew at still higher game. Amongst the multitude of congratulatory odes called forth by the birth of the Crown Prince was one which the *Stockholm Post* thought worthy of the honour of a criticism, and a criticism it accordingly received which could not have been very

pleasant reading for its author. It is true that neither wit
nor imagination was denied him; but his wit was compared
to a will-o'-the-wisp, and his imagination to the delirium of
fever. He was also taken to task for the obscurity, exaggeration, and bombast of his style. The young poet Leopold,
a graduate fresh from the University of Lund, at once
engaged in a polemic with his austere critic, which raged
fiercely through sixty-three numbers of the *Stockholm Post*,
and resulted in a drawn battle. Both of the combatants
acknowledged in later years that they had gone too far.
Leopold himself conceded the point in dispute by excluding
the ode in question from his collected works; whilst Kellgren
apologised for his boyish impertinence in laying so much
stress upon faults which, real or imaginary, were scarcely
discernible; opened the columns of the *Stockholm Post* to his
former foe, whom he also introduced to Stockholm society;
and we shall presently see the two poets, as firm friends
and fellow-academicians, fighting side by side under the
same banner against a common foe.

But some years elapsed before this literary feud ended
in brotherly love, and in the meantime it involved Kellgren
in another contest with a still more formidable antagonist,
who suddenly raised the standard of revolt against the
critical supremacy of the *Stockholm Post*, fiercely assailed
the infallibility of its editor, and succeeded in dividing the
Swedish literature into two irreconcilable camps.

One of the most fervent admirers of Leopold's ill-fated
ode was another young student named Thoren, who had
come up to the capital the year before from Upsala. This
youth had already resolved to make a noise in the world;
but until he had quite made up his mind as to whether he
should reveal himself to his generation as the sublimest
of poets or the most profound of philosophers, he was
content to remain "holy, pure, and glad in an eternal union
with moderation," or in plain English, to live in a back
attic in the poorest but most picturesque suburb of Stockholm, on a hardly earned threepence a day. Thoren had
read deeply (much more deeply than most of his contem-

poraries), anu ιιιs taste was more catholic than theirs.  He admired Racine, Boileau, and Voltaire much, and Goethe, Klopstock, and Lessing still more; but Shakespere and Ossian he loved best of all, though with characteristic perversity he placed the latter very far above the former. An ecstatic enthusiasm for the beautiful and the sublime in Nature, especially in their wildest and most fantastic forms, and a boundless self-worship which frequently bordered upon insanity, were the characteristics of this strange, irrepressible being, who was nothing if not superlative, and whose veriest commonplaces were shrieked forth with oracular ecstasy and oracular obscurity.  Thoren's pride had long been secretly chafing and fretting beneath the yoke which, in his opinion, Kellgren had laid upon the free development of the national literature, and like a second David he burned to defy and challenge the presumptuous Goliath of the *Stockholm Post*.  The wished-for opportunity came much sooner than he had dared to expect.  A few months after the duel between Kellgren and Leopold, the Literary Society, *Utile Dulce*, offered a prize for the best Swedish poem, and Thoren at once sent in an ode on "The Passions," in six cantos, the success of which he never doubted for an instant. "The best heads," wrote he to a friend, "call it excellent; some think it incomprehensible.  It contains the full force of my philosophy and all the splendour of my imagination.  Unrhymed, ecstatic, marvellous."  Three days later an advertisement in the *Stockholm Post* announced that the Society's grand prize had been bestowed upon N. L. Sjöberg for his "Ode to Agriculture;" but that an "Ode on the Passions," by a student named Thoren, had been deemed worthy of a lesser, accessory prize; indeed, the Society freely admitted in its report, that in spite of much that was wild, extravagant, obscure, and turgid, Thoren's poem displayed sufficient genius to have entitled it to the first prize, had he not put himself out of court by using an unrhymed dactylic measure at variance with the canons of polite literature, and which the Society could not but regard as a hazardous and unnecessary innovation.

Now, although the qualifying comments which garnished
this eulogy gave it a somewhat sub-acid flavour, it was
nevertheless no mean distinction for an obscure young
author, scarcely out of his teens, to be saluted and crowned
as a genius of the first rank by the highest literary authority
in the land.   Thoren, however, chose to regard as a slight
and a disgrace what any one else in his position would have
considered the highest honour.   So far from feeling flattered
by the notice of the Society, he was deeply offended, and let
all the world know it.   He forthwith addressed a long letter
to the *Stockholm Post*, declining the prize awarded him, and
suggesting that it should be bestowed upon the author of the
best dissertation on the "Origin and Real Value of Canons
of Taste in the Fine Arts."   He was grateful, he said, to the
Society for its good opinion, but self-respect forbade him to
accept a half-reward, meet only for mediocrity.   The Society
had a perfect right to its opinion, but it had no right to brand
him with failure by proclaiming that he had competed for
the first prize in vain.   His poem had been called a hazardous and unnecessary innovation, simply because it happened
to be in blank verse!   Hazardous, however, it could scarcely
become in a false and corrupt age, which took polished platitudes in jingling verse for poetry, though, for his part, he
would blush to be hailed a poet simply for his rhyme's sake.
Still less fairly could his blank verse be called unnecessary.
"Does," cried he, "the zither make the harp unnecessary,
or the flute the French horn?   Because there are some
people who . . . have learnt to dance incomparably well in
fetters, is it therefore unnecessary to look upon the freer
and certainly nobler movements of nature? . . . One who
sits in the tribunal I address as an irresistible, enchanting
versifier" (here Kellgren is meant).   "He has the right to
exalt rhyme: he has not the right to make it arbitrary in the
world of melody."

Whatever may be thought of the style and tone of Thoren's
epistle, it must be admitted that he had a just ground of
complaint against the Society.   To pronounce his poem a
masterpiece, and to condemn it in the same breath because

it happened to be written in one style of verse rather than another, was a very puerile and paltry proceeding. Thoren had a right to complain of such treatment, and had he complained with becoming modesty and tact he would have carried every sensible person along with him. When, however, instead of merely criticising his critics, he proceeded to dictate to them in language of unheard-of arrogance, the public overlooked the main issue, and began to ask each other not whether the young man was right, but whether he was sane. Kellgren saw his opportunity, and made the most of it. In an anonymous letter to the *Stockholm Post* he defended the conduct of the Society, and after lecturing Thoren as an angry schoolmaster might lecture a clever but conceited pupil, expressed his doubts whether a person with so little common-sense and so much vanity could really be said to possess any genius at all. If, however, Kellgren fancied that this rebuke would silence the audacious rebel he was grievously mistaken. Thoren was irrepressible. In a still longer reply to the *Stockholm Post* he not only explained and defended his æsthetic principles at great length, but accused his critic of narrowness of taste and a slavish worship of form. " It is unnecessary ai d too late to dispute my *genius*," he concluded, "and my conduct will show whether I lack common-sense."

Such language was something new and strange. Addressed by a very young author to the literary oracle of the day, it sounded almost blasphemous to many delicate ears. Thoren was in high glee. He had commenced what he called a tournament of wit, a battle with the whole literary world, and he invited his country friends to come up to town to see the fun. Kellgren, on the other hand, seems to have been much irritated by the pertinacity of his opponent, and in his irritation he for once forgot that native chivalrousness which rarely forsook him in his most bitter polemics. He resolved to crush a foe who refused to take a snubbing quietly, forgetting that if it is excellent to have a giant's strength, it is tyrannous to use it as a giant. He allowed Thoren, indeed, to have the last word on the prize poem sub-

ject, but soon afterwards, when during a heavy thaw the
Stockholm municipality issued an order for the removal of
the snow and slush from the congested streets, there appeared
in the *Stockholm Post* the complaint of a "householder"
against the order in question, in which Thoren's peculiar,
extravagant, aphoristic style was parodied to the letter. A
roar of laughter resounded from every corner of the land.
In the stilted phrase, the lofty affectation, the air of conscious superiority, the incoherent exclamations, the bizarre
reasoning, and the raving paradoxes of this clever parody,
every one recognised at once the peculiar style of the author
of the "Ode to the Passions." To a man like Thoren, whose
self-conceit almost amounted to monomania, it must have
been peculiarly galling to have been thus exposed to the public
ridicule in Kellgren's satiric pillory. To do him justice,
however, he kept his temper admirably, and a sort of tacit
truce ensued between the antagonists. Kellgren threw the
*Stockholm Post* open to Thoren and his friends, and Thoren
responded to this courtesy by warmly eulogising Kellgren's
"Ode on the Death of the Queen," exalting it above the odes
of Pindar and Horace. But this suspension of hostilities did
not last long. In 1783 one of Thoren's numerous disciples
—for he had gathered round him all those who had ever
smarted under Kellgren's lash—one of Thoren's disciples
sent to the *Stockholm Post* a short Anacreontic poem in blank
verse, so utterly absurd, that Kellgren could not resist the
temptation of parodying it in the following number with his
usual matchless skill. Thoren, who had in the meantime
changed his name to Thorild (Thor's fire, *i.e.*, thunderbolt),
was not the man to sit still and see his favourite blank verse
delivered over to the ridicule of his foes through the bungling
of his own followers. He at once rushed to the rescue, and
covered the retreat of his discomfited disciple by a sharp
attack upon the "*bel esprit* of the *Stockholm Post*," who
could not open his mouth without lolling out his tongue, and
whose highest wit was a smart grimace. Finally he expressed
the opinion that Kellgren could not write rhymeless verse
without drifting into prose. The taunt was a rash one, and

Thorild was now to learn to his cost that the arrows in his opponent's satiric quiver were not only manifold but multiform, for his challenge drew from Kellgren the exquisite little satire, "A Fresh Essay in Blank Verse," directed against "the Cossacks of literature," and ridiculing Thorild's "epileptic style" in Thorild's own favourite metre, the rhymeless Anacreontic. The poem describes how the new Icarus, after disencumbering himself of the solid fetters of commonsense, and snapping asunder the silken, flower-embroidered bands which Good-taste and her younger brother Rhyme had wound round his wings, ascends into the high heaven of Bedlam, to the amazement and admiration of the whole world, but comes to grief among the starry spheres, and falls back earthwards a mangled, shapeless mass.

Every one now thought that Thorild had received his *quietus*, or, at any rate, would think twice before he again fell foul of an opponent who had so easily worsted him with his own chosen weapons. But Thorild was rather wounded than disarmed. So far from being cowed into submission, he vowed from henceforth a war of extermination against Kellgren and his school, and opened the assault with what he triumphantly described to his friends as "a gallery of Tartaric pictures," but which to all but a handful of zealots has ever appeared a stigma on the national literature—his too celebrated *Straffsang* (the Vengeance Song), or *Henrik's Kaakstrykning* (Henry's Whipping-Post), which had to be printed privately at Strengnäs, for not a single Stockholm bookseller had the courage to publish it. Nor is this at all surprising, for in the whole wide range of polemical literature it would be difficult, if not impossible, to put one's finger upon a squib which shows such a thorough command of the vocabulary of vituperation, or such a cynical recklessness in the use of it. In this "somewhat high-toned badinage," as Thorild in his cooler moments pleasantly called it, *Kältring* (an abusive play upon Kellgren's name, meaning scoundrel), is apostrophised as "the lap-dog of letters," "Voltaire's pretty ape," "a rhyme hopper," "a jingle despot," "a chicken-brained marmot," "a monster of spite," "the behe-

moth of absurdity," "the pigmy of immortality," "the Beel-
zebub of baboons," "the cherubim of the whipping-post,"
"a toad," "a sparrow," "a fool," "a monster," "Satan's
own spawn "—to say nothing of a hundred other epithets
unfit for publication. The common people and Thorild's
own clique roared with laughter at this farrago of Billings-
gate; but all friends of good taste and good breeding stood
aghast at the virulence and indecency of the attack. Kellgren for once in his life was absolutely dumb. He seems
to have been shocked, almost stunned, at the savage cruelty
of his opponent, and he must have felt that his keen and
polished stiletto was useless against an antagonist who pelted
him at a distance with garbage snatched from the gutter.
Rumpled and mud-bespattered, therefore, the refined and
exquisite critic retired for a time from the contest, leaving
the enemy in possession of the field. Henceforth the position of the combatants was reversed. Thorild became the
aggressor, while Kellgren stood strictly on the defensive.

Thorild's next step was to start a newspaper of his own—
*Den Nyare Granskaren* (The New Examiner), which died
four months after its birth, but which during its brief career
persistently pursued, or rather persecuted, "the little West
Goth who has learnt to rhyme, who cringes for the alms on
which he lives, and whose little sterile soul . . . derives its
nutriment from the dregs of French newspapers!" Kellgren treated this fresh outburst of virulence with contemptuous silence; but the Government shortly afterwards
stepped in and suppressed the ribald print.

Thorild now threw himself into politics (the Riksdag of
1786 had just met), and addressed two memorials to the King
petitioning for the abolition of the censorship. Gustavus III.
was charmed with the young petitioner's eloquent style and
brilliant play of fancy, but put him off with a pretty compliment or two. Thorild was, however, informed officially that
his memorials contained so many weighty truths that they
ought to remain concealed in a great man's desk for at least
fifty years to come. A simultaneous proposal of his to Parliament to translate the works of Tacitus at the expense of

the State was also rejected. Filled with disgust, Thorild suddenly made up his mind to turn his back on a land of "beasts," in order to teach freedom and political science to another nation which had more life, spirit, and power than his own, *e.g.*, to the English. But first the self-appointed apostle posted off to the University of Upsala to win the doctor's degree in two faculties (law and medicine), so as to increase his credit and authority with his British friends. As, however, he objected to submit to the previous ordeal of a regular examination, he was obliged to quit the University, after a year and a half's residence, without obtaining either of the coveted degrees. It was during his stay at Upsala that he enjoyed what was perhaps the greatest triumph of his life. In March 1788, Gustavus III., with a brilliant suite, visited the University, and in the presence of the King, the court, and the full consistory, "the mad *magister*," as Thorild was now called, defended his *Kritik öfver Montesquieu* (Critique of Montesquieu) against fifteen opponents, including the eloquent Leopold, now poet-laureate, the witty, incisive, Secretary Schröderheim, the brilliant and dashing Armfelt, and the Crown Prince's Governor, the subtle and erudite Rosenstein. The disputation, which began early on the 22nd of March, lasted all morning, and it was the general opinion that Thorild was more than a match for all his fifteen opponents put together. Let us hear what Armfelt, one of the chief participators in this intellectual revel, thought of it :—

"The last day of our visit at Upsala," he writes, "a disputation, which lasted three hours, engaged the attention of four hundred spectators, and provided us with a real treat. A person named Thorild, whose mania it is to be unlike every one else in everything, defended a thesis in public. . . . His genius, his declamation, his eloquence, and the fire which animated his looks and gestures, excited general admiration. To these qualities he united a pungent wit, frequently discharging the most cruel epigrams—in short, he made us all laugh till the tears came into our eyes. Even portly Schröderheim, whose repartee seldom fails him, was hurled to the ground by a fulminating comparison with the *Venus aux belles fesses*, and ever since has gone by the name of the *Venus d'Upsale*." On the following day Armfelt waited upon the victorious disputant in his humble attic, congratulated him in the King's name on his brilliant defence, reminded him that so long as Gustavus III. held the sceptre, genius would always take precedence of rank and wealth, and invited him to try his fortune at court. But nothing, not even the prospect of becoming jester in ordinary to Gustavus III., could keep Thorild back any longer from his proselytising mission across the seas. So to England he went, and there conducted himself with characteristic extravagance. During his sixteen months' residence in London, he learnt English so thoroughly as to be able to write pamphlets which have a ridiculous resemblance to some parts of *Sartor Resartus*, and poems which Walt Whitman might have thrown off in his least lucid moods. His object, so far as he understood it himself, seems to have been to agitate for a politico-social revolution which was to spread from England all over the world; but finding himself treated more as a lunatic than as a high-spirited fellow, his admiration for perfidious Albion subsided into unutterable contempt, and he took leave of her in a fiercely denunciatory address, which is a fair specimen of his English, commencing thus : "And this is glorious England ! . . . so high in spirit and so low in fact ! whose boasted eminence is to pronounce proudly the weighty syllables of [*sic*] CON-STI-TU-TION—a word as mystic [as] Abracadabra, and at last [? after all] even as idolatrous and dull ! Constitution without public principle and a true national sense is but a stupid idol, good [only] for court popery and a staring, devout mob." "Oh, glorious England !" so concludes this diatribe ; "dost thou deserve a smile of disdain or still a tear of pity ?"

Thorild had no sooner got back to Sweden than he again took up his old quarrel with Kellgren, whom he reviled in his "Criticisms of the Critics, &c.," addressed to the reviewer of the *Stockholm Post*, which the editor, with rare courtesy, published in its columns, but without comment. In truth,

the great poet, wearied with many labours, and already
stricken by that fatal malady which was soon to cut him
off in his prime, yearned for repose, and left it to Leopold,
now his most brilliant and faithful follower, to defend his
principles against his irreconcilable foe.  Into the history
of the contest between Thorild and Leopold we cannot now
enter.  We need only say that it was on the same lines
as the previous contest, that the champions were equally
matched, and that mutual exhaustion finally put an end to
the indecisive duel.

It is difficult to assign to Thorild his true place in the
republic of letters.  Comet-like, he flashed across the
horizon of the Swedish literature, a wonder and a prodigy,
scattering showers of meteors on every side of his erratic
course, but having no abiding place like stars of more
constant if less dazzling ray.  His most ardent admirers
are the Swedish romanticists, who hail him as their prophet
and precursor, though he had very little of that tender
religiosity which is the distinguishing mark of their school.
In truth, Thorild's lawless, convulsive, fragmentary genius
forms a type apart, somewhat akin, especially in its eccen-
tricities, to Jean Paul Friedrich Richter's or our own Carlyle's,
though incomparably inferior to them both in humorous as
well as in poetic power.  His ideas, though vast, original,
even tremendous, were too nebulous and fleeting to be
reduced to a system, and his utterances were always so
obscurely oracular as to be practically unintelligible.  Yet
his influence upon his contemporaries, and especially upon
his opponents, was undeniably far-reaching.  He enlarged
their whole mental horizon, and opened up before them unex-
plored tracts of which they had had no idea before.  Kellgren,
in particular, *after* his duel with Thorild was quite a different
man from what he had been before it.  It may be that such
an essentially expansive and receptive nature as Kellgren's
might have gradually and completely emancipated itself from
French influences independently of Thorild; but the significant
fact remains that it was only after his collisions with " *the mad
magister*," that Kellgren began to write blank verse as exquisite

and as faultless as his former rhymes, and that he who had once spoken unadvisedly of "Shakespere's delirium," "Goethe's convulsions," and Ossian's "eternal sameness," began to study with increasing admiration, and even to translate for the admiration of others, the masterpieces of the German and even of the Danish literature. At all events, Kellgren was undoubtedly one of those continually progressive geniuses whose ideal of excellence is "ever in advance of their ever advancing powers."[1] The idyll, the erotic lyric, and the satire continued to the last to be his chief studies; but between his earlier and his later pieces there is a vast difference. The form and style indeed is pretty much the same in both, perfect from first to last; any change in this respect could only have been a change for the worse. It is the tone which has changed and become sweeter, yet more manly and more earnest than heretofore. For all their laughing grace and witty sparkle, the earlier satires (e.g., *Mina Löjen*), had been frivolous, flippant, and often daringly profane. The later satires, notably *Man eger ej snille för det man är galen* (Madness is no Mark of Genius), and *Ljusets fiender* (The Enemies of Light), in which, with equal moral and political courage, he attacked and exposed the spiritualistic jugglery and imposture of his day, and scotched the monster on the very steps of the throne, glow with a nobler indignation, a more sublime scorn. Even more remarkable is the awakening sense of religion apparent in his later idylls, elegies, and odes, especially in that great descriptive masterpiece "The New Creation," in which it has been finely said, "Kellgren's muse ascends up to heaven." The joyous delirium of the poet's youth is here exchanged for a calmer and purer philosophy, across whose shadowy pantheism gleams the ray of a more comforting and more hopeful creed. It is true that in this, as in his other pieces, the scepticism of his youth breaks forth again and again, but it has lost its fierceness and its fervour. In the very passage in which he utters a villainous half-sneer at the miracle at Cana there is a sincere confession that the fear of God is the highest virtue,

[1] I borrow this felicitous phrase from a sermon of the late Canon Burrows.

and that thereon depends all our temporal and eternal welfare. What Kellgren might have become in time we cannot tell, but it is probable that we possess but half of him (and that half not the best half) in the little' he has left behind him.

Kellgren's last request to his sorrowing friends (he died at forty-four, in 1795, three years after his royal friend) was characteristic of the man. "Let there be no tolling of bells over me," he said; "that sort of music has never pleased me, and I will not plague others with it."

It must have been some consolation to the dying poet to know that he left the principles for which he had all his life contended in the safe keeping of a champion equally zealous for French classicism, and equally able to defend it. This was no other than Leopold, with whose name we are already familiar, and who now received the literary sceptre of Sweden from the failing grasp of his friend and master.

Carl Gustaf Leopold was born on the 2nd April 1756. His parents, middle-class people, could give him no more than an excellent education, and at the age of seventeen he commenced life as a tutor in the Douglas family, at Stockholm. Subsequently offered an assistant-librarianship at Upsala, he qualified himself for the post by taking his degree at the University of Greifswald, but remained for some time longer in Swedish Pomerania as chief librarian at Stralsund. It was not till 1784 that he returned to Sweden and was installed at Upsala, where his famous dispute with Thorild drew the attention of the King to him. Gustavus at once made up his mind that such a clever young man was thrown away upon the University, and invited him to court. He came, and was introduced into the presence by the favourite Armfelt. Gustavus, who was writing at his desk, kept the poet waiting for a few moments, but suddenly starting from his seat when Leopold least expected it, came straight towards him, measured him from head to foot, and then asked with an inquiring smile, "Well, young man, what is your opinion of the *Fideicommis?*" It was a captious question, for this particular poem was by the disgraced ex-minister

Liliestraale,[1] whose works were therefore the fair prey of courtly witlings. So far, however, from losing his head, Leopold made a reply which showed him to be a man of character as well as a man of talent. "Even in the *Fideicommis*, your Majesty," he replied, "there are fine passages."

"You don't say so!" cried the King, ironically. "Pray, let us hear one!"

"Take, for example, these verses," replied Leopold, and he quoted from memory the following lines:—

"To rise upon another's fall, to no man do obeisance,
And in thy monarch's sight beware of fawning, false complaisance!
His rank and place, to loyal eyes, should ever sacred be,
And truth's the first and highest debt that's due to him from thee."

The King, equally delighted at the *sang-froid* and the candour of this reply, clapped Leopold on the shoulder, exclaiming, "Bravo, bravo! my friend," at once assigned him apartments in the palace, paid his trifling debts, and relieved him of all pecuniary anxiety for the future by appointing him his librarian and private secretary.

The acquaintance thus begun was of the most cordial and familiar description. Not even Oxenstjerna, with rank, birth, and an illustrious name to set off his genius, was so intimate with the monarch as was Leopold. Even the strict requirements of etiquette were relaxed in his favour, and the plebeian poet, as the King's personal friend, took his place as an equal among the highest dignitaries of the realm. Nay, even in the midst of his Russian campaigns Gustavus could not dispense with his favourite poet, and Leopold, sulky and enraged at having to exchange the delights of the capital for the perils of the camp, was forced to tune his reluctant lyre with the din of battle ringing in his ears. Perhaps, however, the following anecdote will best illustrate the familiar footing on which Leopold stood with his sovereign.

Leopold had an intimate friend named Örner, who one day paid him a visit, and was persuaded to stay with him all night. At midnight the friends were suddenly aroused

[1] For an account of Liliestraale's political services, see vol. i. chap. x.

from their slumbers by a violent knocking; it was a royal courier summoning Leopold instantly to the Palace of Haga. Leopold was much annoyed, but there was no choice in the matter, and for company's sake he took his friend along with him. On arriving at Haga, they found that the King, as usual, was in the little Turkish pavilion, and thither went Leopold, leaving Örner promenading in the park in the bright moonlight. In about half-an-hour Örner returned to the carriage to await Leopold. The candles had just been lighted in the royal pavilion. Örner from where he sat could easily distinguish everything that was going on, and what he saw quickly filled him with a curiosity which speedily became alarm. In the middle of the room stood the King, apparently in a frenzy of rage, addressing Leopold with a menacing gesture, the poet all the while regarding the monarch deprecatingly, but without daring to open his mouth. Exhausted at last by the violence of his emotion, Gustavus fell into a chair gasping for breath. Leopold, seizing his opportunity, came slowly forward, took and kissed his hand, and appeared to be imploring pardon. At last he was successful. Gustavus's features brightened, the smile returned to his lips; he rose from his chair, paced up and down, and presently beckoned the poet to his side. Then they walked up and down together for about an hour, when the King affectionately embraced his secretary, and retired for the night. Örner, much disturbed by what he had seen, rushed towards Leopold as he quitted the pavilion, exclaiming with a terrified look, " In God's name, what have you done ? Are you guilty ? " " Guilty, guilty ? " inquired Leopold, in amazement, "what do you mean ? " " I mean," replied Örner, " that the King was about to kill you just now. I saw him raise his hand to strike you in the face, but fortunately you just managed to step back in time to avoid the blow." Leopold burst out laughing, and thus explained the scene which had so disturbed his anxious friend. The King had been describing some court theatricals, and at Leopold's request had recited some dozen verses of the tragedy which had pleased the audience most, selecting the scene in which the hero falls into a violent rage. " In a moment," continued Leopold, " he entered into the spirit of the thing with his usual ardour. He was perfect. I stepped back so as not to disturb his declamation, merely throwing in an occasional approving nod, or an expression of wonder and delight. At last, overcome with fatigue, he flung himself into an arm-chair. I approached, congratulated him, and kissed his hand; . . . and now, my dear Örner, you have the full explanation of a scene which has made you tremble so much for my poor person ! "

In Leopold, Gustavanism in literature (*i.e.*, French classicism as adapted to Swedish tastes) found its ultimate expression : if Kellgren was its apostle, Leopold was its pope. During the last twenty-five years of his long life his decisions in all matters relating to literature were regarded as infallible. His contemporaries looked up to him as the *ne plus ultra* of good sense and good taste, as the most poetic of philosophers and the most philosophic of poets ; less brilliant, indeed, but also less bitter, than Kellgren ; not quite so original, perhaps, as Oxenstjerna, but certainly more equal and more correct. When, however, the anti-Gustavan reaction set in, and the iconoclastic Phosphorists, headed by the inexorable Hammarskjöld, took the Swedish Parnassus by storm, their first act was to depose Leopold from his lofty pedestal. His triumphal odes, which the last generation had thought so sublime, were contemptuously rejected as empty and servile bombast ; his tragedies, even *Odin*, the best of them, for which the poet had received from his royal protector a laurel branch plucked from Virgil's grave and attached to a diamond carcanet—even *Odin* was declared to be without a single spark of dramatic genius. His comedies fared even worse, being dismissed with the curt remark that the time employed upon them was so much time wasted. But Hammarskjöld and his school undoubtedly went too far. It would indeed be absurd to treat Leopold as a poet of the first rank ; but it would be unjust as well as absurd to deny him the name of a poet at all. Leopold certainly lacked the fire, the imagination, the passion, the

spontaneity, the originality, which we regard as the first
requisites of a great poet. What gifts and graces he had
he owed rather to education than to inspiration. His strong
points were a keen judgment, a sparkling wit, a light and
delicate fancy, and a natural good taste cultivated by a
careful study of the best French models. He excelled,
therefore, in the higher kinds of satire, the didactic tale, the
descriptive idyll, where his refined wit, full of Voltairean verve
and gaiety, could move about at its ease. His poetic satire,
*Den Vackra Bedjerskan* (The Fair Worshipper), a model of
grace and elegance, seasoned with the most piquant irony,
in which the peculiar conjugal relations of his age are merci-
lessly ridiculed; his moral ode, *Vänskapen, eller hvad man-
vill* (Friendship, or what you will), which even found favour
with the austere Hammarskjiöld; and above all, the delightful idyll, "Egle and Annette," in which the empty pleasures
of society and the great world are contrasted with the humble
but enduring delights of a domestic rural life, and the blithe
naïveté of which has been well compared to a "mischievous,
truant sunbeam playing upon a sombre pasture"—these
charming pieces sufficiently vindicate Leopold's poetic talent.
And even in those branches of literature most foreign to his
genius, the grace and elegance of his style have been admitted and admired by his most severe critics. Hammarskjöld himself allows that the tragedy *Odin* contains
passages of real poetic worth, and that the Swedish Alexandrine is here to be seen at its very best.

It was thus in the genial sunshine of a brilliant court
that the French school reached its highest perfection, and
produced an abundant and enduring harvest. But the French
school, although preponderant during the Gustavan era, by
no means represents the whole literary activity of that fruitful period. Along with, but independent of it, an original,
purely national literature was springing up, and it says as
much for the catholicity of Gustavus's taste as for the fervour
of his patriotism, that he whose sympathies and education
were so thoroughly Parisian should have enjoyed and appreciated better than any one else the products of the national

school, and should have stood on terms of the closest intimacy with its leaders—Bellman, Lidner, Hallman, and Kexel.

In a little out-of-the-way lane in Stockholm there stood, towards the end of the last century, a shabby little tavern, the favourite resort of the lower classes of Stockholm. A stranger happening to drop in any evening when the fun was growing fast and furious would have noticed a long, lean, haggard, middle-aged man, in a shabby blue coat and cape, and the remains of a once-splendid scarlet waistcoat, sitting at a side table with an empty pipe lolling out of his mouth, and a half-filled glass of punch before him, gazing listlessly at the bacchanalian scene before him. If our stranger, tempted by curiosity, had asked those about him who this threadbare, slipshod, drowsy-looking individual was, he would have been told, not without a contemptuous shrug at his ignorance, that it was Carl Michael Bellman, Sweden's sweetest singer, whose enchanting lyre put all others to silence, and whose name was mentioned with equal enthusiasm in the market-place and the palace. Possibly the stranger would have remained somewhat incredulous; but had the fine weather and his good genius tempted him that same evening to an excursion along the romantic shores of Lake Mälare, tones of an unearthly, pathetic sweetness would have drawn him irresistibly to the little Swiss châlet that then stood on the Djurgarden Island, round which he would have found a motley crowd listening with rapt attention to the music of a lute accompanied by the richest of human voices, and would have heard each one whispering to his neighbour in the intervals of silence that Bellman was at his best that night.

It is difficult for any one but a Swede to appreciate, still more to define, Bellman's genius. We may describe him as one of the few great lyric poets of the world, as the prince of improvisators; we may compare him to Anacreon, to Pindar; but to understand his songs we must not merely read them, we must hear them sung.[1] As Kellgren has so well remarked, one can only know half the worth of these poems if

---

[1] Bellman, by the way, improvised the music to his own songs.

one only knows them as poems.   Never yet were music and
poetry so closely wedded to each other.   It is not so much
the words that are set to music as the music that is set to
the words, words and music being so indissolubly inter-
blended that it is impossible to even imagine which of the
two would lose the most by a separation.   Indeed, an absolute identity of verse and melody is of the very essence of
these poems, and whoever leaves this fact out of sight cannot
comprehend, and therefore must not presume to sit in judgment upon them.

  And if the form and melody of Bellman's verses approve
him a great poet, their subject-matter shows him to have been
an equally great humourist.   It is true that he stooped low
enough for his material, for he chose the heroes and heroines
of his cycle of bacchantic idylls (Movitz, Mollberg, Sten-
dicker, Agrell, Ulla Winblad) and their fellows from among
the motley crew of tipsy loafers and " pot-house Phrynes "
around him, types one might have thought altogether incapable of æsthetic treatment.   But genius, as it has well
been said, is a chemist who separates spirit from matter,
gold from garbage, who can extract perfume from the most
poisonous flowers, and make the foulest and most offensive
objects endurable and even agreeable to the most delicate
organs.   Bellman was such a chemist.   He swept into his
magic crucible what appeared to the rest of the world a
mere mass of moral putrescence ; evaporated all that was
pestilential, corrupt, and degrading; and precipitated a something altogether new and different, a something that was
all flowers and fragrance, mirth and joy, music and the
songs of birds.   Not one of the doubtful, disreputable figures,
the half-tipsy satyrs, and roystering bacchantes which underwent this chemical process is now unfit to take its proper
place in the bizarre and fantastic picture-gallery which Bellman thus created, and when he presents them all to us in
a purely comic light, with the enchanting scenery of Lake
Mälare for a background, and a soft, melancholy colouring
overlaying the whole, then, indeed, we are forced to laugh
and rejoice with him in spite of ourselves.

Bellman's humour is noisy and broad, hearty and uproarious, as was naturally to be expected of one whose favourite theme was the feasts and frolics of Bacchus and of Venus. But the bray of his clarions and the clatter of his kettledrums often seem rather to drown sorrow than to express joy, and a current of elegiac pensiveness runs beneath the wild, bacchantic revelry. It has been finely said that his muse approaches us with twirling thyrsus, holding a comic mask before her wine-flushed face; but her wild *evœ!* often ends in a "plaintive, tremulous wail," and if we approach near enough we perceive that her melancholy eyes are filled with tears.

But even in Bellman's best poems we only possess a faint shadow, a dim reflection, of Bellman himself. Most of his songs were improvisations, the best of which were never put upon paper at all. When the spirit came upon him, he would seize his cithern, strum softly upon it till he was lost to the world around him, and then pour forth his soul for hours together till he collapsed like an exhausted Pythoness. We should also not forget that Bellman's recitals owed perhaps their most subtle charm to his wonderful mimetic powers, which were of the highest order, and of practically unlimited range. Sometimes, with voice and fingers simultaneously, he would imitate every conceivable musical instrument, accompanying his mimicry with the momentary inspiration of his muse. Once, in the presence of the King and a brilliant suite, he improvised a dramatic opera in which Gustavus's two Governors, Counts Tessin and Carl Scheffer, men of totally different characters, were imitated to the life, to the delight and amazement of all who heard him. On another occasion he extemporised an outgoing voluntary, supposed to be played at a country church, allowing his audience to plainly hear through the melody how the people banged to their pew-doors, shuffled down the aisle, and took leave of each other in the churchyard outside. We can readily understand, therefore, that it is one thing to hear Bellman's melodies executed even by the most accomplished artists, but quite another thing to have heard them rendered by the master himself.

Bellman's best friend was Gustavus III., whose piercing eye could detect genius under the most shabby, threadbare guise, and who loved and valued it wherever he found it. A large volume might be compiled from the anecdotes of the intercourse between the poet and the prince, but a couple will suffice to show how intimate that intercourse really was.

One day Gustavus, himself the prince of dandies, was walking in the streets of Stockholm, when he suddenly came upon his slipshod poetical friend in an even more reckless *déshabillé* than usual. "Bellman," said the King, reproachfully, "you really should finish dressing before you leave the house." "I venture to assure your Majesty," replied Bellman, with a shuffling bow, "that at the present moment I carry the whole of my wardrobe upon my back."

On another occasion Gustavus, as he was taking his customary morning walk in the Haga Park, perceived Bellman sitting on a chair apparently the worse for liquor; on the grass, in front of the poet, lay a labourer sound asleep. "Mon Dieu! Bellman," said the King, stopping short, "I really believe you are drunk already." The only answer Bellman gave was to point at the slumbering peasant and murmur the following impromptu : —

> "To think that such a lout should use so well his time,
> That e'en at eight o'clock he's drunker far than I'm."

Next after Bellman, the place of honour in the Swedish school undoubtedly belongs to Lidner.

Lidner was one of those vagabond geniuses apparently without either soul or conscience, whose art is as disorderly and irregular as their lives, and who make us wonder how the sacred fire of poetry could ever have found its way into vessels of so vile a clay. From the very first he seems to have been incorrigible. While still a student at Lund, he naively confesses, in some of his earliest verses, that "Astrild's" (*i.e.*, Venus's) laws were the only laws in which he had undergone a strict examination; and even in those days the ink-horn and the brandy-flask were always to be found

side by side upon his table.   His relations sent him to the
Cape of Good Hope to get rid of him, whence after a year
he returned to his native land, obtained a subordinate post
in the War Office, and published his *soi-disant* fables (they
are rather satiric allegories than didactic apologues), which
were well received on account of their epigrammatic bitterness and extraordinary purity of style.   About this time,
too, Fortune took pity on him, and gave him one of those
golden opportunities which happen only once in a lifetime.
He was strolling one day in the Royal Museum, looking at
some antiquities lately arrived from Paris, when the King
unexpectedly made his appearance.   Lidner respectfully
drew back into a corner, whilst the monarch, stopping short
before a bust of Trajan, gazed long and admiringly at the
effigy of the noblest of the Cæsars.   Turning at last to his
suite, he exclaimed, with a sigh, "Oh! if only I were a
Trajan!"   Seized by a lucky inspiration, Lidner at once
stepped forward and addressed the following impromptu to
the King :—

> " Explain, great King ! if thou art able,
> The sigh that rends thy heart so sore !
> Thou wouldst thou hadst been born a *Trajan ?*
> Thou art a *Gustaf*[1]—that is more !"

The felicitousness of this apostrophe, even more than the
compliment it conveyed, could not but excite the attention
of one who was himself the Prince of Wits.   Gustavus asked
the shabby youth his name, and discovering from subsequent
inquiries that he had fallen into bad company and was rapidly
going to the dogs, he sent him to Paris as an *attaché* to
Ambassador Creutz, hoping that, once separated from his
disreputable associates, young Lidner would develop his
genius and become an ornament to literature and society.
But Lidner had already sunk too deeply into the moral
slough to ever live respectably.   Creutz, the most amiable
and indulgent of men, was at last obliged, in self-defence, to
rid himself of a secretary who not only pawned his books

[1] Gustavus.   Gustavus III.'s admiration for his great namesake was notorious.

and filched from his wardrobe, but even appropriated the finest passages from his manuscript poems and plays. So Lidner returned to Stockholm a ruined man, and eked out a miserable existence by writing epitaphs and epithalamia, and giving desultory instruction in foreign languages. The bounty of the King, however, was his chief resource. Gustavus, indeed, had now abandoned all hope of reclaiming the prodigal, yet he did not altogether withdraw his protecting hand, for the good-natured Prince could not bear to see genius, however disreputable, in distress. Lidner, on the other hand, regarded the bounty of his royal friend as a matter of course, and the ingenious impertinence with which he demanded alms of him is almost incredible. Thus he once placed himself in Gustavus's way, so that the King could not avoid him, and exclaimed, as he approached :—

> " Go on thy way, great King. I'll not disturb thy leisure !
> I to the tailor go that he may take my measure :
> But who's to pay the score ? Ah ! Heaven alone may know it!
> Yet Gustaf is my King, and I am Gustaf's poet."

But though the royal *largesse* was frequent and abundant, it helped Lidner but little. He was saddled, moreover, with an amiable weakness, even more injurious to a man of his character than all his vices put together, that is to say, with a soft-heartedness which could never say no to the appeals of poverty and distress. Thus, one summer, as he was returning from an interview with the King at Drottningholm, a poor widow met him, who bewailed her misery and begged for help. Lidner at once loosed the gold chain from the watch which the King had just given him, took off his silver knee-buckles, added thereto all the money he had about him, wrapped them all up together in his silk neckcloth, and bade the poor woman take the parcel to buy bread for her starving children. The King and Queen, who had witnessed this scene through the window, sent two servants to bring Lidner back just as he was. The King asked him if he knew the person to whom he had been so lavish. Lidner replied that she had seven small children; he had no need to know more. " It is certainly a fine thing to have a good heart," said the King, "but to give away your clothes to the first beggar you meet is going a little too far." He was then dismissed with two rolls of ducats, and a warning to be more careful in future.

Lidner's genius was like his character, irregular, disorderly, fitful, and eccentric, but decidedly original. He is at his best in his tender and pathetic moods, when he weeps over the trials and miseries of human life. Then, indeed, he goes to the very bottom of the human heart, and no Swedish poet has ever sung with simpler yet deeper and truer pathos. His tragedies, " Medea " and " Spastara," and his oratorios, " Messiah in Gethsemane " and " The Destruction of Jerusalem," were read with rapture by his contemporaries ; but in these, as in all his works, we find the sublimest thoughts and the most daring images side by side with the most trivial commonplace and the feeblest platitudes. All his pieces, moreover, except his shorter elegiac poems, are without definite plan or system, slovenly, vague, and shapeless. Poetry with him was an instinct, not an art.

The dramatists of the popular or national school were Hallman and Kexel.

Carl Isreal Hallman enjoys the distinction of having been more successful than any one else in the attempt to found a purely national comic theatre in Sweden. The drama, strange to say, has never flourished on Swedish soil, and this is the more remarkable and surprising, as on the other side of the narrow Sound we find among a people of the same stock (and practically of the same tongue) as the Swedes one of the most vigorous and independent dramatic literatures of modern times. Even the Gustavan drama was rather a splendid gift from the Prince to the people than the creation of the people itself—a delicate exotic, carefully reared in the artificial atmosphere of a court, not a genuine product of the soil. Hallman first showed that a purely native comedy was at least possible ; but the single fact that he found no followers nor imitators only shows how little individual genius can do when it is out of sympathy with

the national character. All Hallman's plays are farces or
low comedies bearing more or less upon the national vice—
drunkenness. The dialogue is always brisk, vigorous, and
full of genuine humour, and the situations are highly ingenious and original; but the characterisation is weak, and the
fun far too coarse and outspoken for the more refined taste
of our own day. Hallman was still more successful as a
parodist. Count Creutz used to say that he would rather
have written Hallman's parody of his own *Zephir* than that
beautiful elegy itself, while Gustavus actually preferred Hallman's parodies to his original plays. On one occasion Count
Gyllenborg, who had little sense of humour, bitterly complained to the King that Hallman had parodied his, Gyllenborg's, play *Berger Jarl*, and begged that the poet might be
taken to task for such an act of presumption. The only
reply Gustavus made was to send for the comedian, and
command him, by way of penance, to parody the opera
*Thetis och Peléc*, with which, as the reader may remember,
the King himself had made his *début* as a dramatic author.

Amongst Hallman's coarse-grained, strong-flavoured
tavern dramas, "like a violet in a bed of onions," is a bright
little comedy-vaudeville, entitled *Tillfälligheten gör tjufven*
(Opportunity makes the Thief), round which has arisen one
of the fiercest literary controversies of modern times. The
real author of this charming little trifle was young Armfelt,
who, desiring in everything to be the shadow of his King,
dashed it off for one of the court entertainments, and acted
the leading part himself, while the comic *rôle* of the market-
crier was improvised by Bellman. Five years after the death
of Armfelt, and nineteen after the death of Hallman, when
for no less than thirty-six years it had passed for the
former's, Hammarskjöld, that bitter enemy of everything
Gustavan, surprised the public with the discovery, based
upon very doubtful hearsay evidence, that Armfelt had
bribed Hallman to write the piece for him, and had afterwards taken the credit of it to himself. The influence of
the Swedish Aristarchus was such that the public accepted
his dictum implicitly, and all the successive editions of Hall-

man's plays included *Tillfälligheten gör tjufven*. It is impossible, however, to believe that Hallman's coarse hand could ever have fashioned such a delicate toy; and later critics have severely criticised Hammarskjöld's criticism, and revindicated Armfelt's authorship, the only point that still remains unsettled being how far Armfelt received aid from others. The most probable conjecture seems to be that Armfelt, after drafting the comedy from some unknown French original, called in the aid of his royal friend, or perhaps of Kellgren. Others have fancied he had the help of another dramatist of the Swedish school, Olof Kexel.

Olof Kexel is far less original, but far more polished and graceful, than his friend Hallman. The plots, and no small part of the dialogues of his dramatic works, are borrowed from French or English sources, but the best of his skilful adaptations far surpass their originals. His dialogue is always easy and natural—neither stilted nor vulgar—and his humour savours far less of the tavern and the gutter than Hallman's. Kexel is also remarkable as the first who attempted the novel in Swedish; but the best of these sketches, the historical story *Zamaleski*, for instance, is too evidently a piece of patchwork to deserve to be more than mentioned. Kexel was much sought after by the high society of his day. His fine presence, beautiful voice, ready wit, above all, his perpetual good-humour (which the most grinding poverty was quite powerless to affect) made him the most delightful of companions. He also prided himself on being a beau, and none could boast of such fine and well-starched sleeves, or of a more splendid dress. The world was not to know that the coat he had on was the only one he possessed, and that his days were equally divided between the debtors' prison and the green-room.

It was no mere accident that the period of Sweden's greatest literary productivity should exactly coincide with the reign of Gustavus III. Gustavus III. has often been described as the "living sun" of the men of letters of his day, and the description is in no wise an exaggeration. He was not only the poetical example, but the earthly providence of his poets and his playwrights. He was not only a guiding light to their feet, but a genial, nourishing warmth in their hearts. He not only showed them the way to mount Helicon, he furnished them with provision by the way. He placed too high a price upon genius to allow it to be harassed and hampered by material cares, and he bestowed his bounty with such grace and delicacy that no man ever blushed to be his pensioner. With his death there fell upon the Swedish literature a corroding blight, a long darkness that was to be felt. The Gustavan era might have had more glitter than gold about it; but there could be no comparison between that joyous picturesque period, which has been so aptly compared to a picture by Watteau, and the leaden age which succeeded it, when beneath the tyrannical sway of the feeble Prince-Regent and his brutal minister Reuterholm, the Swedish Academy was closed, literature and the arts were banished or persecuted, and the sweetest of the Gustavan songsters were left to starve— only a sorrowful little remnant gathered round Leopold to bewail in secret the " Royal Charmer," and hope and pray for better times.

# INDEX*

## A.

*Abo, Peace of*, 1741, i. 11.
*Accord System*, explanation of, i. 175.
ACTON, *General*, i. 271.
*Act of Unity and Security*, terms of, ii. 66 ; adoption, 70.
ADDISON (Joseph), ii. 235.
ADLERBETH (Gudmund Göran), *Count*, i. 260 ; ii. 57 ; touching appeal to Gustavus III. in 1789, 69–70 ; 71, 249, 262.
ADOLPHUS FREDERICK, *King of Sweden*, elected Crown-Prince, i. 11 ; character, 20 ; accession, 21 ; humiliation, 1756, 21–22 ; abdication, 1768, 46–49 ; death, 57.
AHLMAN, ii. 51.
AIGUILLON, *Duc d'*, intervention on behalf of Sweden, 1773, i. 152–154.
*Aix - la - Chapelle*, centre of *emigré* activity in 1791, ii. 118.
*America*, war with England, i. 210 ; treaty with Sweden, 254.
ANCKARSTRÖM (Jacob Johan), character, ii. 156 – 157 ; first three attempts at regicide, 158 ; 189, 190, 191, 194, 195, 196, 201, 202, 207, 210.
ANHALT, *Prince of*, ii. 91.
*Anjala, Confederation of*, ii. 28.
ANNE, *Tsarina*, death, i. 10.
ARIOSTO, ii. 221.
*Armed Neutrality of the North*, i. 210–211.

ARMFELT (Carl Gustaf), *Baron*, character, ii. 21 ; drawn into treason, 1788, 25–26, 28–29.
ARMFELT (Gustaf Mauritz), *Baron*, character, i. 261–263 ; loyalty, ii. 24–25 ; General of the Dalesmen, 37, 59, 83 ; storms Elgsö, 88 ; valour, 90, 91 ; 101, 119, 150, 160, 162, 171, 173, 178, 184, 190, 196, 197, 198, 199, 200, 206, 210, 211, 212, 213, 252, 284, 285, 288 ;—as a dramatist, 300–301.
ARTOIS, *Comte de*. See Charles X., King of France.
ATTERBOM, ii. 223.
*Austria*, alliance with Russia in 1782, i. 256.

## B.

BAGER, ii. 276.
BAGKOV, *General*, ii. 91.
BARNAVE, ii. 119 ; champions royal cause, 133 ; 134, 135.
*Barö Sound, engagement of*, ii. 88.
BAILLY, ii. 114.
BELLMAN (Carl Michael), peculiar genius, ii. 293 ; intimacy with Gustavus III., 295–296 ; 300.
BENGTSON (Jan), ii. 73.
BERGHMAN, ii. 172.
BERGSTEDT, ii. 118, 148.
BERNIS, *Cardinal*, i. 269.
BERNSTORFF (Andreas Peter), *Count*, foreign policy, i. 159.

* All headings other than personal headings are in Italics. The more usual forms of personal names are used, even when less correct, thus—Mirabeau, *not* Riquetti ; Montesquieu, *not* Secondat de Montesquieu.

303

U